COMPLETE

ATHLETE

...

MEN'S
FOOTBALL

2018

© 2018, Complete Athlete, LLC

Front cover photo: Allan Russell

ISBN·978·0·9990217·8·1

The purchase of this book entitles the buyer to reproduce student activity pages for single classroom use only. Other use requires written permission of publisher. All rights reserved.

Printed in the United States of America.

At the time of this book's publication, all facts and figures cited are the most current available. All telephone numbers, addresses, and website URLs are accurate and active. All publications, organizations, websites, and other resources exist as described in the book, and all have been verified. The authors and Publisher/Complete Athlete, LLC make no warranty or guarantee concerning the information and materials given out by organizations or content found at websites, and we are not responsible for any changes that occur after this book's publication. If you find an error, please contact Complete Athlete, LLC.

Complete Athlete, LLC
660 Newport Center Drive
Suite 200
Newport Beach, CA 92660
Phone: (714) 949-3845
www.mycompleteathlete.com

*To every young man aspiring to be a **Complete Athlete** in every aspect of your life—this book is for you.*

TABLE OF CONTENTS

FOREWORD

ARSENE WENGER

My childhood is a little while ago now, but don't worry, I remember it well! It was the same for me as for boys all over the world—most of my best memories from growing up have to do with football. In my village, back in the 1950s, we played and we talked and we watched the game constantly. Hour after hour, day after day.

I don't think the idea of becoming a professional player ever crossed my mind. Growing up in a little French village—so small and surrounded by farmland —you could never have imagined that a scout from a professional club would find his way to our football pitch to discover one of us boys. Perhaps it's different today. Growing up now, anywhere in England, you can be sure that a young player who shows promise will soon be spotted by someone.

So, for me and my friends, football was all about playing for fun, for the simple enjoyment of the game. And that love of football was enough, eventually, to give me a career in football, first as a player and since as a manager. Was I a good player? I would say I wasn't bad! I eventually played in a team that won the league title in France: RC Strasbourg in 1978/79. That was the peak for me as a football player. And I have no regrets. To be honest, though, by then I had already set out on another path, towards becoming a coach.

I started as a coach with Strasbourg in my late 20s; in my career, I have coached and managed in France, in Japan and in the English Premier League.

In that time, I have worked with hundreds of young players at different clubs, watching them develop and helping them, whenever I've been able, to fulfil their potential and to realise their own dreams in the game. It's a responsibility I take very seriously.

Young players need many attributes if they are to succeed: athletic and technical ability and an understanding of football, of course, but also things which are to do with their character as a young person, like desire, attitude and behaviour on and off the pitch.

TO GET TO THE TOP IN FOOTBALL, PLAYERS WILL NEED TO HAVE OUTSTANDING TALENT.

They will also need to work incredibly hard in order to make the most of the opportunities which come their way. I have said before that to build a young player is a little like building a house. Between 7 and 14, the foundations go in: mastering the ball, learning and practicing the fundamental technical skills. If you don't have those in place by the time you're 14, it will be even harder to become a professional player.

After that, between 14 and 17, on the first floor of a career, I think you discover whether or not a young player will have the necessary physical attributes: will the player be quick enough? Strong enough to survive at the top level? Above that, at around the same age, the player will need to prove themselves tactically. They will need to learn to become a team player, a player with a real understanding of how the game works and of the importance of vision and movement.

Finally, from 18 or 19 years of age and upwards: will the player have the desire, the commitment and the single-mindedness, to make a success of their career? Will they be able to make the necessary sacrifices and devote themselves completely to the game?

Of course, many young players have talent and many are prepared to work hard, too. But very few will reach the top in football. In fact, very few will be able to make any kind of living from playing the game. But it is important to know that having ambition in your life, **WANTING TO BE THE BEST YOU CAN BE**, can bring you rewards other than the ones you had your heart set on.

If you are one of those who makes a career as a professional footballer: congratulations and I look forward to watching you play! I know you will have a lot to thank the game for.

If your life takes you in another direction, though—working somewhere in football like I have or doing something else altogether but playing with your friends in the park every weekend—I hope you will still be grateful to the game and grateful for what it has taught you. And, more than anything, I hope you'll still love football with the same passion you had when you were young discovering how to play for the very first time.

—ARSENE WENGER

COMPLETE ATHLETE

CONTRIBUTORS & INFLUENCERS

TONY CARR Tony Carr, MBE, was a product of West Ham's youth system, but his playing career was cut short by injury in the early 1970s. He joined West Ham's staff as Director of Youth Development in 1973 and spent the next 40 years bringing through young players who went on to excel for club and country such as Frank Lampard, Joe Cole, Jermain Defoe, Michael Carrick, Glen Johnson and Rio Ferdinand. Celebrated by his peers as one of the most respected and successful figures in youth development in the country, Tony left his post as Academy Director at West Ham in 2014.

IAN MARSHALL, Chairman of Ridgeway Rovers FC, has spent nearly 30 years working as a coach and volunteer in grassroots youth football. Several professional players, including two England captains, David Beckham and Harry Kane, had their first experience of football at the Chingford-based club. Rovers were recognised as the Essex FA's Charter Standard Club of the Year in 2015 and Charter Standard Development Club of the Year in 2016. Ian was named Essex FA's Charter Standard Volunteer of the Year in 2015.

TONY ROBERTS, Born on Anglesey and a Wales youth international, Tony Roberts went on to become the first Welshman to win senior caps for his country at both full- and semi-pro levels. He played over 120 times for Queens Park Rangers and nearly 450 times for Dagenham & Redbridge FC during 26 years as a professional goalkeeper. Since retirement, Tony has worked with young goalkeepers at both QPR and Arsenal and is currently 1st Team Goalkeeping Coach at Swansea City. In 2016, he also became National Goalkeeping Coach for Wales.

JOHN FOLWELL is based at St George's Park, where he works for the Football Association as National Participation Manager for Youth Football. His role is to oversee the participation and development of youth football across the country for both boys and girls, with the stated aim of 'inspiring every young person to fall in love with the game.' John is also a volunteer coach with an Under-9s and Under-12s grassroots team at Mountsorrel Juniors FC in Leicestershire.

PAUL DAVIS played 450 times for his boyhood club, Arsenal, wining League, FA Cup, League Cup and European Cup Winners Cup medals during the 1980s and 1990s. After retiring as a player, Paul gained coaching qualifications up to UEFA Pro Licence level and worked as a youth coach at Arsenal's Academy for seven years. He then joined the PFA as a coach educator. In March 2016, he was appointed as a senior coach and coach educator for the Football Association. Paul is also an ambassador for both 'Kick It Out' and 'Show Racism The Red Card' Programmes.

PAUL CLEMENT played non-League football while working as a PE teacher in South London. His career as a full-time coach began at Fulham's Academy in 2000. He moved to Chelsea's Academy in 2007 and began coaching the first team at Stamford Bridge under Guus Hiddink in 2009. He worked as assistant to Carlo Ancelotti—with several of the world's greatest players—first at Chelsea and then at Paris Saint-Germain, Real Madrid, and

Bayern Munich. Having managed in the Championship briefly with Derby County, Paul was appointed Head Coach at Swansea City in January 2017.

TERRY BURTON captained Arsenal's FA Youth Cup-winning side in 1970/71 but wasn't offered professional terms at the club. He played non-League football, worked in schools while gaining coaching qualifications and returned to Arsenal as Youth Team Coach in 1979. He later went on to coach and manage at Wimbledon, Watford, Cardiff City, West Bromwich Albion, Sheffield Wednesday, and Reading. One of English football's most respected developers of young talent, Terry was recently appointed Head of Academy Recruitment at Southampton FC.

MARK CHAMBERLAIN & WENDIE OXLADE-CHAMBERLAIN Wendie Oxlade Chamberlain is a professional physiotherapist. Mark Chamberlain played 8 times for England over the course of a 20-year playing career and has coached at both Southampton's and Portsmouth's Academies. Wendie and Mark have two sons: Alexander, an established England international player, came through the youth system at Southampton before joining Arsenal in 2007. He moved to Liverpool in August 2017; Christian is five years younger and graduated from Portsmouth's Academy. He signed his first professional contract at the club in 2016.

LOIS LANGTON is a Partner in the Family Department at leading law firm Howard Kennedy. She specialises in all aspects of family law including divorce, financial remedy, civil partnerships, pre- and post-nuptial agreements, co-habitation, separation and child-related work. Lois is also the joint head of the Sports Individuals team and visits professional academies on a regular basis to advise young players on issues related to family law. She currently chairs the Arsenal Independent Supporters' Association.

KYLE PHILLIPS is a Senior Associate in the Business Crime and Regulatory Department at respected law firm Howard Kennedy. He represents individuals subject to investigation for a range of business crime-related issues as well as continuing to represent clients investigated for general criminal matters, including drug offences, sexual offences, theft, and assault. Kyle currently sits on the disciplinary committee for the Surrey FA and regularly visits professional Academies to advise young players on matters related to criminal law.

ROSSI EAMES grew up as a gymnast, winning medals at the British Championships before retiring at the age of 21. He played non-League football before studying for a degree in Sports Science at Leeds Metropolitan University. He coached at Leeds United's Academy before joining Barnet FC in 2009. He worked with several age groups in the club's academy before becoming Academy Manager. After two spells as Interim Manager and still only 32, Rossi was appointed Barnet's Head Coach in May 2017, becoming the youngest manager in the English professional game. He recently stood down from that role to become the club's Head of Player Development.

TROY TOWNSEND was released as a teenager by Millwall and then Crystal Palace before coaching and managing in non-League, youth, and grassroots football. As Education Manager for 'Kick It Out', he delivers the *Equality Inspires* programme into Premier League Academies and works as a life skills tutor in

Academies across the three divisions of the Football League. In 2013, he was named one of the FA's 150 Grassroots Heroes, receiving his award from Prince William at Buckingham Palace. Troy's son, Andros, plays for Crystal Palace and England.

STEADMAN SCOTT & TONY GOLDRING founded Afewee in 1997. Based in Brixton, Afewee Urban is now a community-run sports charity specialising in football and boxing. The project began life as a grassroots football club based at Crystal Palace Sports Centre, before moving to Streatham Common Park two years later, holding regular Saturday morning training sessions that continue to this day. Steadman and Tony eventually rented a space at the Brixton Recreation Centre, paying for it with their own money, and began working with local disadvantaged youngsters. They were and are determined to use competitive sport as a way to change lives for the better. Thirty Afewee alumni have gone on to become professional footballers, including Nathaniel Clyne of Liverpool and England. There are currently nearly 40 more recent graduates signed to professional academies in the Premier League and Football League.

JERMAIN DEFOE was a schoolboy at Charlton Athletic before joining West Ham United as a 16-year-old scholar. During a club career spanning nearly 20 years and more than 650 first team games for West Ham, Spurs, Portsmouth, Toronto FC and Sunderland, he has scored upwards of 270 goals. Jermain has been capped by England 57 times, scoring 20 goals. Now 35, he joined AFC Bournemouth—where he first played on loan in 2000/2001—in July 2017.

ANDRE GRAY was released by Wolves when he was 13 years old, but won an Academy Scholarship with Shrewsbury Town, earning his first professional contract at the club in 2009. After several years playing non-League football, he signed for Luton in 2012 and subsequently moved to Brentford and then Burnley, where he was voted Championship Player of the Year in 2015-16 as Burnley won promotion to the Premier League. He joined Watford in August 2017 for a club record fee.

TOSIN ADARABIOYO is the only player in Manchester City history to join the club as a 5-year-old and subsequently play for the first team, his youth career having spanned City's transformation, on and off the pitch, over the past decade. He made his senior debut in February 2016, playing against Chelsea in the FA Cup. He has since appeared for City in the League Cup and the Champions League. Tosin has played for England up to Under-19 level. His older brother, Fisayo, plays for NAC Breda in Holland.

ADAM LALLANA began his schoolboy career with Bournemouth before joining Southampton's Academy in 2000 and making his first team debut in 2006. He went on to play 235 times for Southampton, as they climbed from League One to the Premier League, before being transferred to Liverpool in 2014. Having won his first international cap while still at Southampton, Adam has played for England 33 times and, in 2016, won the England Player of the Year award.

ALLAN RUSSELL was born in Glasgow and came up through the ranks at Glasgow Rangers. He played in the top three divisions in Scottish football and in the English

Football League before joining Carolina Railhawks in the United States in 2010. He enjoyed 5 successful years in the U.S. before returning to the UK where he became a coach specialising in striker training, with his own company, Superior Striker. He was recently appointed to the staff of the England national team to work with the squad's attacking players ahead of the World Cup in Russia in 2018.

TOM WATT, an actor, broadcaster, and film-maker, has been writing about football for the past 30 years. His books on the game have included ghost-writing David Beckham's autobiography, *My Side*; an award-winning book about football and childhood around the world produced in co-operation with UNICEF, *A Beautiful Game*; *The Greatest Stage*, the official *History of Wembley Stadium*; and in 2010, the official legacy book of the 2010 World Cup in South Africa.

INTRODUCTION

Do you dream of becoming the next Jermain Defoe? The next Adam Lallana? Or the next Andre Gray? Or are you already sure you can become the first... A one of a kind? Whoever you're modelling yourself on, what could be better than to imagine playing the game you love and earning a living from doing it?

The idea of becoming a professional athlete and getting paid to play is very exciting. Who wouldn't want to walk out at Wembley in an England shirt in front of 90,000 fans? Who wouldn't want to take a seat in the first team dressing room of their favourite team? The truth, though, is that fewer than 1% of elite schoolboy players will ever take the field as full-time professional footballers. Significantly fewer than that 1% will actually play a first team game at a professional club.

That's the harsh reality, but it definitely doesn't mean you should give up on your dream.

If you're determined to shine in front of coaches and scouts in order to become a professional footballer, **COMPLETE ATHLETE** can help show you the way. This book will help you prepare to play football at the highest level and to have a potential future as a name on the team sheet for professional and semi-professional managers. Just as importantly, it will also make sure that—however far you're able to go in the game—you'll play at the very top end of whichever level your footballing talent can take you, whether that's Premier League, Football League or Sunday League.

COMPLETE ATHLETE emphasises the proven fact that success isn't just dependent on your natural ability. Your footballing future will be influenced by your attitude and behaviour and by how you treat yourself and others on and off the field. Guidelines, suggestions, inspiration, and real-life stories are provided throughout this book by our team of contributors and influencers from across the football world.

Our intention and our commitment is to help you find your own pathway and **TO SUCCEED IN BECOMING THE VERY BEST PLAYER YOU CAN BE.**

LEVELS

A young player who is hungry and determined to become a professional footballer needs to become a **COMPLETE ATHLETE**. We've mapped out 5 levels on the path to becoming a **COMPLETE ATHLETE**. Generally speaking, the 5 levels correspond to the following (although there may be some overlap depending on maturity, life experience, and ability):

LEVEL 1 – 7 to 9 years old, playing 7 v 7 football

LEVEL 2 – 9 to 12 years old, playing 9 v 9 football

LEVEL 3 – 12 to 16 years old, playing 11 v 11 football

LEVEL 4 – 16 to 18 years old, Academy/College Scholar Years 1 and 2

LEVEL 5 – 18 years and older, Professional/Semi-Professional/Senior Football

A **COMPLETE ATHLETE** will need to achieve the highest level in 5 different categories:

ATTITUDE refers to how you behave as a footballer. For instance, listening quietly while the coach is talking, showing respect for opponents and match officials, being positive in what you do, and working hard for your team-mates are all qualities which demonstrate that you have a good attitude.

PREPARATION refers to off-field activities, such as keeping your boots, kit and equipment well maintained. It demands a willingness to learn everything you can about the game and to practice at every opportunity.

FITNESS refers to the physical fitness and strength needed to compete and excel as a footballer.

TECHNIQUE revolves around acquiring skills, including mastering the basics and, eventually, specialising in a particular position.

LIFESTYLE refers to how you look after yourself, including eating well and getting enough sleep. It also includes getting good grades at school and being a solid member of your family and community.

THE COMPLETE ATHLETE MATRIX

ATTITUDE
- Respect
- Sportsmanship
- Teamwork
- Professionalism
- Leadership

PREPARATION
- Practice
- Nutrition
- Hydration
- Recovery
- Mentality

FITNESS
- Lower-Body Strength
- Upper-Body Strength
- Flexibility/Mobility
- Core Strength
- Speed/Explosiveness /Agility
- Endurance

TECHNIQUE
- Foundational Ball Skills/Dribbling
- Passing
- Ball Control
- Finishing
- Heading

LIFESTYLE
- Family
- Academics
- Social Life
- Role Model
- Living Your Sport

Each of the elements combine to create a young man's character which will also define their success and development as a **COMPLETE ATHLETE**.

If you study the **COMPLETE ATHLETE** matrix carefully, you'll see several categories have attributes that relate to your decisions and behaviour away from football. What you do off the field directly affects what you do on it. For instance, maintaining good fitness will make a big difference in your ability to consistently exploit the technical qualities in your game, helping you to succeed at the highest possible level.

It's worth remembering that just because someone is a professional player in the sense of being paid to play football, he isn't necessarily a professional according to the **COMPLETE ATHLETE** matrix. The day you stop learning and the day you stop giving of your best to the game is the day you are finished as a player, however far you've managed to come so far.

The next few sections of this book will discuss what you need to know, do and be at each succeeding level in order to become a **COMPLETE ATHLETE**.

PLAYER » *If you'd told me, when Frank Lampard was 15, that he would win 110 caps for England and have this amazing career, become Chelsea's record goalscorer, I'd have said, 'Are you sure? That's quite a big ask!' But he's the best kind of example; a fitness fanatic with mental resilience like very few others.*

His dad, Frank Sr, had a part in that. He drove Frank on when he was young. Drove him to distraction sometimes, I think. 'Come on, let's go out running. Let's train!' And when Frank was younger, he was quite small, not particularly quick. He grew outwards before he grew upwards, too. We'd tell him, his mum and dad would tell him, 'Don't worry, Frank. Your body's still growing.'

And, sure enough, he had a growth spurt later in his teens. But, by then, he'd made himself so strong mentally, and he took that into the rest of his career: every day, he'd try to be faster, stronger. Always trying to make himself a better player. A fantastic attitude. How can you not admire that?

As a youth coach, all you're trying to do is help players develop good habits. Think about his game at Chelsea; ball played out wide and he'd be off, getting into the box, between the centre halves, arriving late and scoring.

I can remember him doing exactly the same thing when he was a boy at West Ham. You'd hear his dad on the touchline, 'Get in the box, Frank. Get in the box!' But really it was all about Frank's instincts and his enthusiasm.

The other thing with Frank was him always being ready to get on the ball. The Premier League did a short film, just focussed on Frank on and off the ball in a match. It was incredible. He was like a traffic policeman or something: constantly scanning the pitch, aware of what was going on around him. I asked him to come along to a presentation I did in Manchester when he was playing at City, and I showed this little film.

Frank was amazed, not even aware that was what he did in games. But that's instinct, learning good habits from a very young age. And it's not just doing what a coach tells you. It's about taking ownership, taking responsibility, for your own game as well. —Tony Carr

DEAR PARENT,

YOU HAVE MORE POWER THAN YOU THINK.

This can be difficult to believe sometimes, especially during a boy's challenging teenage years, when your son seems determined to question or contradict nearly everything you say. But if you ever start to doubt how much influence you still have over your child, just pay attention the next time he pulls off something special or makes a crucial interception during one of his games. Where is the first place he'll look to for a reaction?

Chances are, it will be to wherever you're watching from.

Chances are, too, that you'll be reacting to whatever just happened. You should know that your reaction—whether you're cheering, grimacing, clapping, shouting, looking proud, looking embarrassed or looking angry—may very well shape the way your son approaches the rest of the game; how he reacts to winning or losing; how he behaves on the drive home; how he views the game he's just played and football in general. It may even have an impact on how he feels about himself and his future.

We all want the best for our children, and we all want our children to be the best at what they do. But what is best for one child may not be what's best for another.

COMPLETE ATHLETE offers you a guide to managing expectations, whether your son is a stand-out player dreaming of a future as a pro or happy being part of the supporting cast, playing the game he loves with friends and team-mates. Our children, for sure, were born to surprise us.

Often a boy can accomplish much more than we ever imagined him capable of; at other times he may prove far more fragile than we suspected. It's worth stopping to consider how you, as a parent, are reacting to each success and each disappointment.

As you read and explore each level with your son, think seriously about what your role is in helping him grow into something more than just a good footballer. What are you teaching him about responsibility when you make a consistent effort to get him to training on time each evening? What are you teaching him about respect in the way you speak to and about his coaches, team-mates and their families? What will you teach him about resilience when he faces defeat? Or about humility when he performs to his maximum and has a big win? How important are these lessons to be learnt from football which he'll carry out onto the pitch and on into the rest of his life?

Sometimes the right answer is obvious. Sometimes you may not have any clear idea as to what you should say. That is where **COMPLETE ATHLETE** can help. In these pages, we'll suggest some clear guidelines with regards to the appropriate skills, game knowledge, health and nutritional demands, and personal and emotional maturity needed at each stage of a young player's development.

You'll be able to access tips, examples, ideas, and real-life applications both in the book and via the app. This is an interactive, multifaceted, in-the-moment approach to investing in our children's futures both as footballers and as young men to be proud of.

At each stage of his journey—whether your son is just starting out or on the verge of turning pro at an established club—you will be your son's most important and influential supporter. You will always be the person who loves your son most and most unconditionally.

And you'll remain the person he looks to first for advice and guidance. More than his coaches, more than his team-mates, how you choose to act and the values you pass on by word and deed will be the foundation for the man your boy will eventually become.

It's a responsibility and a privilege.

You have more power than you think.

PARENT >> *My parents split up when I was quite young. But neither of them used to come and watch me at training or in games. I was playing alongside Teddy Sheringham: his dad was always there, watching, talking to the coaches. My dad never saw me play once. At the time, I didn't think I cared. I was off playing the game I loved.*

But it must have had an impact because now, with my own family, I've worked really hard to always be there. If I was off coaching somewhere, my wife would go. Five children: girls who love dancing, boys who love football and athletics. We'd make sure they all came along to support their brothers and sisters. I give workshops and talk to parents now about it because I think it's easy to underestimate how much it means to a kid having that support alongside you.

I remember an Under-18s game when we had an accident on the way over and got to the game 15 minutes late. It was 1–0 already and Andros had scored. End of the game, I said, 'Well done. Good goal'. He said, 'How do you know? You weren't there!' You assume a boy would just be focused on the game. But he knows if you're watching. A little support? A comfort? Don't underestimate how important that is.

I talk to parents now and they say, 'Oh, my boy doesn't care if we're there or not.' I tell them, 'Oh, yes he does!' Your body language is important: if you're disappointed by a pass or annoyed by something he does and you're shaking your head, he'll know. Even in the midst of a game, he'll pick up on it. —Troy Townsend

DEAR PLAYER,

You have big dreams and the desire to make them come true. How do we know this? Simply the fact that you have picked up this book and are reading it tells us that you're a young man who wants to do more than just the minimum. You're someone who wants to continually develop his game and push the limits of his potential. You're already demonstrating one of the most important qualities you'll need if you're going to turn your dreams into reality: the player who's willing to learn, hungry for coaching, and open to new ideas will always achieve more than the player who thinks he already knows it all. Always.

PLAYER >> *If you want to make the best of yourself as a footballer, at whatever level you're playing at, you need to know that the drive is going to have to come from you. You may have parents and coaches around who really support you or you may not. Either way, that desire to be better than you are at the moment—to get to the next level—will have to come from inside yourself.*

There are so many knocks and disappointments along the way that, if you don't have that determination, you'll never move forward. You'll never get to the highest level you can play at, whatever level that might be. Your attitude is what can take you as far as your ability will allow. The moment you sit still is the moment you start going backwards. —Paul Davis

COMPLETE ATHLETE is strategically designed to guide you through your career as you evolve and grow, both as an athlete and as a person. As well as helping you with Fitness and Technique, we emphasise three key elements: *Lifestyle*, *Preparation*, and *Attitude*, which are all essential in developing and maximising your talent. Before we begin, however, it might be useful to consider how each of these elements impacts on your character. And to ask yourself some questions:

LIFESTYLE means your commitment to making good decisions about the way you live. Are you eating healthy food? Are you sleeping as much as you need to? Are you as focused on your school work as you are on your training? Are you avoiding illegal drugs and alcohol? Are you spending time around positive people and in healthy relationships that won't get you into trouble? If the answer to any of these questions is "no," then you must ask yourself if you are ready to make the necessary changes today to set yourself on course to becoming a **COMPLETE ATHLETE**?

PREPARATION is about your willingness to do the work needed to be ready, mentally and physically, every time you step onto the pitch. It requires dedication to learning rules and practicing drills so you master the fundamentals of the game. It also means that you arrive at training or games with your boots and kit clean and organised, with your head in the right place to learn and improve yourself as a player. Do you have what it takes to do the necessary work and study of the game to develop and grow, even when that preparation amounts to something tougher than easy fun?

ATTITUDE has to do with your maturity, in terms of how you approach and respond to others, as well as how you handle yourself. Showing respect for your parents or guardians, for your coaches and for your team-mates can be a really significant part of what makes you an appealing prospect for the team or club you aspire to play for.

Progress isn't just about how talented a player is. If he refuses to listen to instruction, talks back, or stirs up trouble between other players, no coach is going to want him on the team sheet or around the dressing room.

A player who is willing to work hard and is eager to learn, and who approaches the game and other people in a positive way at all times, will eventually grow into a leader and dominant player, no matter where he is within the pecking order of the squad at any particular time. Your attitude matters because it demonstrates to other people how you interact with the world around you. More importantly, it represents the clearest evidence possible as to how you think about and value yourself.

Can you be confident without being arrogant? Can you handle disappointment without beating yourself up? How will you react if you don't put that chance away? If you don't get picked for the team? If you don't receive a contract offer? And how will you react if you do? How you behave in those situations tells others a great deal about who you really are, and who you will become in the future.

If you are serious about your career as a footballer, you need to be the person who takes charge of the journey. And you need to take charge of it now. Your parents, guardians, and coaches can play their parts in helping you achieve your full potential, but, ultimately,

IT ALL COMES DOWN TO YOU.

Are you willing to put in the time and show the dedication needed to succeed? No one else can do it for you. You must have the courage and integrity to consistently make the right decisions about how you live, how you prepare, and about your attitude—both when every eye in the stadium is on you and when no one else is looking. Are you ready to become a **COMPLETE ATHLETE**?

DEAR COACH,

The name of this book—**COMPLETE ATHLETE**—is no accident. Although your primary responsibility is to develop the boys and teenagers under your care into the best footballers they can be, you also play a hugely important role in helping them mature into rounded and complete young men. Whether you're an experienced professional, coach or parent volunteering in the role, you are in a position to contribute so much more to a player's life than just teaching him the fundamentals of the game.

As you read this book and review the accompanying app, we hope you'll recognise how they can complement what you're trying to achieve both on and off the field. For example, it's important for coaches to communicate clearly with parents about what they can reasonably expect their child to learn during each session and over the course of every season. This book provides a clear set of guidelines as to how best to outline those points, helping the entire group—players, coaches, and families—to work together in a positive and mutually supportive way to enable each player to reach his full potential.

During the hours, weeks, and months you are teaching your players the fundamentals and finer details of football, you are also passing on lessons in the fundamentals and finer details of being a good citizen and a responsible individual. Your attitude and the example you set can show the player both the importance of being a good teammate and the satisfaction that can come with self-reliance. The way you talk about and interact with parents, match officials and other coaches is as important in that respect as how you communicate with the players themselves.

Please don't let this extraordinary opportunity slip through your fingers or become lost amidst the noisy clamour of competition. It's easy for coaches to fall into the habit of making the game about themselves, rather than about their players. Victories and defeats can become personal—seen by you as a reflection on your abilities, rather than being used as teaching opportunities for your players. Every training session, every game, every single conversation can be a chance to influence these children and young men for the better. A good coach prepares players for the game. A great coach prepares them for life. We're excited to be given the chance to walk alongside you as you train, push, encourage, discipline, nurture, mentor, and celebrate every member of the team you're responsible for. Thank you for your commitment to coaching and thank you for your dedication to these special young individuals. We share your ambition: to help every player make the most of his talents and opportunities; to guide him toward becoming a **COMPLETE ATHLETE**, a credit to himself, to you, and to the game.

COACH >> *Building a team involves teaching skills which are also going to be useful in every other area of a boy's life. You have the outgoing boys, the extroverts; you have the boys who are quieter and less sure of themselves. You rein the loud ones in a bit for the good of the team and help the less confident ones come out of themselves. If they can find a balance amongst themselves, a togetherness as a group, that's when they'll be successful. And that process of team-building will relate to so much else in their lives, too, even though most of them won't end up playing football for a living.*
— *Ian Marshall*

IN LEVEL 1

Every footballer, even if he now plays for one of the world's greatest clubs and appears on the game's greatest stages, started out on his journey as a raw beginner. In many respects, the beginner's level can be seen as the most important: it's time spent training your mind and body to master basic techniques and awakening the ability to make decisions. Whatever the amount of experience you've gathered so far as an aspiring young footballer, it's vitally important that you meet the standards outlined in this chapter.

1.1 ATTITUDE

A **POSITIVE ATTITUDE** is essential to an athlete's development and success, on and off the pitch, especially if you are to move on toward the higher levels of elite football. It's one of the absolutely necessary attributes which scouts and coaches look for when recruiting a player.

A positive attitude is a quality that can be developed and improved with practice, just like any other skill. In this case, it's a matter of training your brain. A **COMPLETE ATHLETE** makes a habit of demonstrating the following five attributes:

RESPECT

SPORTSMANSHIP

TEAMWORK

PROFESSIONALISM

LEADERSHIP

PLAYER » *To be the best you can be you need passion, energy, enthusiasm. Desire. We had a week's training camp with Wales recently at Vale do Lobo in Portugal, before a round of international games. Cristiano Ronaldo's got his own villa there on the complex. I got talking to the guy working in the gym, I asked him if Ronaldo ever came in and did anything when he was on holiday here. He told me that Ronaldo —the best player in the world, by the way—would be in the gym from 9 til 11 every single morning. Then he'd go up to the football pitches with a bag of balls and practice for an hour on his own.*

This is Ronaldo when he's on holiday! That focus and dedication and drive: nobody's given that to him. That's come from inside and the result is that he's got the best body, the best technical skills, the best mental attitude. The guy's scored 600 goals but, every day, he wants to be better. If I see a boy with a bit of that energy and enthusiasm in him, I think he's maybe got a chance. With goalkeepers, I can see it in a second: whether or not they've got the right attitude to their work.

—Tony Roberts

PARENT » The right attitude isn't just about what your son demonstrates on the pitch. Think about being at home, ready to get into the car or onto the bus to head off to training or a game. Before you even get to the ground, your son's frame of mind is either focused on getting the maximum from his game or session or it's not.

With younger players, if they've been harassed by their parents for being disorganised or in a rush, they'll often get out of the car angry, flustered, and frustrated, less able to focus on performing, learning and enjoying himself. As a parent, it helps if you can teach your son the importance of being organised, properly prepared, and on time.

It's actually a good feeling: being ready will allow him to fully focus on being at his very best. A positive attitude means he'll then step onto the pitch composed and clear-headed, ready to improve himself as a player and make a positive contribution to his team.

COACH » Every player will make a mistake at some point in a game. Every player will struggle to master a particular drill at a training session. What's certain is no young player ever deliberately makes a mistake or finds a drill difficult on purpose.

With this in mind, you need to focus on a boy whose head has gone down because he's made a mistake or is struggling to master a particular skill. Look the boy in the eye and remind him of the positive and influential things he's done in the match; remind him of the skills he's already taken on board and made part of his game. It's crucial to explain to the player how much value he adds to the group, and that mistakes are just a part of the game. We learn from getting things wrong as much as we learn from getting them right. What's key is to continue to believe in yourself, to stay confident and to recover from setbacks.

Take that time with the individual, and you'll have a more confident player whose renewed sense of self-worth will help the team and add value to your training session.

Academies are signing players at Under-9s, which means Under-8s are seen as the next age group on the 'production line'. So, at that age, boys are often going from club to club, deciding which will be the right one for them. All the clubs are vying for the same promising players from the same pool of talent in their areas.

My opinion is that, below those ages, definitely, the game should just be about fun. Don't over-coach; just let them play. You can give games a particular theme if you want the boys to practice particular skills. Do your drills, devise a game, but don't be starting and stopping all the time. 'You should do this. You shouldn't do this.' Let them play. Let them learn. Let the game itself be the teacher. —Tony Carr

RESPECT

RESPECT means talking to and behaving toward other people in ways that show they have worth and value in your eyes. At Level 1, young footballers should always treat their coaches with respect. These are people who have sacrificed valuable time, studied, and worked hard in order to create an environment in which young players can learn more about the game at the start of their football journeys.

PLAYER >> HOW TO DEMONSTRATE RESPECT FOR YOUR COACHES

- When you arrive at training or a match, always greet your coach politely with a firm hand shake.

- Find out how your coach likes to be addressed, whether it's by first name, Mr or Mrs, or simply as 'coach.' Then always speak to your coach using the term he or she prefers.

- Listen carefully and don't fidget or become distracted when a coach is speaking.

- When a coach speaks directly to you, always maintain eye contact with them and don't interrupt their sentences.

- Don't talk back to or disrespect your coaches, match officials, or other players.

- Follow instruction without complaining. However if you didn't hear or don't understand an instruction, it's important to ask the coach to repeat or explain it.

I think respect is an important part of what the young player needs to bring to his work. I will talk to a 16-year-old, for example, as a young adult, not as a child. He needs to talk to me as his coach. That's something I learnt as a gymnast: respect for your coach.

The boy needs to buy into what we're doing at the club; he needs a willingness to learn. I've had to explain to boys that they're un-coachable at a particular time because they don't want to listen. But if you're 15 or 16, and you already know everything about football, why aren't you playing for our first team? Why aren't you playing for Chelsea or Real Madrid?

At that age, you only know a tiny part of what you're going to need to know. Respect your coach, respect the club, respect the environment and then you've got a chance of making progress in the game. —Rossi Eames

SPORTSMANSHIP

Good **SPORTSMANSHIP** starts with respect for your team-mates, opponents, coaches, and officials. It also includes playing with integrity. Playing with integrity means respecting and following the rules of the game without cheating. At Level 1, a young player should be familiar enough with the basic rules of the game in order to abide by them.

(To review the basic rules of football, see APPENDIX 1.) He should never try to bend the rules or cheat; he should always respect what coaches and officials say in terms of decisions on free kicks, throw-ins, and penalties and not

argue with them. After all, coaches and match officials have been involved in the game and learning the rules a lot longer than he has.

PARENT >> *We hold a parents' evening at the start of every season, to explain what we're doing at the club. What our aims and ambitions are. What we expect from parents, and what we hope we won't see. And we send them home with a printed copy of our code of conduct, trying to give an idea of how we want them to behave. It's necessary. Some of the things that go on at games are unbelievable, and I don't know how much more the clubs or the FA can do.*

If anything, the problems are getting worse at the younger age groups, where the games aren't even supposed to be about winning and losing: shouting abuse at kids, at other parents, at coaches, at referees. Violence, too. We're all volunteers. We want kids to have fun and develop. Why should we have to deal with all that other stuff as well? Why should the children have to deal with it? —Ian Marshall

RESPECT for match officials and coaches is essential. At the youngest ages, players at Level 1, the example is set almost entirely by a boy's parents. Unfortunately, we all know shocking behaviour can be witnessed at children's football matches all over the country every weekend. Who are parents on the touchline attacking the most? Referees. All you hear is, 'That was a foul, ref!' 'That was offside!' 'Are you serious, ref?' 'That was a shocking decision!'

Often those exclamations are accompanied by the kind of foul language nobody would endorse using in front of their children at home. Parents lose control and vent their frustrations by abusing match officials. The worst side-effect of this behaviour is that youngsters witness it and start to assume it's normal. Soon they're assuming it's OK to start disrespecting match officials themselves.

If there was one thing I could say to all parents, it would be: don't ever contradict the coach during a game or a training session. There's a reason I ask a boy to do something or not to do something. I train with him. I know what he can and can't do. And I trust him. If I say one thing and then his mum or dad is shouting something else from the touchline, it'll just confuse him. Maybe even upset him.

If a parent has an issue with anything I'm asking for from a player, I always say to take it up with me off the pitch and after the session. And then I'll always listen and try to explain what I'm trying to do. —Ian Marshall

Nobody would ever suggest it's OK for a parent to walk into their son's school and start yelling at teachers because they don't agree with a decision to give their son a C on a test instead of an A.

Most of us realise we need to remind our children that a teacher is someone whose decisions you ought to respect even if you don't always agree with them.

THE WORLD OF FOOTBALL IS A DIFFERENT KIND OF CLASSROOM, where coaches are teachers devoted to helping boys make the most of their talents as players.

In that context, parents have to set the example, reacting to decisions, right or wrong, in as positive and unaggressive manner as possible. Players need to understand that a coach—like the referee—is no different than a teacher, a policeman or any other figure in authority. If you disagree with something he's doing —or with a decision made by a match official, for that matter—let your coach know but don't try to affect the situation by losing your temper in front of your son.

PARENT » From the earliest days of his involvement with football, your behaviour and attitude will set the example your son is most likely to follow. If you demonstrate respect for match officials and coaches, it will become second nature for your son to do the same. That attitude will help define his reputation. On the other hand, if you're constantly questioning a coach's instructions or disagreeing with every refereeing decision, your son will assume that's what he should be doing too.

Those bad habits will stay with him—and undermine him—for the rest of his journey as a player. A bad reputation will follow a boy around. No parent wants their son to be known as a kid with a bad attitude toward coaches, match officials and team-mates. And, as a parent, you can help make sure that doesn't happen. Please consider your son's future next time you feel tempted to shout abuse at a referee or to confront a volunteer coach.

COACH » *Coaches are role models. Coaches are mentors. If young players get on with a coach and trust him or her, as opposed to having someone standing on a* *touchline barking at them, then they'll be more receptive to ideas and develop faster. That's what coaching is, after all: passing on ideas. If kids listen and buy into those ideas, work at putting those ideas into practice, they'll improve as players.*

It's as simple as that. It's probably why coaches do it, especially youth coaches: you communicate and they listen; you watch players improve and a team develop. Even with the youngest, 5- and 6-year-olds, you show them a step over or a drag back and then you watch them do it in a game, it's a huge satisfaction. —Ian Marshall

One of the most powerful and positive messages you can pass on to a young player is that sportsmanship matters. From as young as possible, it's important he understands that sportsmanship is a part of the game and should become a part of his character, on the pitch and off it.

More than good manners, sportsmanship defines young players as young men: teach them to shake hands with their opponents after every game, no matter the result. Make sure it becomes second nature to show respect for every single player in the opposing team; to acknowledge match officials and thank them for refereeing the game.

This is when outstanding team leaders can be vital, leading by example and helping to reinforce the core values of sportsmanship and respect you, as a coach, instil in your players. And that they express after both heart-breaking defeats and uplifting victories.

JOIN THE CONVERSATION!

For more coaching tips, be sure to check out the **COMPLETE ATHLETE** app.

TEAMWORK

TEAMWORK means working together as a group to achieve a shared goal. In football, players contribute their individual efforts and abilities to the structure and identity of the team in the hope that this will allow them to dominate and win games.

Players at Level 1 should be focused very much on mastering skills and techniques as individuals. And, just as importantly, focused on having fun. But part of that enjoyment can be the earliest experience of working together as a team, recognising what can happen when you're performing not just on your own but also as part of a collective. This awareness becomes increasingly important as a player moves through the Levels on the way to becoming a **COMPLETE ATHLETE**.

By the end of Level 1, a young footballer should be starting to learn to make decisions during games about the best times to keep individual possession of the ball and the best times to pass the ball on to a teammate. He will also start to learn how to communicate with team-mates and help them by making himself available for a pass. He will learn that it's important to support team-mates before and after games as well as during them.

The ability to work as a member of a team will also help a young player take on board the basic outlines of a plan determined by a coach. At these early ages, this plan should be designed to allow every member of the group to participate and make a contribution irrespective of his level of technical ability or physical development.

COACH » It's never too early to start introducing the fundamental principles of teamwork to a group of young players, especially as the idea of working and playing as a member of a collective may not come naturally to many boys at this age. There's often one boy on a team whose technical ability or physical development is more advanced than his peers at a particular age.

His instincts may well push him towards dribbling the ball around an entire team on his own every time he gets possession. Left to his own devices, whether he ends up scoring or not, he'll just repeat the process over and over again. In training and before games, it can be very useful to introduce the idea that the group—and therefore each individual within the group—will achieve more by working together.

Passing to a teammate 10 yards away can often achieve as much, if not more, than running those 10 yards with the ball at your feet. Give every boy the chance to experience the unique satisfaction of cooperating successfully with others. You can show as well as tell: take one pencil and ask a player to break it. It's easily done. Then ask him to break a bundle of seven pencils. That's impossible! Young players need to learn these lessons. Maybe their parents do, too.

PROFESSIONALISM

Obviously a young player developing at Level 1 and just discovering the game isn't a 'professional' in the sense of being paid to play football, even if—for some—that's already an ambition. However, developing what could be described as a 'professional' attitude is already important.

Good habits, strong mentality, positive outlook and enthusiastic work rate will help a boy move up through the Levels and age groups better able to express himself and to excel at every stage of his journey. Look at a lawyer in court: smart and well-presented in suit and tie. Look at a doctor: a pristine white coat.

These are professional people who you can trust and take seriously on first impressions. A young footballer at Level 1 should already be arriving on time for his sessions or games, well turned out with clean kit, boots properly tied and any other equipment he's going to need ready to hand, such as shin pads for a game or trainers if the coach is going to have to take the session on a hard court instead of on grass.

Part of being professional in your approach to football is to be properly prepared and to always look the part. Being professional, though, runs deeper than that. It's good if a young player arrives outwardly ready for training for a game. But it's never too early to begin making sure you're inwardly ready as well.

How much you'll take from a session or from a game is entirely up to you and will depend on the frame of mind you bring to football. Are you focused? Are you determined? Do you know what you want to achieve, as well as looking forward to having fun and playing with friends? Some boys will find this kind of attitude to football comes naturally. For others, it may be an attitude acquired with conscious effort and over time. Either way, it'll stand you in good stead if you want to progress as a player.

PLAYER >> *The boys who come out of our community and have success in football all share certain qualities. He has a winning mentality. He's selfish in the sense that he knows what he wants. And he doesn't need a lot of talking to. Boys like Nathaniel Clyne—or most of those who have gone on from us to join professional academies—you never have to raise your voice to. They just want to learn.*

There are other boys, though, boys with talent, who want to fight you all the time. Because of that, they don't reach the same level of success. You argue with them, you ban them for a week, for two weeks. They come back again. You're just trying to break them down a little so you can talk to them. Teach them to listen. To give them a chance at a club.

Still, it'll always be difficult for those boys to mix with their peer groups or be willing to take on instructions. A boy who you have to argue and fight with? Well, the odds are he's not going to make it. What coach or manager at a club is going to put up with that? He'll just say, 'I don't want to listen to that. Get out of here.' —Steadman Scott

LEADERSHIP

A good leader has the ability to inspire and motivate, to breed confidence in others and help a group to perform at ever-higher levels. Developing **LEADERSHIP** skills at Level 1 will benefit a young player not only in the context of football but also in his school and family life.

At these early ages, it wouldn't be expected of a young player to display all the obvious traits of a leader. However, by watching and listening to his coach lead, organise and motivate the group, a boy will begin to develop an instinctive understanding of what leadership means and what a leader can do to help a group achieve. This focus on the coach can also be a first step towards becoming a leader himself, inspiring other boys with his attitude to learning from a senior figure.

COACH » One strategy to think about using, even at Level 1, is one that's used by many professional academies and also in high-level business environments outside football: shared responsibility.

This is a concept that can be put into practice in football in very simple ways. Start by asking different players to act as captain or team representative at tournaments and at football-related events. Even at ages 7 and 8, shared responsibility is a proven way of building confidence and cohesion amongst a group of players.

To achieve this, the coach needs to make sure that all members of the group are aware of what you're doing and why. You will also need to outline what will be expected of each individual when they put on the captain's armband or step forward to represent the team. For example, you might want the captain's responsibilities to include:

- Being positive when communicating vocally to team-mates.
- Being respectful when speaking on behalf of the team to match officials.

- Leading by example regarding work rate and team spirit.
- Being ready to pass on a coach's instructions to team-mates on the field.

A really important thing about leadership: leaders don't come first. If I lead, it's not for me. It's for you. That's why other people follow you: because you're doing what you're doing for them, not for yourself. That has to be true of us, as coaches, too.

Parents look at what we do: we discipline their kids, we teach them. We shout at them when we need to. We love them and nurture them. But we aren't getting paid to do that. It's not about us. Parents see that: everything we do is about their kids, helping their kids to achieve their dreams. —Steadman Scott

1.2 PREPARATION

PREPARATION is vital if you're going to get the best out of yourself as a player. Being prepared covers quite a lot of different aspects to the game. It's about practicing your technical skills. It's about eating the right kind of food at the right time of day and staying hydrated. It's about getting rest and optimum sleep. It's about soaking up detail and examples of what the best players do from anywhere you can—books, the internet, TV, and going to watch professional games.

Preparing properly for training and games will give you confidence. You will know you're ready, mentally and physically, to perform at your very best. When you properly prepare, you know there's no reason you can't give your all in the session or the game. The old saying is true: **FAIL TO PREPARE, PREPARE TO FAIL**.

PLAYER >> *The difference between kids who are going to be your best players and those who are along for* *the ride, there just to take part and enjoy themselves? The best kids will always be the ones who go away and practice on their own.*

The kids who simply participate—and there's nothing wrong with that—will say goodbye at the end of a training session and then simply turn up again the following week. It's like they're attending a school lesson or something, whereas the kids who are aspiring to go to the next level are always looking to improve. They drive themselves: something you can actually spot at quite a young age. So much of it is about attitude. You can coach skills, of course, but you can't coach attitude. —Ian Marshall

A **COMPLETE ATHLETE** prepares to perform consistently well on the field by paying attention to, —and improving on—the following aspects of his life and work as a player:

PRACTICE

NUTRITION

HYDRATION

RECOVERY

MENTALITY

JOIN THE CONVERSATION!
More nutrition advice and tips are available in the **COMPLETE ATHLETE** app. —download today!

PRACTICE

PARENT>> *For youngsters getting involved with football for the first time, the number one thing has to be enjoyment of the game. I think everybody would agree on that. Enjoy playing football, enjoy watching it, enjoy talking about it. It might just be you, kicking a ball against a wall. It might be with a mate in the garden or with friends after school. It's all about trying things, using your imagination, being creative.*

I can still remember when I was that age, going downstairs at the flats where I lived and kicking a ball around for hours at a time. I got so much enjoyment from that, 5, 6, 7-years-old: **THAT'S WHEN YOU CAN DISCOVER FOOTBALL***. Experiment, invent games. You don't need a coach coming in and telling you what to do and what not to do. That can actually block a young player's development at that stage.*

The other thing that's necessary for a young player is somewhere safe to play, of course. That may be something a parent or a teacher needs to find out about. Well, find that somewhere but then just leave him to it. You don't even need to stand around watching! Make sure he's safe, but then just let him play. Of course, that's not as easy as it used to be.

People aren't so comfortable letting their children disappear off with a football for hours at a time and, if parents want to take their boy along to a club because they feel he'll be safe there, that's fine. But it's important that the coaches at the club recognise the importance of just letting the kids express themselves, try things, and enjoy what they're doing.

I know that in the professional game—and even in grassroots football—there's a move to have kids involved in organised football from as young as 6- or 7-years-old. For me personally, I'm not sure about that at all. I don't really think kids are best being 'coached' at that sort of age, even up to 8- or 9-years-old. But I'd hope that those clubs, at whatever level of the game, are letting boys play: just setting them up for 4 v 4 and then walking away and letting them get on with it! Letting them develop by playing. —Paul Davis

Level 1 is where the foundations for becoming a **COMPLETE ATHLETE** are laid. It is important at this level to train a young player's mind and body to love and master the football. At this age, every experience a boy has with a football should be fun but should also be directed toward developing the fundamental skills needed to become completely comfortable with the ball at his feet. It can also be a boy's first experience of working and contributing in a team environment. Training—and playing—as often as possible will help young players develop agility, balance and coordination, building base strength and resilience in their bodies while performing the functional movements that football demands.

He'll need all those qualities as he moves through his life in football. Working on them will also mean he's less likely to pick up injuries. He'll get the maximum time possible for progression on the pitch.

PLAYER ›› *It's a team game but football is 1 v 1's all over the pitch. So, we start with the basics: beat a player, take the ball off a player. Like they work to become basketball superstars in America. One against one is the key to becoming a star in football, too.*

We start with you and the ball. You own the ball. Your feet have to work like your hands. The football stadium is your stage. People are watching you. You have to show me why I'd want to see you play. How you touch the ball, how you move: up on your toes, like you're stepping across a minefield.

Once a boy's mastered the football, then we play two against two, three against three—no more than that. Working around the pitch in triangles, learning to make decisions. Everything we do is focused on footwork, which, of course, is different than at the academies, where right from the start it's all about passing the ball.

But I think that will always come naturally enough. There'll be enough teachers telling you how to pass. What you have to start with is footwork, the basic tool. You have to learn that if you're ever going to be a footballer.

—Steadman Scott

With pre-academy players, you'll watch them in a game and it might just be one thing that catches your eye: a boy drops a shoulder to beat an opponent; a boy plays a first-time pass because he's already seen a team-mate available; a defender beats a striker for pace and slides the ball out of play.

Or it could just be enthusiasm: you see 6- and 7-year-old boys who are natural competitors, urging their team-mates on, chasing up and down the pitch. You just need to see one thing and then you invite them in to train and see how they get on around boys at the same standard. But it's that one thing, whatever it is, that first catches your eye: something natural, something instinctive, something that hasn't been coached. —Tony Carr

HOW MUCH TO PRACTICE

How much training is enough? How much is too much? There is plenty of debate as to how much time a young player should spend practicing. Some experts in the field of elite performance believe it is better to practice with full engagement, challenging yourself to acquire new skills, for a shorter period than to practice for longer and risk a drop-off in the quality of the training session.

Practical experience, though, would suggest that any time a boy spends with a ball at his feet is time well spent. In an informal setting—the park, the garden, the street; with parents, siblings, or friends—a boy can never play too much football if playing football's all he wants to do.

PARENT » *With football—and with anything else, really—what mattered to us was that they were enjoying what they were doing and doing it the best they could at whatever level. We're competitive, we want to see them trying, but we're not parents to scream and shout at our boys. If they seemed to be unhappy with it, under pressure, we'd pull back and let them take a break from things.*

Boys develop at different speeds and over different timeframes. If a boy is driven, wanting to play all the time, you can push him and push him. But one boy might be like that at 5 or 6. For another, it might not happen till he's 9 or 10. And I don't think it's ever going to be too late. Look, a parent has to have the drive as well as the boy: someone's got to take him everywhere for training and games! But it's got to be all about their son's dream, not their own. —*Wendie Oxlade-Chamberlain*

At the elite level, the ability to perform actions and movements subconsciously—instinctively—is the key to consistency, and, therefore, the key to success. If someone asks you to pick up a glass of water and then place it back down, you perform the task easily and with precision because it feels natural. You don't have to think about it; it's something you've done hundreds and thousands of times before. It's an action you can perform without needing to engage your conscious mind. It's instinctive.

However, if someone asks you to pick up the glass with your non-dominant hand while rolling a ball from left foot to right foot at the same time, you will only be able to do this slowly at first. Mind and body will need to work together to figure out how to complete the task. It'll feel unnatural at first. Only by practicing will you be able to speed up and perform the actions with ease. At that point, they'll have become instinctive. You won't need to be conscious of what you're doing. You'll be an elite level picker-up of the glass! With a ball at his feet, a young player can master technical skills by practising on a daily basis, even if that's only for a few minutes each day. The key is repetition: mastering one skill and then moving on to the next, he will eventually start to perform those skills subconsciously and at a very high level.

PLAYER >> *For this generation, our generation, and generations before us it's been the same: it's how kids discover football. In the garden, in the park, out in the street: they've got a ball. Find a wall, something to use as a goal. They play and they practice.*

You know, on your own, you start just by practicing mastery of the ball. Keepy-uppys! How many can you do?

10? Now try and do 20. Or 50. Or 100. And that can start at any time. Younger or older. Whenever you get that spark. Start just by dropping the ball onto your foot and then catching it. Then doing the same with your other foot. Work up to being able to keep it in the air and close to you, being able to transfer it from foot to foot. It all starts with mastering the ball. —Terry Burton

HOW TO PRACTICE

- Create training content that allows you to work on skills you really need to improve on, making sure you try to master them using your weaker foot as well as your stronger one. Improve the skills you've already mastered by challenging yourself with the tempo and quality of your practice.
- Ask your coaches to provide a training programme for you, perhaps asking them to suggest which skills they feel you should be practicing in order to improve.
- Work on the skills you've been introduced to at training sessions. Think about things in games or sessions that have let you down or held you back. Try to think up or find routines to work on those particular skills. Repetition will help your weaknesses to become strengths.
- Watch one of your favourite players. Make a note of four skills he uses that you think make him stand out as an elite player. Practice those skills and include them as part of every practice you do on your own.

PLAYER >> *With young goalkeepers, I'll show them the first team keeper in action and then all their work is about learning to do what the senior guy can already do. Physically, they might not be strong enough, might not be able to reach the top corners yet, but we break down all the different processes, work on all the details.*

The first team is where they all want to be, isn't it, even though very few of them will ever make it to that level? But it's good to show them what you want. In that way, the internet can be a great tool. I use it myself: if I want to find an example of a particular technique or if I want to get an idea to work on in a session, I'm straight on YouTube! A kid can do that, too. He can have his heroes, but he needs to find his own character as a keeper: he can look at what the greats do—how they take off for crosses, how they kick the ball, how they set themselves for one-on-ones—and take bits from all of them.

—Tony Roberts

SAMPLE TRAINING SESSION

- Warm up and stretch
- Drill 1
- Drill 2
- Drill 3
- Cool down and stretch

NOTE » It is very common for young players to get frustrated, to look for excuses and to quit early while trying to master certain skills and techniques. If this is happening, it's best to either take a break from the particular drill altogether or perhaps try to break the drill down and practice in stages. Those component parts can be mastered before trying to put the whole together again in one drill. The effort made to stick with acquiring a skill that's proving elusive—or the strategy of breaking that skill down into component parts—will encourage persistency, resilience, and a strong mentality.

You refuse to give up or you find a new solution to a problem: either way, these are approaches which will stand young players in good stead if they are to overcome adversity and achieve their goals in football and in life.

COACH » *There's always been a discussion about drills for younger age groups and people often say that young English players have shorter concentration spans and so drills aren't so useful for us. Personally, I still think there's a place for them. It depends on the standard kids are at and on the environment and circumstances you're in: there's not much point in getting kids standing around, passing a ball 10 yards back and forth between themselves, if there's a driving wind and pouring rain.*

It seems kids from places like Italy and Germany and Spain will quite happily stand and pass a ball 10 yards over and over again, whereas in England we feel as if we need to motivate our boys by mixing things up all the time and working in short bursts. But how about challenging boys to focus in, for five or 10 minutes, on a basic technical skill? To be able to concentrate like that is perhaps building mental strength as much as anything else. —Paul Davis

PARENT » At Level 1, boys may already be practicing with a team or a club two or three times a week. They may be playing football at school, at after-school clubs, or socially with friends.

That still leaves plenty of time, if their desire to play and improve still isn't satisfied, to follow an individual programme suggested by a coach, or to create games and drills with the help of their parents or on their own.

Games that boys and their friends make up will, by definition, be fun—they're designed for play. Any adult input should be conveyed with this in mind: the goal of improving skills and technique must be realised at the same time as the boy is enjoying himself, playing the game he loves. The moment football feels like a chore as opposed to a challenge, your son will very quickly lose interest and find something else he has more fun doing.

PRACTICE GAMES TO DEVELOP SKILLS

1. Try playing **ONE BOUNCE** to encourage soft touches and balance while cushioning a ball that arrives slightly above ground level. It can be done with a parent or a boy can do it on his own against a wall. Count how many successful repetitions he can achieve and then challenge him to go past that mark.

2. SHOOTING PRACTICE will always engage a boy's attention: it's the excitement of working on the skill that wins games. Put yourself in goal and see how many times your son can score from 10 efforts with you alternately feeding passes on the ground and off the ground, the challenge being to keep shots with both the rolling ball and the bouncing ball on target. Raise the stakes by getting your son to use alternate feet to fire in his shots, too.

3. The **FIRST TOUCH GAME** is great for encouraging young players to work on a soft first touch in a confined space. Set up four markers to make a grid—a square small enough to be testing, but big enough to keep the game fun—and feed the ball in to the player from outside the grid. Use different angles and different speeds. How many times in a row can he control the ball with a soft enough touch to make sure it doesn't leave the grid?

I grew up with it and it still works now: squash with a football. You just find a bit of wall and set chairs or something on each side to make goalposts so the ball has to hit inside. You can play on your own, of course. Maybe left foot then right foot. Volleys or half-volleys. But it's better with someone else. There's an element of competition, and you're going to need to adjust your body to deal with the ball coming back to you off the wall from an opponent's shots. It works just like squash, but you're moving and striking the ball at different angles just as you would in a game. —Terry Burton

If you're a parent working on these drills with your son, try to encourage consistency and focus. Just push a little in order to up the number of repetitions each time a skill's practiced. And when mistakes are made, react with a positive attitude—you're hoping to challenge him, not to frustrate him, after all. It's time to enjoy: instilling a love of the ball and the game. You'll share memorable moments together doing something that gives you both enormous pleasure.

NUTRITION

NUTRITION plays a key role in athletic function and performance. Young footballers' bodies are trying to build muscle and core strength whilst burning calories and going through a succession of growth spurts.

This means they need to properly fuel and hydrate their bodies at optimum times in order to make up for the calories and fluids they're losing during training and matches, as well as in general exercise during school hours and after school playing with friends.

An active youth footballer needs to consume **PLENTY OF HEALTHY FOODS AND DRINKS** in order to:

- Replenish his energy supply
- Maintain hydration
- Obtain the vitamins and minerals needed to support metabolism, tissue growth, and repair
- Prevent injuries and/or illness
- Perform at his best both on and off the field

NOTE >> All of **COMPLETE ATHLETE**'s sports nutrition guidelines have been developed and set out by Courtney M. Sullivan, founder of *NUTRITION FOR BODY AND MIND*.

Sullivan is a Registered Dietician certified by the Academy of Nutrition and Dietetics, and a Certified Personal Trainer recognised by the National Academy of Sports Medicine. APPENDIX 2 provides more detailed guidelines as well as suggested meals and recipes developed by Sullivan specifically for optimal health and football performance.

FOOTBALL-SPECIFIC NUTRITION GUIDELINES »

- All athletes should consume 5 or more balanced meals spread across the day, every 3 to 4 hours.
- Pre-match and pre-training meals should be eaten 2 to 3 hours before activity, and snacks eaten 1 to 1.5 hours before activity.
- Eat when you're hungry to prevent lean-muscle breakdown. Stop eating when you're full to prevent feeling sluggish.
- Eat breakfast within 30 minutes of waking up to prevent lean-muscle breakdown, increase energy and concentration, and maintain good blood sugar control.
- Choose whole grains, fresh fruit, and lean protein for breakfast.
- Eat well-balanced meals and snacks, consisting of carbohydrates, lean proteins, and heart-healthy fats.
- Drink a protein shake or eat a snack or meal that has the right balance of protein and carbohydrates within 30 minutes of completing training or games.
- Choose fresh whole foods when possible (instead of processed foods which have been packaged or refined to increase nutritional value. Avoid foods that are high in sugar and either saturated or hydrogenated fats.

LEVEL 1 ATHLETE NUTRITIONAL GUIDELINES »

Each young player will have his own specific nutritional requirements depending on age, height, weight, activity level, metabolic rate, and genetic background. Therefore, the following suggestions for daily nutritional proportions are guidelines based on the average age and activity level of a Level 1 player:

- 60 percent carbohydrate
- 15 percent protein
- 25 percent fat
- No more than 7 percent saturated fat
- No trans fat
- 25 grams of fibre per day
- No more than 150 calories per day from sugar
  (37.5 grams or 9 teaspoons)

TO FULFIL THE NUTRITIONAL NEEDS LISTED ABOVE, TRY TO EAT A DIET BASED ON »

CARBOHYDRATES High-fibre foods such as whole-grain bread, brown rice, whole-grain pasta, beans, starchy vegetables such as corn, peas and potatoes, quinoa, and cereals.

PROTEINS Chicken, turkey, or fish, especially wild salmon, tuna, trout, mackerel and sardines, which are all high in heart-healthy omega-3 fatty acids.

FATS Low-fat cheese, nuts and nut butters (preferably without added sugar or salt), avocado, seeds, and heart-healthy oils such as extra-virgin olive oil, rapeseed oil, sunflower oil, and peanut oil.

FRUITS/VEGETABLES Any and all (leafy green vegetables are of particular value); raw vegetables and fruit are highly recommended.

PARENT » In tournaments or at all-day events, children may play several games or engage in several activities over the course of five or more hours, with a lunch break in between. Parents will often take their children to the nearest place to eat.

There's every chance that will mean heading for a fast food outlet. When the players return for the afternoon session, they'll seem mentally and physically sluggish. Even running's an effort! What's certain is that sluggishness isn't the result of tiredness after the morning games or session. Unfortunately, it's due to them having eaten high-sugar, high-salt, high-fat food at the franchise you went to.

Players at this age (7 to 9 years old) probably aren't yet ready to take on full responsibility for fulfilling their dietary needs. It's the responsibility, instead, of a parent or guardian to be prepared with a healthy lunch and snacks to sustain your young player through the whole day and to replace calories and fluids after it. Healthy hydration doesn't mean high-sugar sports drinks.

Water's always the right choice. The quality of food and hydration for athletes is paramount in them performing their best. The choices you make for them now can become the decisions they make for themselves later on. Good habits will be crucial as they develop as young footballers and young men.

PLAYER » *You need to do everything you can, don't you? Be fitter, be stronger, look after yourself better. I think back to when I was a young pro at Arsenal, age 20 or 21. I was doing stuff that other players would laugh at or not see the point of.*

For example, in the '80s, long before nutrition had come into English football, I got hold of this book from somewhere about nutrition and diet. Drinking water, eating particular kinds of food. I read it, and it made sense to me. So I took it upon myself. I took the book into the club and showed the other lads. They just thought I should chuck it away.

But I went along with it. I wanted to do whatever I needed to do to be better at football. I would go out and look for ways to improve. I'd make whatever sacrifices I needed to in order to get to where I wanted to go in the game. I learnt to solve my own problems. And that's the best feeling: working something out for yourself. —Paul Davis

HYDRATION

An athlete needs to drink water before, during and after training and games. This is particularly important on summer days when temperatures are high. If a footballer does not drink enough water he could suffer from dehydration. The warning signs of dehydration include:

• Thirst
• Irritability
• Headaches
• Weakness
• Dizziness
• Cramps
• Nausea
• Increased risk of injury

HOW TO MAINTAIN PROPER HYDRATION »

- Drink 16 to 20 fluid ounces (450 to 550 millilitres) within a 2-hour period before exercise.
- During exercise, drink 4 to 6 fluid ounces (120 to 170 millilitres).
- After exercise, you'll need to replace 24 fluid ounces for every 1 pound (0.5 kilos) of body weight lost during exercise.
- 5 fluid ounces equal half a cup, 20 fluid ounces there fore equal a couple of cups.

NOTE » These figures are approximate. If you feel thirsty at any point, drink water!

* Adapted from guidelines provided by the American College of Sports Medicine (ACSM)

PARENT » Even at this early stage in your boy's football journey, good lifetime habits are what you're trying to instil. Young children give themselves over completely to a game or a training session and get excited before it.

They won't necessarily think about hydration and may well ignore feeling thirsty. That puts them at risk of the side effects of dehydration noted previously, especially if the weather's warm. (Remember to always check the forecast.)

Hydration isn't about guzzling down a bottle of water just before stepping onto the pitch. That's likely to lead to stomach cramps and even vomiting. It's all about taking on liquids regularly before, during, and after exercise, using the above list as a guideline. Hydration will keep your son feeling comfortable during games and will be hugely important in his preparation and recovery phases.

RECOVERY

Young footballers need to eat and drink within 30 minutes of training and games to make up for the calories they're burning and the fluids they're losing. Replenishing calories and fluids also aids in muscle recovery and repair.

HOW TO REPLENISH CALORIES AND FLUIDS >>

- Drink 24 ounces of fluid (not sugary drinks) for every pound of body weight lost within a 2-hour period of training or a game. As a guide: 20 fluid ounces is about 1 pint or 2 cups. Look to drink that amount (or more) after your session or match. Remember: water is always a good choice!
- Consume 5 to 10 grams of protein plus an equal amount of carbohydrates within the 30-minute recovery window. As a guide: 10 grams of protein is equivalent to about half a chicken breast or half a can of tuna. 10 grams of carbohydrate is equivalent to half of a slice of bread.

SLEEP

Just as increased activity creates a greater need for calories, it also creates a greater need for **SLEEP**. Recovery also means allowing the body to rest and heal from the demands of training and games.

According to the National Sleep Foundation, a Level-1 footballer should get 10 to 11 hours of sleep each night to ensure proper growth and development. If that's not possible or practical for whatever reason, or if a young footballer needs additional recovery time, he can take short naps (no longer than 30 minutes at a time) or engage in quiet rest periods (lying down, watching football on TV, or reading).

PARENT >> At this age, you will play a key role in helping your son develop good professional habits as regards preparation, punctuality, presentation, and nutrition. That responsibility applies, as well, to his need to sleep, rest, and recover.

For example, if a young player is wanting a sleep over with his mates the night before a game, either try to avoid or reschedule this or, at least, have it at your own home to help you control the sleeping arrangements and monitor the hours of sleep he gets.

When players are recovering between games in tournaments or between sessions, make sure recovering is what they're doing! Don't let them run around like crazy with team-mates and sap their energy levels. If it's a hot or humid day, find somewhere in the shade or in an air-conditioned environment for them to recover and allow core body temperature to cool down.

MENTALITY

Being a **COMPLETE ATHLETE** doesn't necessarily mean just training harder or longer. Of course, a young footballer needs to spend time physically preparing his body for action. Likewise, though, understanding and committing to the right kind of mental preparation will also help him perform at his highest level.

JOIN THE CONVERSATION!
Step up your mental game with more tips in the **COMPLETE ATHLETE** app!

- Take a few minutes to think about the training session or game you're about to take part in.
- Try and think about the good things you did at your last session or game.
- Think about being able to influence the game with:

  - Good passes
  - Inventive tricks
  - Scoring goals
  - Dribbling and beating opponents 1 vs 1
  - Creating chances for your team-mates to score
  - Working as hard as you can to support your team

- Celebrating with your coach and team-mates after you win a match.

At Level 1, a young footballer should be playing for the love and enjoyment of the game. While he will already possess an instinctive competitive spirit, it's important to remember, that every training session and every game is also about having fun, developing and mastering skills, and enjoying being part of a team. If, for whatever reason, football isn't enjoyable for a young Level 1 player, he probably won't be able to achieve elite levels of performance. If he's playing football to please his parents rather than because he's self-motivated, he may well fall out of love with the game altogether. Certainly he won't fulfil his potential under that kind of parental pressure.

PARENT >> *I'll never forget, when I was working at Southampton, we had to sit down with one boy's parents and tell them we were releasing their son. They were upset—'What are we going to do now? What's going to happen to us?' My assistant, an older guy and more traditional, perhaps, said to them, 'All I'm hearing is "We". It's not "We". It's not you. It's all about the boy.'*

You definitely see those situations where the parents' ambition is greater than the son's. For me, you have to look at the boy. Does he want to do this? And, if he does, how can I help him? You assess what he needs from you. Does he need pushing, mentally? Does he need to be left to get on with it himself? You have to go along with the boy and what he needs. Every boy's different.

You can't push an introvert the same way you can push an extrovert. You have to try and give them the kind of support they need and always remember it's not about you. It's about your boy. —Mark Chamberlain

COACH >> It's really important not to over-coach, not to tell young players what to do. Let the game be the teacher. A coach can set up the game, and then afterwards, ask the players to think about how they might do things differently next time. After all, eventually, you're looking to develop players who can make decisions for themselves.

Boys that age are just enjoying playing but, of course, for some, the dream is already there. Don't get me wrong: it's great to have a dream, to imagine yourself as the next Harry Kane or Alex Oxlade-Chamberlain. But one of the biggest challenges we face in youth football is to do with where that dream comes from.

Is it the boy's dream? Or is it his parents'? If it's the parents forcing that dream on a talented boy, then that brings an awful lot of pressure, doesn't it? We see that happening even at 5 and 6 years old when, really, at that age, it should all be about them just enjoying the game.
—John Folwell

1.3 FITNESS

The **FITTER** you are, the **BETTER** you will perform. It's as simple as that. A footballer needs to develop strength and speed to play the game effectively and limit the chances of picking up injuries. One of the keys to maximising strength and speed is mobility.

Mobility is being able to move efficiently through a full range of motions. To achieve his goals as a player, a **COMPLETE ATHLETE** will always develop and maintain high levels of:

LOWER-BODY STRENGTH

UPPER-BODY STRENGTH

FLEXIBILTY/MOBILITY

CORE STRENGTH/BALANCE

SPEED/EXPLOSIVENESS/AGILITY

ENDURANCE

LOWER-BODY STRENGTH

LOWER-BODY STRENGTH is necessary for almost every athletic activity, but is especially important in football. A great deal of the power and momentum used for kicking, accelerating and decelerating comes from the gluteal muscles, from the hamstrings and from the quadriceps. Young footballers can always be encouraged to do balance exercises and strength exercises using their own body weight, which are designed to develop these key muscle groups.

Many simple exercises which involve focusing on a single leg can help with muscle development and the improvement of balance and posture. Others can help determine whether one leg is significantly stronger than the other. Broad jumps, on the other hand, are a great exercise to aid development of explosive strength, balance, coordination and cohesion between upper- and lower-body movements in young players.

SINGLE-LEG SQUATS »

- Balance on one slightly bent leg while your other leg is positioned slightly in front of your body.
- Using your arms to help you balance, start to bend your standing leg slowly, going as low as you can while still maintaining balance and control.
- Slowly return to the starting position and repeat.
- It's important to know that a player actually builds more strength on the way back up to his starting position than he does on the initial descent. (That's why control on the return to the starting position is vital.)
- Make sure you try the exercise with both legs in turn.

UPPER-BODY STRENGTH »

Flexed-arm hang of 15 seconds
25 push-ups in 60 seconds

FLEXIBILITY/MOBILITY »

Sit-and-reach test score of at least 32 centimetres
90/90 test is pass or fail

CORE STRENGTH/BALANCE »

Plank for 2.5 minutes
Single-leg balance on each leg for 30 seconds
Standing overhead 6-pound medicine-ball throw of at
least 4 yards

SPEED/QUICKNESS/ENDURANCE »

5-10-5 shuttle run in 6 seconds
30-yard sprint time of 5.3 seconds
Beep test minimum score of 5/2 to 6/4 (number of
levels/number of shuttles completed)

SINGLE-LEG WALL SITS »

- Stand with your feet shoulder-width apart against an
  upright wall with a smooth surface.
- Slowly slide down the wall until both your knees and
  hips are at 90 degree angles.
- Slowly lift one foot off the ground and hold it for as
  long as possible.
- Put that foot back on the ground, rest for 30 seconds
  and then raise the other leg.
- Count how long you can hold on each leg.

UPPER-BODY STRENGTH

At the ages of Level 1 players, development of **UPPER-BODY STRENGTH** is often overlooked or sometimes avoided altogether due to a popular belief that it is bad for younger boys. Certainly, at this point in a player's physical development, it's too early to be using weights or exercise machines. It's never too early, however, to be trying exercises which rely entirely on a boy's own body weight for their effect. These exercises are called Calisthenics.

As a player's body grows and develops through the levels outlined in **COMPLETE ATHLETE**, we'll constantly test the ability to lift your own body weight using simple exercises like push-ups and pull-ups. These exercises develop upper-body strength in exactly the same ways as many natural activities done in the course of general children's play. Upper-body strength is developed in two distinct ways:

PULL EXERCISES are exercises which involve pulling your body weight toward an object and are good for increasing back strength and mobility. A good example is a pull-up or partial pull-up.

PUSH EXERCISES are exercises which involve pushing your body weight toward something and are best for increasing strength in your chest and arms. The simplest example is the push-up.

It's important to remember that these body weight exercises aren't designed to increase size or build bulk in young players. Instead, they build core and muscle strength, muscular endurance, and mobility.

BENT-ARM PULL-UP »

- Grip an overhead bar with underhand grip (your palms facing toward your body).
- Try and pull your body up slowly with the aim of getting your chin above the bar. The emphasis should be on using your arms and back to lift your body. Don't use your legs to give momentum.
- At the highest point, with your chin above the bar, your legs should be hanging straight down.
- Hold for 2 seconds and then lower yourself slowly with control and composure.
- Get an adult or older sibling to take partial weight if necessary and to encourage good line.

PUSH-UPS »

- Lie face-down with your palms under or slightly wide of your shoulders. Make sure fingers are straight and legs are straight and parallel.
- Straighten your arms, pushing your upper and lower-body up together in one smooth movement, back and knees straight throughout.
- Push up until your arms are straight then slowly lower again until your face, chest, and knees are an inch or two from the floor.
- Perform as many controlled repetitions as possible before resting.
- Be very careful not to let your back arch as this will put strain on your back muscles and can cause injury.

FLEXIBILITY/MOBILITY

High levels of flexibility and mobility add to better technique and performance on the pitch and help prevent injury. The sit and reach test is used as a marker to assess and improve a young footballer's hamstring and lower back flexibility.

SIT AND REACH TEST »

You'll need a box measuring 8 to 12 inches high. A shoe box is perfect. Use a ruler to mark out inch-divisions across the top of the box to measure your reach.

- Place the box against a wall with the top of the box facing upward.
- Sit on the floor with the soles of your feet flat against the side of the box.
- Keeping your legs straight and flat on the floor, slowly stretch forward with straight arms and try to reach the box.
- Do this slowly and with control three times then, on the fourth stretch, reach as far as possible and hold for at least three seconds.
- Note the distance you reached using the inch marks on the box. Reach further next time!
- Be aware of the difference in strength between the dominant and nondominant legs. Ideally, you'll be able to hold each leg off the floor for similar times (you're working on strengthening the planted leg). Any significant difference between the two can be worked on by doing extra reps on the weaker leg.

BROAD-JUMPS »

- Stand behind a marked line on the ground with feet slightly apart.
- Raise both arms forward in front of you.
- Swing them back behind you, and at the same time, start to bend your knees. Then, as your arms swing back in front of you, leap forward.
- Jump as far as possible, landing as softly as possible, with knees bent and both feet aligned.
- Your knees should never travel forward ahead of your toes. This causes instability and can cause injury.

CORE STRENGTH/BALANCE

Core muscles provide strength, power, and stability across the full-range of functional movements in football: kicking, jumping, sprinting, and protecting the ball. Developing **CORE STRENGTH** amounts to much more than just endless sit-ups and crunches. The core muscles wrap around your body, in your abdominal area, lower back, and glutes. Plank exercises are excellent ways of improving core strength and stability.

PLANK »

- Lie face-down on the floor. With elbows bent at a 90-degree angle, hands in a fist and shoulder-width apart, on the floor facing forward, lift your body to balance on your arms and toes.
- Your body should be completely level and straight, at roughly shoulder height.
- No sagging or arched back as this puts concentrated strain on other areas.
- Think of the flat shape of a plank of wood.
- Now squeeze your stomach in and tighten while in plank position, keeping your body level.
- Hold this position for as long as you can.
- If you're unable to perform the plank as described, try the beginner's version, which is exactly the same sequence but with arms straight rather than bent at 90 degrees.

FUNCTIONAL PLANK »

- Follow the same guidelines as above.
- Once in the plank position, slowly bend your left knee out beside you and move it up toward your left arm. The moving leg never goes above shoulder height.
- Slowly move back into original plank position then repeat with your right leg moving toward your right arm.
- Repeat on both sides as many times as you can.

SPEED/EXPLOSIVENESS/AGILITY

The main types of speed and explosiveness in football are straight line speed and lateral (side-to-side) speed. **STRAIGHT LINE SPEED** is your ability to get from point A to B as fast as possible. **EXPLOSIVE SPEED** is how quickly you can take off in the first 5 yards of a sprint (explosive speed in football is multi-directional). **AGILITY** is your ability to get from point A to point B moving in multiple directions.

STRAIGHT-LINE SPEED: 30-YARD SPRINT »

- Place two cones 30 yards apart.
- Run from cone 1 to cone 2 as fast as you can.
- When doing sprint work, it's important to rest for 8 times as long as the action has taken (for example, after a 6-second sprint you should rest for 48 seconds before going again).
- Time your sprint or get a friend or parent to time it so you can chart your improvement.

The aim here is train your mind to tell your body to run faster. This will only happen by continually sprinting as fast as you can. As the body becomes used to moving at a speed, it'll then be possible to want to move faster. This will only be effective with the appropriate rest times of 8-to-1. If you don't rest appropriately, you risk the sprints becoming just an endurance drill.

This is counter-productive as your sprints will become slower the more you do. Our purpose is training the mind to recognise, get used to, and then increase the body's maximum speed.

EXPLOSIVE SPEED: 8- OR 10-YARD MULTI-DIRECTIONAL SPRINTS »

- Practice 8- or 10-yard sprints in different directions by placing cones 8 to 10 yards away from you at different angles.
- Start each sprint by getting your body low and gradually raising it toward the end of the sprint.
- Choose a spot in the distance and focus on this point while sprinting.
- Keep your body in line, arms pumping in a straight line faster than your legs (the faster your arms pump the faster your legs will move), and keep your head as still as possible.
- Don't let your arms and head flop side-to-side as this will reduce the efficiency of your explosive movements.

JOIN THE CONVERSATION!
Get the latest advice from your coach and the pros in the **COMPLETE ATHLETE** app!

AGILITY: 5-10-5-5-10 SHUTTLE RUN

- Set up 5 cones or markers, each five yards apart, in a symmetrical shape as below.

Δ

Δ   Δ   Δ

Δ

- Start in the centre and sprint 5 yards to the right cone.
- Then turn and sprint 10 yards to the furthest left cone.
- Sprint 5 yards back to the middle and then 5 yards running backward to the bottom cone.
- Then explode 10 yards through to the top cone.
- Rest for six times longer than it takes you to complete the drill. Then repeat drill with your first sprint going to the left cone.
- When you get close to each cone in turn, try to start getting your body low to prepare it for a change of direction.

ENDURANCE

Endurance is the ability to sustain a high standard of performance until the final whistle or throughout a training session. **ENDURANCE** is a function of your heart/cardiovascular system working to supply your muscles with enough oxygen to keep you running without fatiguing or breaking down. Low levels of endurance will result in lower amounts of oxygen in your blood and an inability to sustain high levels of performance.

The classic test of endurance even for Level 1 players is the Beep Test. It is an endurance test—a series of shuttle runs between markers 20 metres apart, each run starting on a beep. It begins at level 1 and ends at (an impossible!) level 20. There are around 8 to 10 runs per level with the gaps between beeps gradually getting shorter, giving you less time to make it to the 20-metre line before the next beep. For example, level 1 (a walk, really!) has 10 runs and you have 8 seconds to complete each one between beeps. At level 10, you have around 6 seconds between beeps to complete each 20-metre run. If you fail to complete the runs at any level in sync with the beeps, you will have failed that level. Note the last level you completed: that's the level you achieved in the test.

To provide your beeps, you'll need to download a Beep Test application to your phone or tablet. You'll also have to be able to measure, accurately, the 20 metres between lines for the runs.

BEEP TEST >>

- On a non-slip floor surface, place cones or simply mark lines 20 metres apart.
- After you press start on the Beep Test app, the recording will sound a beep for each 20-metre run and then sound a sequence of beeps to advise that you are moving up to the next level and that your speed will need to increase.
- Make sure one foot touches the line before each turn. And do not start to run until the beep has sounded.
- You should stop when you fall short of the 20-metre line 2 beeps in a row.
- Remember to note your last completed level (not the one you failed to complete).

LEVEL-1 PERFORMANCE TESTS

LOWER-BODY STRENGTH »

- Single-leg wall-sit on each leg for 30 seconds.
- Sequence of 4 broad jumps, each at 62 inches or more.
- Single-leg squat on each leg for 30 seconds.

UPPER-BODY STRENGTH »

- Bent-arm pull-up for 15 seconds.
- 30 push-ups in 60 seconds.

FLEXIBILITY/MOBILITY »

- Sit and reach test of at least 1.5 inches.

CORE STRENGTH/BALANCE »

- Static plank for 2 minutes.
- Functional plank for 8 reps on each side.

SPEED/EXPLOSIVENESS/AGILITY »

- 30-yard sprint in 5.3 seconds
- 8-yard multidirectional sprint in 1.5 seconds.
- 5-10-5-5-10 shuttle run in under 6.5 seconds.

BEEP TEST »

Achieve score of level 9.

1

2

3

4

5

1.4 TECHNIQUE

In every sport, including football, there are fundamental **TECHNIQUES** which represent the core skills an athlete must master in order to excel. These basic skills are the foundations on which the highest levels of performance are built.

In football, a **COMPLETE ATHLETE** not only masters the basic and advanced skills needed to thrive on the pitch; he also understands the roles and responsibilities of every position and how all the positions work together to continually improve, perform, and win games as a team unit. Much of that work will come later, but it does no harm for it to be in the back of a player's mind now, as well as being part of a coach's vision. But first things first. The basic skills and techniques of football include:

BALL CONTROL

BALL MASTERY & DRIBBLING

PASSING

SHOOTING

HEADING

AWARENESS

PLAYER » *It's all about you and the ball. Look: football is a team game but it's also an individual game. Every person in a team has to do his job, be in charge of his position. If you can't do that, there'll be someone else* *ready to take your place. That's even more true now when players are focused from very early on playing a particular position. But, if you look back at great teams of the past—Brazil or Holland in the '70s, for example—their players could play anywhere.*

So before we teach a boy how to play a position, we teach him how to play football. Beat a player, take the ball off a player. That's the basics of football. Master those skills. From then on, it's about mentality. Do you think like a striker? Or do you have a defender's instincts?

A good coach will look at his players and recognise their individual qualities and work out where they can best fit in a team. Or, if one player is like a Raheem Sterling or a Gareth Bale, who can beat an opponent on both sides, you don't tie him down in one particular position. You let him have a free role. —Tony Goldring

PARENT » *I don't know what's going on with the youngest players at professional clubs, but I would hope that at that level, like at every other level, they're just being given space to play. When I was a kid, I seem to remember coaches just left us to it. But coaching's an industry now, isn't it? I just hope that doesn't mean kids, at those youngest ages, get over-coached.*

For example, I wouldn't want 6 and 7 year olds to be playing one- and two-touch. It's taking so much creativity out of the game at that age. Yes, to play one-touch you have to have your head up and see things, and there's creativity in that. But what about dribbling or trying tricks? One- and two-touch is taking those things out of the game. —Paul Davis

COACH >> *Our first phase, the Foundation phase, is ages 5 to 11 but, of course, we tend to break that down. So much happens during those years. The fundamental thing, early on, is that coaches and parents create an environment in which kids can have fun, get engaged, and try new things. Experiment with no constraints put on them.*

The key things, physically, are around the ABCs: agility, balance and co-ordination. Those things aren't football specific at the youngest ages: coaches should be able to use other sports, other balls, whatever helps to develop those core physical skills. Technically, it's about mastering the ball. You hear coaches on touchlines saying, 'Pass! Pass! Pass!' But those youngest players should be left to keep the ball. Let them decide when to pass. That'll come as they get older. —John Folwell

BALL CONTROL

- First and second touches
- Controlling with all surfaces of the foot
- Direction of touch
- On the ground
- Bouncing
- On the full
- Controlling under pressure

TECHNICAL TIPS »

- Lower your body and bend your knees slightly to encourage a soft and precise first touch.
- Do not lunge and stretch onto the ball as this will inhibit balance and quality of touch. Invite the ball onto your foot (or any other part of your body) rather than meeting it with a stiff approach.
- Always try and get your body behind the ball. This will help you protect the ball, stay balanced, and keep your body in line within the width of your hips.
- When making contact with the ball, don't have your foot raised too high or it will connect with the top of the ball, pushing it into the ground. Don't have your foot too low, either, or it will connect underneath the ball and lift it into the air without you controlling it.

BALL MASTERY/DRIBBLING

- Try keeping the ball within 5 inches of your foot as you move with it. This will allow you to change direction quickly in tight spaces without surrendering control.
- Try dribbling with the ball at different speeds. Draw in your opponent then beat him!
- Dribble with your head up, if you can, so you can see what else is going on around you.
- When you have the ball under control, try to manipulate it by touching it with all the different areas of your foot.

TECHNICAL TIPS >>

- Close control is paramount when you need to change direction quickly, under pressure, or in a tight situation. Remember that 5-inch rule!
- Vary the speed and direction of your dribbling. This breaks up your opponent's stride pattern and undermines his balance. Those are the weaknesses you can capitalise on to beat him.
- Try and be aware of where you're taking the ball in order not to lose it and in order to use your skills most productively.
- Running too quickly with the ball can sometimes mean you lose control of it. Focus on control first and build up your running speed as you develop.
- Dribbling with your head down can take you into a crowd of opponents or even off the pitch altogether!

TECHNIQUES TO MASTER »

- Cruyff turns
- Drag backs
- Drag back and push
- Step overs
- Snakes
- Touch, fake step, and push
- Touch roll, drag, step over, and push
- Triple-pace, multi-directional dribbling

PASSING

- Inside foot pass
- Driven pass, high and low
- Curved pass, high and low
- Half-volley pass, inside foot, high and low
- Half-volley pass, driven with laces, low
- Volley pass, high and low

INSIDE FOOT PASS

- Try to make a good, clean, firm connection with the soft instep of the foot with your hips guided toward the target.
- For a low pass, keep your follow-through low. To play a pass through the air, raise your foot on your follow-through.
- To keep the pass controlled, try to strike the ball with the soft instep so it doesn't clip your heel or your toe.

1

2

3

4

5

DRIVEN PASS

- Connect with laces tight against the ball. Short, punched follow-through with your hips facing the target.
- If you chop underneath the ball, you'll find it slices off in another direction than the one you intended.

CURVED PASS

- Connect with the ball using the inside of your foot on the outside of the ball. Shape your follow-through to describe the shape you want the ball to make as it travels.
- Always lift your follow-through to lift the ball off the ground. Keep your follow-through low if you want your pass to travel along the ground.
- Twisting your hips too sharply will make your follow through take the pass beyond your target.

HALF-VOLLEY PASS

- Connect with the ball when it's just off the ground, within 2 inches of it bouncing, to give yourself maximum control over the pass.
- If you mis-time the connection and the ball is too far off the ground when you strike it, you'll hit underneath the ball and the pass will either slice or go too high.

VOLLEY PASS

- Get your body over the ball and connect in the middle of the ball, your laces guiding it downward to keep the pass controlled. Standing foot and hips should be pointed toward the intended target.

- Let the ball come onto your foot. If you connect too early, you'll hit the bottom of the ball and slice it. If you connect too late and strike the top of the ball, you'll push it into the ground instead of towards the intended target.

SHOOTING

- Inside foot
- Laces strike
- Curve
- Volley
- Half volley
- Knuckle ball

INSIDE FOOT

- Body behind the ball and make a good strong connection with the inside of the foot. Transfer your weight through the ball with your hips angled toward the corner of the goal.
- Over-rotating your hips will tend to guide your shot toward the centre of the goal instead of the corner.

LACES STRIKE

- First point of contact with the ball should be your laces right against the centre of the ball. Keep your follow-through below knee height and guide it toward your target.
- If the ball's first point of contact is the front of your foot and not your laces, this will mean you don't get a clean strike away, and the ball will usually rise over the crossbar.

CURVE

- Similar to the curve pass, for a curve shot you need to connect on the outside of the ball with the inside of your foot. Shape your follow-through to describe the same shape you want your shot to make on its way to the target.

VOLLEY

- If possible, let the ball drop to knee height before striking it and connect with laces tight against the centre of the ball. Follow through on a high-to-low arc to keep the shot under control.
- Connecting underneath the ball—as you often do if the ball doesn't drop to knee height or below—will mean your shot flies up over the bar.

HALF-VOLLEY

- As with the half-volley pass, it helps to strike the ball when it's as near to the ground as possible to ensure a clean, controlled connection.
- Allowing the ball to rise more than a couple of inches before striking it makes the shot much more difficult to keep low and on target.

KNUCKLE BALL

- When connecting with the ball for this kind of shot, make contact with the 'knuckle' of your foot striking the lower part of the ball. Aim for the least possible amount of follow-through as you punch the ball towards goal, keeping the connecting foot flat and straight. (The intention is to make the ball move

laterally in the air and dip without warning by striking it with an uneven part of the foot, the 'knuckle.')
• The trick is to connect with the 'knuckle' of your foot. Striking with the inside of the foot will not give the ball swerve and dip in the same way.

NOTE >> It's very important not to spend too much time on heading repetitions at the age of Level 1 players. There are health and safety and developmental issues that need to be respected as regards young footballers and frequent heading of the ball. Any heading drills, therefore, should be condensed so that players are only heading short distances. The focus should be on timing and point of contact rather than power and distance.

HEADING

INTRODUCTION TO AGE APPROPRIATE HEADING TECHNIQUE >>

• Cushioned pass headers
• Heading at goal
• Defensive clearance headers

CUSHIONED PASS HEADER

• As you approach the ball (or the ball approaches you), try to keep your eye on it and concentrate on making contact with your forehead. This will help you to avoid mis-timing connection and making connection with the top of your head.
• Don't follow through with too much momentum. The intention is to cushion the ball in the direction of the intended area or target.

HEADING AT GOAL

- When moving toward the ball with the intention of heading it, it's important to arrive at the point of contact with some momentum if possible.
- Always keep your eye on the ball. Use your neck muscles as your forehead connects with the ball to push the ball downward, toward the corners of the goal.
- Try to keep your eyes on the ball as you travel toward it. This gives you the best chance of connecting with your forehead rather than the top of your head, which would result in the ball bouncing upwards and over the bar.

DEFENSIVE CLEARANCE HEADER

- Try and get a run up toward the ball to generate some momentum.
- Keep your eyes focused on the ball at all times and lift one arm in front of you to protect your face.
- Try to generate power from the waist and spine, putting your whole body weight through the ball when connecting. This will guide the ball upward and away from you.
- Practice the timing and control of your jumps. Try to make sure you don't close your eyes. This is very important if you're going to avoid the ball hitting either the bridge of your nose or the top of your head.

PLAYER >> *Andros is a very determined young man. He was a very determined boy, too. I ask young players if they love the game, and it's easy for them to use the word 'love' and say, 'Yes'. But what does that mean? I was a coach so there were always balls around our house. We lived backing onto Arsenal's academy, and Andros used to grab a bag of balls, climb over the fence, and disappear for a couple of hours.*

He'd be there on his own, smashing balls into the goal. I'd go out with him sometimes, get him to work on his right foot. But it was Andros himself who'd developed this dedication by the time he was 11 or 12 years old. He wanted to be the best he could be. It wasn't just training and getting stuff from other people. It was all his spare time, too. That's where you saw a real love for the game. Everything was about football. Just repetition, on his own, until he'd mastered it. He got to know the ball.

—Troy Townsend

COACH » *With the very youngest goalkeepers, 6 or 7 years old, I just want to see them working on the basics, like everybody else: controlling the ball, passing the ball, heading the ball. For goalkeepers, you start by working on the four hand shapes you can use for catching the ball: W-shape, cups, hands leading, and scoops.*

So, let's throw the ball in to practice catching with each of those. You dropped six out of 10? Well, next time we'll work on it again and only drop three. Once that's mastered, instead of throwing the ball, we'll kick the ball. Then volley it, then kick it on the full. It's about setting targets for every training session. And I'll try and show him where that skill can be important in a game. Those very early years, 6 years and older, are vital for developing the motor skills you'll need later on. Can you catch the ball? Control the ball? Kick the ball? Those are the basics. We can work on the technical side, decision-making and so on, later on. —Tony Roberts

JOIN THE CONVERSATION!

For more stories and conversations with athletes and coaches, download the **COMPLETE ATHLETE** app!

1.5 LIFESTYLE

The more a young player is enjoying his football —looking forward to every training session, every match and every kick-about with his friends—the more quickly his game will improve. He'll become stronger and fitter. He'll begin to master fundamental technical skills and start putting them into action during games. He'll begin to challenge himself as a player and, in doing so, the demands football makes on his time will increase.

It's important, at this stage, that the young player—and, crucially, his parents—understand the importance of balancing his passion for football with other elements of his development as a boy.

He will still need to commit energy and attention to his school work, to having time with his family away from football, to his hobbies and other activities, and to the enjoyment of a broad social life. A happy and fulfilling childhood will require some time management on his part and some clear guidance on priorities from his parents.

A **COMPLETE ATHLETE** not only excels as a footballer, he also commits to being the best he can be in other areas of his life:

FAMILY

SCHOOLWORK

SOCIAL LIFE

ROLE MODEL

LIVING YOUR SPORT

FAMILY

PARENT ❯❯ *I had applied for a job at Southampton's Academy and got it. At the time, Alexander wasn't really involved in any organised football. He was playing at school, enjoying football and other sports.*

So, after a few weeks on the job, I'd taken a look at the Under-9s and Under-11s and I thought to myself, 'Alexander's as good as these'. He came in for a trial and, after a week or so, they decided to take him. He joined the Under-9s. He was so keen to do it: we couldn't have held him back. That was his first connection with professional football.

For a boy, it's great: you get school—the hard part of your life!—out of the way and then you're off to training. It's football. It's fun. For parents, it can be quite a commitment, though. It was easier for us because I was actually working at Southampton at the time. But for most, it'd mean doing a day's work and then getting them to and from training and games. Quite a bit of driving as well as everything else! —Mark Chamberlain

Parents have a huge part to play in the lives of their children. This is particularly true if a son has taken the first steps on his journey to becoming a footballer. Even at Level 1, parents will need to be ready to fulfil a number of roles:

- Taxi-driver: getting your son to and from games
- Financier: paying for boots, kit, team fees, proper nutrition, and more
- Support staff: taking time out of your own schedule to attend training sessions, games, and tournaments

It's perfectly natural for a young footballer to feel the game is the most important thing in his life and therefore that it's the most important thing in everybody else's life, too. His hunger and enthusiasm mean he'll often take for granted that parents and guardians drop everything to accommodate his football activities.

It'll be up to you to remind him that people have other commitments and responsibilities, too: work, paying the bills, the demands of other sons and daughters, caring for elderly relatives, involvement in community activities, and attending to their own personal needs.

Of course, helping their children to realise a cherished dream is one of life's great satisfactions for a parent. Time around football can play a uniquely positive role in developing and sustaining your relationship with your son. The time and effort you'll need to put in to supporting him as a young player may sometimes make the whole business feel like a chore.

And other life pressures can make it very difficult indeed to do as much as you'd like to. Even so, every parent knows that being with your son on his football journey is also a pleasure and a privilege.

That said, it's important for parents to make sure that their son is aware of and appreciates the sacrifices dedicated parents (and volunteer coaches and others) make to support them as they move up through the levels toward becoming a **COMPLETE ATHLETE**. This isn't just something a boy needs to pay lip service to—it's an attitude that needs to be demonstrated by the role he plays in the life of his family. Behaving like the centre of attention is a bad habit that needs to be broken as early as possible. Your son needs to help his family as well as be conscious of how much you're helping him.

PLAYER » Do you behave like you're the centre of attention? Like the whole world revolves around you? Think about your parents: do they get stressed out because you suddenly realise you've got a game, and they have to drop everything to get you there? Think about your brothers or sisters: do they have to change their plans or cancel something because you've just re-membered you have a special training session you have to be at?

If this kind of stuff happens more than very occasionally, you need to stop and open your eyes to what's going on. You need to think a bit more often about the rest of your family. You need to remember that Mum and Dad, your brothers and sisters, have got lives of their own to get on with. You're part of the family, not always the whole point of the family!

It really helps if you can think ahead, discuss plans, and take some responsibility: maybe there'll be a Sunday when you can get a lift to and from training with your team-mate's dad so your parents can both be at your sister's dance show for once.

LOOK FOR WAYS YOU CAN HELP YOUR PARENTS AND SIBLINGS WHENEVER YOU CAN.

Your parents devote an enormous amount of time to taking you to and from games and training, making sac-rifices to buy you what you need, watching you play, and cheering you on. When they get home, they may have other responsibilities waiting: cooking you healthy meals, cleaning the house, doing the laundry, helping with homework, and lots more.

You have to think about being a part of a team at football. You can think about being part of a team at home, too: take on a few chores like making your bed, cleaning your room, or doing the washing up. Not only will you be taking a bit of pressure off your parents' shoulders, those are the kinds of things that will let them know you're grateful for what they do for you. And that you respect their lives as well as your own.

PARENT >> As a parent of a Level 1 player, it's vital to set the best kind of example: how to organise and plan; how to consider others, and how to take on responsibility. Those aren't just skills that will help him make a mark as a footballer, they'll be vital life skills as he grows up to become a young man.

The night before a game or in the morning before training: teach him how to pack his bag, have his kit tidy and ready to put on, and his boots clean. It can become part of his routine to check that he's got food packed and waiting to go in the fridge along with a bottle of water so he can put them in his bag just before leaving home. If nothing else, helping your son to think ahead—and for himself—will ensure he's completely focused when it comes to the training session or the game. Most boys will thrive on the challenge of responsibility. The earlier these things can become routine, the sooner he'll start to feel the benefit of a structure in his journey toward becoming a **COMPLETE ATHLETE**.

Maybe it's a generational thing. We have some boys come to us whose parents are hoping we can put discipline into them. Social and economic pressures make them feel as if they can't always do that for themselves in the way they'd like to. The culture nowadays is that Mum and Dad are more like friends than parents to their children! Boys need to learn about risk—to learn about getting knocked down and getting back up again. But they're held back from that.

Home environment is very important. Support from parents is very important. Often it's a practical thing: we have a young boy here who's a real prospect. Chelsea wanted him to come to their academy. But his older brother, who's not got the same good attitude to learning, was already at Crystal Palace. So Mum decided that the younger boy needed to go there, too: she couldn't be in two places at once. But then, later, Palace released the older brother anyway. What should she have done in that situation?

I know about this from my own life. When I moved up to secondary school, I played for the school team. Played a year up, in fact. I was small, but they could see I had that fighting spirit. One of the teachers, Mr Hodder, had a connection with Southampton and said he could fix up a trial there.

But I spoke to my mum: she was on her own, had to work to put food on the table for me and my three brothers. How could she give me the support? Another boy from my year, whose family were in a position to support him, was able to take up the opportunity, and he went on to play for Manchester United and England: Danny Wallace.

There has to be a parent, or somebody in the family, who can make the sacrifice to take a boy to a club four times a week. But what if both parents have to be working? What if it's a single parent? A boy can't make it through on his own. And remember: there's no guarantee at the end of it that he'll make it as a player, even after 10 years being at a club. —Tony Goldring

JOIN THE CONVERSATION!

Live your sport and join the **COMPLETE ATHLETE** community of athletes, parents, and coaches by downloading the app today!

SCHOOLWORK

Many young footballers—and many parents, for that matter—imagine that, if a boy's making progress at elite football level, his education and grades don't matter. Nothing could be further from the truth.

The chances of a boy who shows promise at Level 1 going on to have a career as a professional footballer at a top club are very small indeed. Making a living from football in the Football League or further down the pyramid is only a slightly more realistic prospect.

FOR THE VAST MAJORITY, playing football will become something they do alongside a career rather than it becoming a profession in its own right. That's the reality and it shouldn't, for a moment, spoil or undermine the journey, whatever the eventual destination in football might be. It should, though, make you and your son pause for thought: who says education and grades aren't going to matter just as much as they do for everyone else? Even at the very top end of the game, football's a short career and involves decision-making skills and business acumen if a player's going to get the most out of his years in the profession.

PLAYER >> Just as not everyone is going to make it as a professional footballer, not everyone's going to leave school with a bag full of A+ grades on their exams. The challenge is to get as far as you can: a young player will practice and take a positive attitude at all times in regards to football. He needs to do the same when it comes to school. His future prospects depend on it, one way or another. Progress in football is all about developing good habits. The same goes for schoolwork and there are simple strategies that can help you get the exam results you deserve.

HAND IN HOMEWORK ON TIME. Most teachers make a mark against you for handing in homework late. You'd never want to be late for training or kick-off, would you?

BE ORGANISED. Having all your books and work organised before school and once you get home will help you get the most out of the school day and get work done on time. You wouldn't turn up for training without boots and your kit, would you?

PAY CLOSE ATTENTION IN CLASS. In training, you focus completely on what your coach has to say. In lessons, you need to have the same attitude toward your teacher: listen to what he or she is saying. Take good notes and follow instructions.

STUDY A LITTLE BIT EVERY DAY. Just as consistently practicing your technical skills will help you perform better as a player, regular study and revision will develop your brain's ability to retain and process information.

ASK QUESTIONS. Remember, like your coaches, your teachers want you to succeed. If you're unsure about anything or are struggling with a particular subject or a particular bit of homework, don't hesitate to ask for help. It's what teachers are there for!

DON'T LEAVE STUDYING UNTIL THE LAST MINUTE. So much of football is about being in the right place at the right time in order to perform at your best. Make sure you're always ready in regards to your schoolwork, as well. Plan ahead. Set yourself a schedule. Don't rush it all at the last minute!

BEHAVE APPROPRIATELY IN CLASS. Every school has different rules, and they have those rules for a reason. Make sure you abide by the school's and individual teacher's codes of conduct. Progress in football will depend on knowing how to make a good impression off the field as well as on it.

PARENT » *There's a lot going on in a young boy's life, in football and outside it. We always focused on the boys doing their best at school along with everything else. One thing that was easy for me was that, because Alexander needed to grow, he'd eat anything I put in front of him: broccoli, spinach, whatever.*

I'd tell him it was all about putting the right fuel in his body. But it's tough mentally, staying strong.

Later, at 15, Southampton was going to release Alexander. They said he wasn't good enough, wasn't effective in games. Mark had to really put his foot down: he knew

they weren't seeing the wood for the trees. And then he was playing for the first team by the time he was 16.

All of that was going on while I was nagging him about his GCSEs and insisting that nothing was going to happen with football unless he studied hard and got the grades he knew he was capable of. Mark was telling him he had to do his best in every game and not go off partying.

We knew he was under pressure. But we also knew that, if he could cope with that pressure, he'd also be able to cope with any pressure that came later. I knew he was bright and could do well academically. Mark was convinced he could have a career. We both said, 'You're good enough. But it's all up to you.' And Alexander responded to that really, really well. —Wendie Oxlade-Chamberlain

SOCIAL LIFE

A rich and interesting **SOCIAL LIFE** can be really important —a huge plus, a great resource for all young people, not just young athletes—as friends give honest advice to one another and help to ease anxiety in times of stress and worry. Young people who are not encouraged to express themselves socially and who don't form good friendships will tend to feel lonely and be less confident as a result.

Both in a football context and in the rest of his life, these are things that can hold a boy back, hamper achievement and result in damaged self-esteem. Making friends and learning about yourself aren't things that only happen around football. It's very healthy to try to maintain a social life away from football, in fact. And strength of character developed in those other environments will make a real contribution to a boy's development as a footballer as well.

PARENT » *It was a conscious decision not to focus in too completely on football. We let the boys try other sports: cricket, tennis, athletics, rugby, anything they showed any interest in. There was so much for them to learn from those other sports: balance, co-ordination, agility, proprioception. It was good for them to mix with different kinds of people, too, so the conversation wasn't always just about football. We wanted them to feel comfortable in all those different environments.*

As well, there are so many ways for boys to be sat still on computers or PlayStation these days. We wanted them to be active, out in the fresh air. We let them try all those different sports until they got to an age where they needed to decide which one they were going to focus on.

I think even now, though, Alex misses playing cricket.

They both do. They follow tennis and rugby: they really engaged with those sports when they were still at school. —Wendie Oxlade-Chamberlain

PLAYER » When you start to make close friends, it's important to treat them with respect and in a way that they feel valued. Strong and long-lasting friendships are a fantastic part of anyone's life. They can be even more important as a boy focuses on a career in football. Remember that friendships made outside football may prove as rewarding as those made with your team-mates in the long run.

And there are things you can do to make sure that your friendships matter and that you'll always have mates you can trust at your side:

- Be considerate of your friends' time and treating their time as being as important as your own. Don't be the one who's always late or cancelling arrangements at the last minute.
- Be there for a team-mate when he's going through a hard time. Pick him up when he is down as well as share the good times together.
- Make sure you don't say or do anything to embarrass your friends in public or in social situations.
- Be loyal to your friends and never talk negatively to others about them behind their backs.

ROLE MODEL

A **ROLE MODEL** is someone who possesses presence and qualities that others admire. He'll possess a strong value system and a standard of behaviour that others feel ready to emulate.

A role model has what we can call leadership qualities. Being a good role model—being ready to take on the responsibilities that come with leadership, demonstrating respect for yourself and others—are qualities that always attract the right sort of attention. Other players want to line up alongside you. A coach wants you on his team sheet. And, one day, an academy director or a top manager might want to recruit you to his club.

Role models demonstrate respect for others and for themselves. You are never too young to start developing and displaying the traits that mark you out as a role model, on the pitch and off it:

- Listen carefully, looking people in the eye when they're speaking and don't interrupt them.
- Address people by their names and greet them with a firm hand shake.
- Learn to value other people's opinions. There's always something to learn.
- Let team-mates know they're appreciated and valued, as players and as people.
- Make a point of never insulting people, making fun of them, or talking about them behind their backs.

PLAYER » *Leadership qualities begin with thinking for yourself, making your own decisions. You can be on your own but you're still a leader. I made my own mistakes when I was young, and they happened because I went along with other people, gave in to peer pressure. Right or wrong, you have to do what your own spirit, your own instinct tells you, not what someone else says you should do.*

If you follow your own instinct, then you will be responsible for your own actions. If you're in an environment—football or any other—where there are people with those leadership qualities, you will pick up those qualities for yourself. Those environments are always disciplined, structured environments: at Afawee, we're always getting older boys to play back a year or two to see if they can be leaders for the younger players: Show us who you really are. And those qualities will be passed on to the rest of the group. —Tony Goldring

JOIN THE CONVERSATION!
Be a team player—join your team-mates in the **COMPLETE ATHLETE** app today!

LIVING YOUR SPORT

Young footballers who are serious about being recruited by an academy, earning an academy scholarship, and, ultimately, being rewarded with a professional contract are willing to take on the challenge to do everything they possibly can to achieve their goals. They will fully commit to training more, doing extra fitness or strength work, and spending more time practicing their skills outside scheduled sessions. They'll watch as much football as they can, talk about the game constantly, and learn from whoever they can. They'll develop a culture of always doing more than is asked of them, doing whatever it takes for them to improve. **THEY LIVE FOR FOOTBALL**.

To live your sport, you'll first learn to love it. That's what the experience of the Level 1 player's all about. It's a time to enjoy football so much you can't imagine life without the game: learning skills and developing a positive attitude which will be the tools you'll need on the journey to becoming a **COMPLETE ATHLETE**.

PLAYER » *I first played in goal when I was stuck there in a match between classes at primary school. Saved a penalty and had everyone jumping all over me, saying 'well done!' And I thought to myself, 'This is good. I like this!' I played local football on Anglesey and ended up at Holyhead United Juniors.*

By the time I was 14, though, I was already playing men's football. I was tall and skinny. Easy games, they'd let me play out on the pitch. Harder ones, I'd be back in goal. As well as football, I played basketball. I played for the County. I played table tennis. Back then, there were no mobile phones, no computers. It was just up the youth club and I'd play any sport going!

That was my pathway: after school, until it got dark, and all day every day during the holidays. Playing football, doing sport. That was all I wanted to do.

They say you have to spend 10,000 hours on your game, but a lot of the skills I needed for goalkeeping— hand-eye coordination, movement, footwork—I was practising when I was playing other sports. The other big thing for me was playing men's football when I was still a boy: you learn the toughness, getting slaughtered for your mistakes, standing up for yourself, facing the physical and mental challenges.

Boys against boys, it's all so quiet in a dressing room! They're not getting challenged in the same way. I was desperate to be a footballer. I got into the Welsh youth teams: the only boy from Anglesey. And I was constantly writing off to clubs, asking for trials. Football was my passion. Nobody had to tell me to write those letters! I always had that drive in me. That and a hatred of losing. —Tony Roberts

PARENT >> *When a boy first wants to join a grassroots club, perhaps the most important thing to remember is that football is something he'll want to do with his friends. Will he have friends at a club or be able to make friends? At those early ages that's more import- ant than parents ferrying children around looking for the 'best' club; 'best' in terms of being successful and winning things.*

When it comes to choosing a club, it's worth asking about their philosophy and about how they measure success. Is it still about enjoyment and developing the individual or is it about winning any way they can? Is the club investing in its staff?

Are volunteers being trained up? Are coaches doing youth module qualifications to ensure they understand what kids need at different stages of their development?

What's the environment like? Are they embracing the 'Respect' programme? Are they developing 'young leaders', getting boys from their older age groups to come and help out with the younger ones? Are players training with a smile on their faces? —*John Folwell*

COACH >> *I see a boy get knocked over during a game and I want to see how he reacts. Does he shrink or does he go back into the game ready to be strong, bringing even more energy into what he's doing? People ask what Afawee is about. I tell them that it's a way of life, taking boys out of darkness and into light. We seek to empower the next generation. We teach boys how to play football. We teach boxing, too.*

But I always say to the boys, 'Coming here, even if you don't make a success of playing football, we're trying to make sure you can make a success of your life.'

You can move amongst the worst people around and in the worst situations but you know how to conduct yourself. You don't interfere with other people. You respect other people. But you stand on your own two feet. Don't let anyone take liberties. You're strong enough to survive in any environment. You work hard and you focus.

We're teaching football lessons. But these are life lessons, too. We have boys who've not made it as players but their experience here has helped them to go out and start businesses, work with young people, or even become football coaches themselves.

—*Steadman Scott*

IN LEVEL 2

Over the course of Level 2, as a young footballer approaches adolescence, he will start to develop his own distinct and recognisable personality, both on and off the pitch. As he continues to master the fundamental ball skills and techniques, he will become aware of the strengths and weaknesses in his game.

He'll begin to have an idea as to what he'll need to work hardest on to improve and to develop into a **COMPLETE ATHLETE**. He'll also become increasingly aware of the ways in which his life away from the sport can affect his involvement with football, recognising that attitude, preparation and lifestyle are key elements in continuing his progress as a player.

Stepping up to Level 2, boys will find greater demands are made of them physically, technically, and tactically due to now playing on a bigger 9 v 9 pitch, with more players in both their own team and the opposition's. There are challenges to be faced, some obvious and some less so, which mean Level 2 players will need the support, guidance, and encouragement of parents and coaches as they seek to move forwards on the journey to reaching their full potential.

It's a good change, I think, that's come into youth football: the size of pitch and number of players have been adapted to the different age groups. I can still remember when you'd see 8-year-old kids on full-sized pitches, some of them hardly ever getting a touch of the ball. As players get bigger, the pitches need to get bigger and the numbers in each team needs to grow, too. Moving up to 9-a-side on a bigger pitch, there's more space to play. More players with more space to play on the pitch means new strategies, more decisions to be made, and more ground to cover. The game starts to change.

Formations become important, and players have to start concentrating more on working with other members of their team. You can start feeding in information, first at 7 v 7 and then, even more, when they're playing 9 v 9. You can start pointing towards things that need thinking about when teams are set up in formations, a little bit of guidance about football being a team game. Structure becomes more important although, hopefully, not at the expense of players' creativity.

Winning and losing have to be managed, as well. Wanting to win is just something that's in all of us, from the earliest age. It's natural, and I don't think we should try and take it away. Winning matters even to the youngest players.

But the challenge is to help young players handle it. You send them out wanting to win but what if they lose? How do you restore their balance? You have to talk about why it happened, perhaps. Suggest ideas. Lift their spirits again. But winning all the time isn't ideal either. If that's happening to my team, much as I might want to see them win, I'd be trying to find a way to challenge them, getting them games against better teams. Because it's losing that often teaches us the most. And learning how to handle getting beaten is an important part of learning the game. —Paul Davis

It's not always simple: he'll make it, he won't. Young players at any age can surprise you. You find yourself thinking, 'Wow! I didn't know he had that in him.' And players can also lose their way and disappoint you. Even boys you thought were 'dead certs'. It can be any number of things: wrong attitude, parents being involved in the wrong way, or a player not enjoying football anymore. Falling out of love with the game.

You have to remember it's not just about ability. As they get older, the physical demands get greater: more ground to cover, being outmuscled by bigger, stronger players. Not getting as many touches of the ball in a game. At that age, too, they're not used to disappointment. You don't always win. You don't always get picked to play. As players develop, they need character and spirit—mental toughness—as well. —Tony Carr

JOIN THE CONVERSATION!

Read more from special contributors in the **COMPLETE ATHLETE** app!

A NOTE ON MATURITY

At Level 2, young footballers begin to be aware of the differences in skill levels amongst individuals in the group. Some players begin to develop high expectations of themselves as well as of their team-mates. Often it'll be the players who've put in the most work in terms of extra training, studying the game, and attention to preparation who will perform at the highest standard.

Young players may be aware of differences in physical attributes amongst the group, too. Some boys who train regularly and are just as committed to their work may not see the benefits immediately. At this age, individual players are already maturing at very different rates, mentally as well as physically. Those differences can have a huge impact on how quickly a boy progresses in terms of coordination, physical strength, speed, decision-making, confidence, self-belief and resilience. Player One is an 11-year-old who is maturing quickly and has the mental and physical maturity of a 12- or 13-year-old.

On the other hand, Player Two, who's also 11, is maturing much more slowly and has physical and psychological attributes common in a 9- or 10-year-old.

Here are two boys, roughly the same age and playing in the same team, but who are at totally different levels when it comes to their mental and physical maturity. At this point, Player One appears to be the star performer while Player Two is lagging behind. Players, coaches, and parents all need to remember that circumstances can change as boys develop.

Player One's obvious advantages will wear off eventually. If Player Two, at a disadvantage right now, continues to believe in himself and work hard at his game, he may be the one who, at 18, earns a professional contract. He will need to learn patience and resilience along the way and will benefit from the support of parents, coaches, and team-mates.

Player One, meanwhile, may be bigger and more mature than some of his team-mates and some of his opponents at the moment but that won't always be the case going forward. With this in mind, it's important he continues to challenge himself technically and tactically and doesn't allow his physical advantages to give him a free ride at this stage. He must continue to develop as a player—standing still will mean going backwards. The role of the coach is crucial here for obvious reasons.

COACH » *Of course football's a team game, but early on, I think coaching needs to be focused on the individual player. A coach needs to be aware of where a boy's at with his physical and technical development. But, as well, he needs to be aware of psychological issues. If a boy is shy, how can we use football to draw him out? He needs to be aware of social issues, too. If a boy's new to the area, how can we use football to help him build a circle of friends?*

I've seen teams who've worked out a way to win games: little Johnny, who's quick, goes up front; a boy who's not great outfield gets stuck in goal and does OK; and the biggest boy gets played at centre half. That works to make a successful team, and they win games, but what's the cost of that? Three or four years down the line, those individual players haven't developed at all. They've stood still—they have not tried different positions, not been challenged in different ways.

They've just got good at doing the same one thing they've always done. Players who've developed holistically might not win everything at first, but, as they grow older, you'll see them start to perform.

There's the challenge, too, of age bias: boys born between September and December tend to be bigger, quicker and stronger than boys in the same school year who were born from January onwards. Those bigger boys are the 'talent that shouts'. You can see them being effective in games because they have those advantages. I'm not sure what we can do to alter the situation but we can try to get coaches to be aware that the late developers are there and they're worth waiting for. The later-born will just need some extra time to deal with the physicality of the game. The physicality is the real issue: technically, socially and psychologically, there's every chance those smaller boys are just as good. And those smaller boys who have to find ways to cope with that physical disadvantage will often turn out to be better players because of it. —John Folwell

PLAYER >> *Football's a great sport. It's also a dream, an aspiration. Talk to a young kid and ask what he wants to be when he's older, the chances are he'll say: A footballer. And if he's got a little talent and people start recognising that, the idea of 'becoming a footballer' can start very quickly to put pressure on him. He'll get asked about it all the time. For him, 'being a footballer' means being a professional footballer, making a living doing it.*

Most boys, probably, know deep down whether they're good enough or not. They can work it out for themselves. But it's important to keep them all involved. You never know: the one who breaks through as a teenager might not be the one everybody thought was going to make it when he was young. —Paul Davis

2.1 ATTITUDE

A **POSITIVE ATTITUDE** is essential to a player's success on and off the pitch, especially if he is hoping to progress to the higher levels of elite football in the future. From Level 2 onwards, a boy's mentality is one of the qualities scouts and coaches will be examining closely when it comes to making decisions about whether or not to recruit a player.

A positive attitude isn't something that can be plucked out of thin air but, once you've recognised it as important, it can be developed and strengthened with practice, just like athletic and technical skills. It's a case of training your brain.

At Level 2, a player will encounter new challenges, both in training and in match situations. 9 v 9 football demands a step up from a young player—physically, technically, and tactically. That step up needs to be accompanied by the development of a strong mentality, a positive attitude which will see the player demonstrating the following five attributes:

RESPECT

SPORTSMANSHIP

TEAMWORK

PROFESSIONALISM

LEADERSHIP

RESPECT

RESPECT means treating other people in ways which show you recognise their worth and value. At Level 1, young footballers should always be reminded to treat their coaches with respect. That does not change at Level 2. Or at any other Level, for that matter. A **COMPLETE ATHLETE** always shows respect toward his coaches.

At Level 2, it becomes more and more important for young players to learn to make a habit of respecting their team-mates, too. As football moves onto bigger pitches and begins to involve more players, a new team dynamic emerges. You become more reliant on your team-mates to achieve the success you're all after. The key, of course, is to treat other people in the way you'd want them to treat you. Respect them and there's every chance you'll get their respect back in return.

- Address your team-mates with the name they want you to use, rather than a nick name you find funny.
- Listen carefully when a team-mate is talking to you (remember respect means showing you value what they say and do).
- Do not insult team-mates or opponents or talk about them behind their backs (and remember today's opponent may well become a team-mate somewhere down the line).
- Be positive and supportive when others make mistakes (remember they'll be feeling bad enough without you making fun of them or getting angry).
- Let your team-mates know they're appreciated on and off the pitch (taking anyone for granted amounts to disrespect).

At 12, you'd hope that boys have developed an understanding of the game. What do we do in possession? What do we do out of possession? Do you have experience of playing different positions? If you prefer playing centre back, the experience of playing centre forward will help you really understand how to play in the position you prefer.

It's only at Under-13 that boys will start playing 11 v 11 and start developing to play in a particular position. Socially, you want players to be able to communicate: give feedback to their coach, to support their team-mates. How can you build resilience in your team when things are going wrong? How do you bounce back after conceding a goal?

We know a lot of coaches focus on the physical and technical aspects of the game: two of the 'four corners'. Those are the obvious bits, I suppose. The bits you can see. But the social and psychological aspects of the game are the ones that will be crucial in the end.

We all know boys who were fast, skilful, powerful, but didn't make the grade because they weren't able to deal with the social and psychological elements: the demands that were placed on them as individuals, like their resilience and decision-making, and the demands that were made of them as members of a group, like their communication skills and their willingness to support team-mates. —John Folwell

SPORTSMANSHIP

Good **SPORTSMANSHIP** starts with respect for your team-mates, opponents, coaches, and match officials. Every player at Level 2 should understand the fundamentals of the Laws of the Game. Every player should be committed to abiding by those laws and inspired to do so by coaches' and parents' examples. Sportsmanship is about knowing what's right and doing it in even the most challenging or competitive of environments. If players can grasp that at Level 2, they'll be sure to take the principle of sportsmanship on into the rest of their careers.

Sportsmanship doesn't just show when you're lined up against opponents. Every player will benefit from learning that it's also important you treat your team-mates with the respect they deserve no matter their size, strength, or skill level. It'll be true of every team you ever play for: you're in this together.

- Never make fun of a team-mate in a way that personally insults them.
- Do not talk about team-mates behind their backs. If you have something to say, have the courage to say it face-to-face when others aren't around to put pressure on the situation.
- Acknowledge anything positive a team-mate does, on or off the pitch, in training or in games.
- Reassure and show confidence in them if they make a mistake.

COACH » It is imperative you teach your team—and the individuals within it—to develop a sportsmanlike attitude to the game. Teaching them how to be good footballers is important, and they will always be grateful for your role in doing that. However, if you teach them how to become respectful, polite, driven, and positive young men as well as capable footballers, you will also leave a significant mark on their growth and development into adults who families and communities can be proud of. Teaching those lessons successfully will probably mean, too, that you remain an important figure in their lives for many years to come.

TEAMWORK

TEAMWORK means working together in a group to achieve a common goal. In football, players contribute their individual efforts and skills in combination with their team-mates to collectively dominate and win games. Each player offers his own qualities to the group. The ideal is for a team to always be more than the sum of its parts.

COACH ›› At Level 2, players should be ready for drills at their training sessions which are designed to show how important teamwork is in making sure the group achieves success.

Take one of your strongest attacking players and give him a ball. Now place 3 of your best defenders in front of him in a triangle shape 25 yards from goal with the point of the triangle facing him.

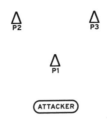

Now ask the attacking player to dribble past all three defenders and create the chance to shoot on goal. Give the attacker five chances to succeed, he probably won't be successful with too many of his attempts.

Now put three team-mates in to help the attacker, creating a 4 v 3 situation against the three defenders. Give the attackers another five chances to score. It's an absolute certainty the four attackers will now have much more success than the lone attacker did. This drill is a good example to use as it avoids highlighting weaknesses in a single player. It simply demonstrates the importance of team-mates and effective teamwork, adding numbers to achieve superiority in both attacking and defensive situations.

PROFESSIONALISM

Of course, at Level 2, a young footballer isn't yet a **PROFESSIONAL** in terms of playing full-time or being paid a salary to play. However, working to build the mentality, habits, attitude, and work-rate of a professional player—a process which began at Level 1—is vital if the young player is to excel at Level 2 and then move up through subsequent Levels. This is the time for a player to put in football foundations which will serve him well, right up to—potentially—a chance in the professional game.

At Level 1, a young footballer has learned the importance of arriving at each game and every training session on time, with kit ready, food and hydration prepared, and a positive mind-set in place. However, it's likely his parents have been helping him with all this by regularly washing, organising, and laying out his training and match kit before he leaves the house.

At Level 2, a young player should start to take responsibility for his own preparations. He knows how a washing machine works and he knows how to tell the time. The ability to take responsibility, think ahead, and be organised beforehand will help ensure he has the same strengths in place once the match kicks off.

COACH » It's vital you start to make your players aware of their off-pitch responsibilities. Make sure they understand how their behaviour can affect the way they perform in training and in games; and how they're perceived by coaches, team-mates and opponents.

It's particularly important to establish good habits in relation to time-keeping. If you can't rely on a player to be on time for training sessions, can you really rely on him to track his runner or get into position promptly at free kicks or corners?

Being on time is a discipline and, without discipline, a player will always come up short. He won't be trusted by coaches or team-mates. Big decisions in games are about making the right choices, often in a split second. Discipline and good habits—good time-keeping, for example—are key if a player's decisions are going to be the right ones more often than not.

I remember one boy who got brought here by his father. The club he was at wasn't really moving him forward, he said. He wanted to try Afawee. So I said to the boy, 'what's your dream?' And he looked at me and said, 'um. umm...' I said, 'that's not a good start, son.'

So I called one of our boys over and asked him the same question, 'what's your dream?' Straight back: 'to be a footballer, Steadman.' So I explained to the first boy, 'if you don't know what you want, there's no point in you coming here.'

Look at me. I'm not smiling. The advice I'm giving you is serious. I'm here to help a boy achieve his dream. If you don't know what you want, you won't cope because this environment is strict, disciplined. I may end up shouting at you and, if you don't really know what you want, you won't be able to deal with that. You will need to have strength of character to handle every football environment you find yourself in. I'm not here to be your friend. I'm here to prepare you to be a footballer.
—Steadman Scott

LEADERSHIP

A good leader has the ability to inspire, motivate, and breed confidence in others, enabling those around him to perform at higher levels.

Developing the **LEADERSHIP** skills discussed at Level 1, taking notice of good examples set by coaches and parents, will benefit a young footballer not only on the pitch but off it. At Level 2, he can be expected to begin displaying some of those leadership skills for himself, integrating them into his life at school and at home, as well as football. He will continue to grow towards becoming a loyal and respectful team-mate, player, and son.

PLAYER >> Leadership qualities can be demonstrated in many different ways, which you will learn throughout the journey towards becoming a **COMPLETE ATHLETE**. There are particular and important leadership attributes you can make your own at Level 2:

- Establishing yourself as a player who is always well-prepared for training and games.
- Setting yourself the highest standards of good behaviour on and off the pitch.
- Helping every team member feel valued and respected.
- Supporting team-mates when things aren't going well and helping them feel free to develop and express themselves as players.

What I want to see from a young player is enthusiasm. I want him to come along to every training session and every game with that enthusiasm, totally committed to that session or to that game. And then, as you develop and become a better player, I want to see you challenge yourself. Don't ever be satisfied. Don't be happy scoring 20 or 30 goals for the Under-12s.

Try to get in the Under-13s and score 10. Don't be happy being the star at your level. Challenge yourself to move up to the next level. Set targets, set goals, and talk to your coaches about them. Be open-minded about what they say to you but recognise it's not just about doing what the coach tells you to do; it's about ownership of your game, deciding for yourself what you need to do. Want to be the best player you can possibly be.

—Tony Carr

PARENT » *I've met quite a few people you might call 'pushy parents'. Look, it's the same with anything: if you're under pressure to do something all the time when you're young, you push back against it. It stops being fun. Same for a coach: I don't tell my players to do something. I challenge them. I ask them if they can.*

It's a great way to coax boys: not, 'Do this!' But instead, 'Can we do this?' The idea of coaching, after all, is to get kids to think for themselves. To make their own decisions and help make sure those decisions are positive rather than negative more often than not. It's the same with parents. I've seen boys pushed until they break, especially academy-level lads whose dads are living their lives through their sons without ever stopping and asking the boy himself, 'What do you want to do?' —Ian Marshall

JOIN THE CONVERSATION!

Don't miss out on all the conversation happening in the **COMPLETE ATHLETE** app. Join today!

2.2 PREPARATION

PREPARATION refers to off-the-pitch activities such as practicing your technical skills, studying top players, eating properly, staying properly hydrated, and getting enough rest and sleep to allow you to prepare for training and games. Preparation gives you the confidence and assurance to perform at the highest level with complete focus.

PLAYER » *I look at some of the senior players at Barnet, players who've had really good careers: Jamal Campbell-Ryce, Michael Nelson. They're in their 30s now, but they still have that fire in their bellies, that drive, that willingness to learn and be open to new ideas.*

And the younger lads, third year pros who I've worked with now for several years, I can see they've become serious about being professional footballers, too: they're

in at half eight every morning instead of 10 minutes before training; they want to prepare, do extra work; they're asking for video analysis; studying GPS data; asking the nutritionists what they should be eating; working on the physical side in the gym. Those are the boys who will push on in their careers. The others won't. It's as simple as that. A coach can create the right environment, can give them the tools, but at some point that won't be enough. The boys will have to do the rest for themselves.
—Rossi Eames

A **COMPLETE ATHLETE** prepares to get the very best out of himself as a footballer by consistently working and improving on the following:

PRACTICE

NUTRITION

HYDRATION

RECOVERY

MENTALITY

At Level 1, a player began learning individual technical skills and mastering the ball. At Level 2, he should be motivated to continue improving those skills on a daily basis, stepping up the amount of time he spends practicing outside formal sessions and games, playing on his own or in small groups with friends or team-mates.

At this stage, too, many young players will also be starting to understand how football works as a **TEAM GAME**.

PRACTICE

At Level 1, a player began learning individual technical skills and mastering the ball. At Level 2, he should be motivated to continue improving those skills on a daily basis, stepping up the amount of time he spends practicing outside formal sessions and games, playing on his own or in small groups with friends or team-mates.

PLAYER >> *Joe Cole was about 12 when he came to West Ham. We didn't have the younger age groups back then. It was amazing: first thing you saw was that he'd get the ball and beat everybody. But when he didn't have the ball, he'd be chasing around, smashing into tackles, trying to get it back. Naturally competitive but unbelievable natural ability, too. I saw him do things that made me wonder. I asked him, 'Who taught you to do that, Joe?' He told me he used to watch European Cup games on TV. He'd see someone do a trick or a skill, then he'd go out into the little yard at the back of where he lived and practice on his own until he'd taught himself how to do it.* —Tony Carr

This is a good time to be tested—or to test yourself—in different positions all over the pitch. You'll end up a more rounded footballer for the experience and will also be better prepared for the challenge of eventually learning to play in your favourite or most effective position. Your love of the game, your individual ability and your willingness to work hard and intelligently will all help you now to become the best you can be.

As at Level 2, the more focused and concentrated you can be during training sessions and informal practice, the more effective your learning in football will be.

The idea is to create a schedule which allows you to attend formal training sessions, but also to practice outside those sessions. Always aim to work intelligently but not necessarily harder or for longer. Choose three specific elements of your game you think you can improve on by working on your own or with friends.

LEVEL 2 SAMPLE TRAINING SESSION »

- Warm up
- Drill 1: Position specific
- Drill 2: Position specific
- Drill 3: Position specific
- Warm down

EXTRA TRAINING SESSIONS

PARENT >> *I think being an FA Charter Standard club, like Ridgeway Rovers are now, is really important: coaches with qualifications, all staff DBS checked, children's safeguarding policies in place.*

You go to almost any local park around London, and you'll get guys who may or may not have done their coaching badges and who could be anybody, really. People are coming up to them saying: I've got my son here. I want to get him some football training. They ask the price and pay the money, without knowing if the guy's qualified, without knowing if he's been checked out, without knowing if he's got even the most basic child protection policies in place. If you haven't got those, you shouldn't be coaching kids at all in my opinion.

As a club, it means we need to tick a lot of boxes but we want to do that. We do more than just tick boxes, I hope. We make sure anyone running a team at Ridgeway has the right qualifications in place. We pay for coaches to do their FA courses if they need to. Look: you don't know who's out there. If your kid was going to a school and the teachers didn't have the right qualifications—if you didn't really know anything about who those teachers were—you probably wouldn't want to send him there. Why should it be different if your son wants to go to a club and play football? You should know that the right checks and qualifications are in place. That's what Charter Standard's all about. —Ian Marshall

At Level 2, a player who is serious about his commitment to improving as a footballer might be looking for ways to do extra training. There are many forms this can take:

PRIVATE COACHING: Training one-on-one with a coach who works purely on improving individual young players technically, physically, and mentally.

PRIVATE ACADEMIES: Private academies normally only provide training sessions and focus principally on the technical development of young players.

SMALL GROUP TRAINING: A group of 3 to 6 players taking part in training sessions will not offer the same individual focus as one-on-one sessions, but will still be detailed and specific enough to help develop an individual's skills. The financial commitment will be significantly less than private coaching.

SELF-DEVELOPMENT: Recognising what you need to improve on and being creative in finding ways to develop your skills. If you need to work on receiving the ball, your first touch, and your passing, a wall is probably all you need by way of a partner. Likewise, accuracy in your shooting can be developed against the same wall, chalking smaller and smaller targets on it as you improve.

TRAINING WITH PARENT OR GUARDIAN: If you have a parent or guardian who is willing to help and spend time with you at a local pitch or in the park or back garden, adding a bit of structure to your play can help you improve as well as being an opportunity to spend enjoyable time together.

PLAYER » *Mastering the football comes from doing the same things over and over again. It's repetition. If you can't do that, you'll never be a footballer. If you just want to have fun, just want something to amuse you and pass the time, then go and find somewhere else to play!*

But if you want to be a footballer, you need to be ready to do these things over and over for days and weeks. Even years. Working in grids, doing the drills, running with the ball, doing turns, and the rest.

It's like the Kumon method in Maths and English for schoolkids. Repeat and repeat until you master one level and then you move on to the next. You see the boys who can focus on that and they're the ones who have the mentality to get to the top. Whatever else is going on around them, they're focused on what they're doing. They're not getting distracted by other people's bad habits. —Steadman Scott

COACH » *There are certain things, I think, while you're growing up, that your body learns by doing over and over again. Until those movements become instinct, second nature. But everybody's different and every boy has his own unique characteristics that will make him whatever kind of footballer he's going to be.*

So, although there may be a technically correct way of passing the ball from A to B, if someone can achieve the same thing in their own individual way, why would you change that? You can always refine technical skills as boys get older. Ultimately, boys will get more from discovering their own way of doing things, finding their own solutions to problems, than by just being shown what people think is the 'right' way.

As older people, I know we always want to impart knowledge to the young, show them the way to do things. Often that's coming from the best of intentions, but often it's not the best way with young players. It can be hard, sometimes, to just stay quiet and let kids find their own way. It can be hard when you see a boy make a mistake to just bite your tongue for long enough, to wait and see, until he sorts things out for himself and finds his own solution. It's about patience. Discipline, even: waiting to see what happens, not interrupting those crucial moments in which a boy makes a mistake and then remedies it for himself. Let him get back up and try it again: that's the way lessons are learned that really stick. That's the natural process, particularly at those young ages. —Paul Davis

PARENT » When I was a teenager, I got to know a goalkeeper a few years older than me, Mervyn Williams. He wasn't a coach then. He was a goalkeeper. But we'd go out together, kick balls, practice things together. He taught me a lot. Nowadays, there are a lot of goalkeeping coaches out there. Almost wherever you are, you'll find that not far away there'll be a coach who's got a little goalkeeping school going where he's working with five or six young keepers. That kind of training is much more accessible now.

Obviously, that's something you've got to pay for, and you've got to find out how good the quality of the coaching is. But if a lad wants to be a goalkeeper, that's something he can say to Mum and Dad, 'Will you find me a coach?' Most of the young goalkeepers who come into a club now will have had coaching like that. Whether it's been the right coaching or not, you only find out when you start working with them. —Tony Roberts

It's important to remember you are trying to help your son learn and develop. He will make plenty of mistakes at this stage of his playing career, and it's important you don't fall into the habit of continually highlighting what he can't do. He's in the process of learning and improving what he can do. That's where your focus should be, too. The reason a young player wants to do extra training is to spend more time with the football, learning what works and what doesn't work in terms of his technique. Be patient and supportive—rather than critical and demanding—and he'll start to figure things out for himself as he becomes more and more comfortable with his own body and what it can do.

NUTRITION

NUTRITION plays a key role in athletic function and performance. Young footballer's bodies are trying to build muscle, burning calories and lurching from one growth spurt to the next. It's hard work!

Boys need to take on the right kind of fuel and to properly hydrate at the right times. They need to replace calories and fluids lost during training and games, as well as during general exercise at school and playing with friends.

Developing as a player will put extra pressure on a boy's body and so a structured and conscious approach to diet is essential. An active Level 2 footballer needs to consume healthy foods and beverages in order to:

• Replenish his energy supply.
• Maintain hydration.
• Obtain the vitamins and minerals needed to support metabolism, tissue growth and repair.
• Help avoid injuries and or/illness.
• Perform at his best both on and off the pitch.

NOTE ≫ All of **COMPLETE ATHLETE**'s sports nutrition guidelines have been developed and set out by Courtney M. Sullivan, founder of *NUTRITION FOR BODY AND MIND*. Sullivan is a Registered Dietician certified by the Academy of Nutrition and Dietetics, and a Certified Personal Trainer recognised by the National Academy of Sports Medicine. APPENDIX 2 provides more detailed guidelines as well as suggested meals and recipes developed by Sullivan specifically for optimal health and football performance.

FOOTBALL-SPECIFIC NUTRITION GUIDELINES ≫

- All players should consume 5 or more balanced meals spread across the day, every 3 to 4 hours.
- Pre-match and pre-training meals should be eaten 2 to 3 hours before activity and snacks eaten 1/1.5 hours before activity.
- Eat when you're hungry to prevent lean-muscle breakdown. Stop eating when you're full to prevent feeling sluggish.
- Eat breakfast within 30 minutes of waking up to prevent lean-muscle breakdown, increase energy and concentration, and maintain good blood sugar control. Choose whole grains, fresh fruit and lean protein for breakfast.
- Eat well-balanced meals and snacks, consisting of carbohydrates, lean proteins, and heart-healthy fats.
- Drink a protein shake or eat a snack or meal which has the right balance of protein and carbohydrates within 30 minutes of completing training or games.
- Choose fresh whole foods when possible (instead of processed foods, which have been packaged or refined) to increase nutritional value. Avoid foods that are high in sugar and either saturated or hydrogenated fats.

HYDRATION

All athletes need to drink water before, during, and after practices and games. This is especially important on days when both temperatures and humidity levels are high. If a youth soccer player does not drink enough water, she could suffer from dehydration.

HOW TO MAINTAIN PROPER HYDRATION* »

- Before exercise, drink 16 to 20 full ounces within the 2-hour period prior to exercise.
- During exercise, drink 4 to 6 full ounces.
- After exercise, replace 24 full ounces for every one pound of body weight lost during exercise.

Adapted from guidelines provided by the American College of Sports Medicine (ACSM)

ATHLETES AND PARENTS » Players should take responsibility for following the guidelines on how much to drink before, during, and after games; parents should be monitoring to make sure it's done the right way. If a player did not hydrate right ahead of time, she is not going to perform her best; if she did, and if she keeps up with her water intake during the game, she should be able to last through the whole game and perform very well.

LEVEL 2 PLAYER NUTRITIONAL GUIDELINES »

Each young player will have his own specific nutritional requirements depending on age, height, weight,
activity level, metabolic rate, and genetic background.
Therefore, the following suggestions for daily nutritional
proportions are guidelines based on the average age
and activity level of a Level 2 player:

- 55 percent carbohydrate
- 20 percent protein
- 25 percent fat
- No more than 7 percent saturated fat
- No trans fat
- 30 grams of fibre per day
- No more than 150 calories per day from sugar
  (37.5 grams or 9 teaspoons)

Just as at Level 1, a young footballer should choose from
the following to fulfil the macronutrient requirements
outlined above:

- CARBOHYDRATES: High-fibre foods such as whole-
  grain bread, brown rice, whole-grain pasta, beans,
  starchy vegetables such as corn, peas and potatoes,
  quinoa and cereals.
- PROTEINS: Chicken, turkey or fish, especially wild
  salmon, tuna, trout, mackerel and sardines, which are
  all high in heart-healthy omega-3 fatty acids.
- FATS: Low-fat cheese, nuts and nut butters
  (preferably) without added sugar or salt), avocado,
  seeds and heart-healthy oils such as extra-virgin olive
  oil, rapeseed oil, sunflower oil and peanut oil.
- VEGETABLES: Any and all (leafy green vegetables are
  of particular value). Raw vegetables and fruit are to be
  highly recommended.

PLAYER >> At Level 2, games last longer and they're played on bigger pitches. This means your body is going to require a lot more fuel to maintain your highest levels of focus and performance. Nutrition is more important than ever now, so you — and your parents — need to focus and plan what you eat and when you eat it; how much you drink and how often you drink it, especially in the build-up to training and games. It's time to start taking the business of nutrition seriously, in a professional manner. Preparation, performance and recovery are words that should be in your head most days by now, helping you plan and organise your diet.

HYDRATION

Regularly drinking water needs to be part of a player's daily routine and not just something he thinks about before, during, and after games. Regularity is the important element: it allows the body to remain hydrated at all times and empowers muscles and vital organs, keeping them healthy and working efficiently on a daily basis and not just in periods around matches and training sessions.

PLAYER >> Everywhere you go you should have a bottle of water with you. A bottle of tap water is just as good as a bottle of expensive mineral water. Sipping regularly will be more effective than glugging a bottle at a time without drinking in between. Remember that feeling thirsty may mean your body is already dehydrated, a situation you're doing your best to avoid.

MAINTAINING HYDRATION AROUND GAMES >>

- Drink 16 to 20 fluid ounces (450 to 550 millilitres) within a 2-hour period prior to exercise.
- During exercise, drink 4 to 6 fluid ounces (120 to 170 ml) and perhaps extra at half-time.
- After exercise, you'll need to replace 24 fluid ounces for every 1 pound (0.5 kilos) of body weight lost during exercise.
- 5 fluid ounces equal half a cup, 20 fluid ounces therefore equal a couple of cups.
- These figures are approximate and, if you feel thirsty at any point, drink.

* *Adapted from guidelines provided by the American College of Sports Medicine (ACSM)*

PARENT >> At Level 2, a young player should be starting to take responsibility himself for following the guidelines on hydration (and diet, too, for that matter). He will, though, continue to rely on you for both advice and practical help. That gives you the opportunity to make sure he's going about things the right way.

If your son isn't being disciplined with his hydration, you can be sure he won't reach peak performance or sustain levels of concentration during games and training sessions. Coaches have a lot to think about before, during, and after games; your son, meanwhile, will be getting swept up in the excitement of playing competitive football.

You can make a huge difference, monitoring what he's drinking during and after exercise. This doesn't mean you'll need to crash the team talk or wander on to the pitch during games, though! Just make sure water is available and make eye contact now and again to remind him he needs to be drinking.

RECOVERY

Young footballers—all footballers—need to eat and drink within 30 minutes of finishing a training session or game in order to replace the calories they've burnt and the fluids they've lost during those intense bursts of physical activity. Replenishing calories and fluids will also help muscle **RECOVERY** and repair.

HOW TO REPLENISH CALORIES AND FLUIDS »

- Drink 24 ounces of fluid (not sugary drinks) for every pound of body weight lost within a 2-hour period of training or a game. As a guide: 20 fluid ounces is about one pint. Look to drink that amount (or more) after your session or match.
- Consume around 15 grams of protein plus an equal amount of carbohydrates within the 30-minute recovery window. As a guide: 10 grams of protein is equivalent to about half a chicken breast or half a can of tuna. 10 grams of carbohydrate is equivalent to half of a slice of bread.

SLEEP

Increased physical activity demands an increased need for calories. It also increases a body's need for sleep. Recovery allows a young player's body to rest and heal after the intense demands put on it by training and games. According to the National Sleep Foundation, a Level 1 or 2 footballer should get between 10 and 11 hours of **SLEEP** each night to ensure his necessary growth and development. If that's not possible, or if a young footballer needs additional recovery time, he can take short naps (no longer than 30 minutes) or enjoy quiet rest periods (lying down, watching football on TV, or reading).

PLAYER >> One of the exciting things about being a young footballer at Level 2 is that you never know who is watching you play. Scouts and coaches attend more matches than you'd ever imagine, another reason why you need to be at your very best each time you step onto the pitch.

Every young player will need luck to be on his side from time to time. But the more professional you are in relation to football, the better prepared you are to take advantage of opportunities when they come along. As the old saying goes: the harder you work, the luckier you get.

Just because you think you're playing a weaker team on Sunday morning and feel confident about winning the game, your preparation shouldn't include a late Saturday night round at a mate's house, eating junk food and staying up till 3AM on the Xbox. The next day, you'll arrive at your game in a weaker physical and mental condition.

Your team might still win but your own game will suffer. The particular game might be the one an academy scout has turned up to watch you play in. If he leaves the game with a question mark against your performance, that first impression will stick with him and may be passed on to other people who ask him about you.

There are thousands of young players waiting for that one chance to get spotted, to get their first break. You never know when the opportunity will come along: make sure you're always prepared to perform at your best, ready to impress.

MENTALITY

PARENT >> *I think it's important that Mark's opinion counts for a lot with the boys. With Alexander and with Christian, he's always been completely honest. He'll never say they've done well when they haven't. Sometimes, I watch a game and, listening to Mark, I think our son's had a terrible game. But then he'll get 'Man of the Match' afterwards. But they know Dad's been there and done it. And they know he's honest with them, so they trust his opinion. If Mark says 'You can do it,' they can say to themselves, 'Yes I can.' My instinct is always to say, 'You're really good.' And, to me, they are really good because they're my sons. But they need to know that when we say something it's because we really believe it. I want to be loving and kind and supportive, but I don't want to give them false hope. That would mean, down the line, if there was disappointment to be faced, it'd be heartbreaking. You have to be realistic every step of the way.*
—Wendie Oxlade-Chamberlain

PLAYER >> *Physical attributes are important. Maybe a boy's slow so perhaps he won't make a footballer. A boy's overweight so he won't make a footballer. But does he have the right attitude to work and train to overcome those things? You have to look the part, look like a player. But mental toughness is what I want to see, too. If you don't fight to win out on the pitch, I don't know what I can do with you. If a boy arrives holding his father's hand and won't let go, it's no use him being here. I'm looking for the boy who, once he comes in to the session, he forgets all about his father. All he's interested in is the ball and everything that's going on on the pitch. Is the boy a* *winner? Is he brave? If he gets taken up to an academy, he'll be the new kid. He'll be a stranger coming into a family and looking to take the place of one of that family. So they're not going to talk to him. They're not going to pass to him. They don't like him. If he's not strong-minded, that boy will lose heart and leave. Physical and mental—those are the attributes a boy needs if he's going to be a success as a footballer. —Steadman Scott*

Being a **COMPLETE ATHLETE** doesn't just mean training harder or for longer. Certainly a youth footballer must spend time physically preparing his body for the demands of training and matches. But engaging in the right kind of mental preparation is also fundamental in helping him to perform to the limits of his ability. It's something practice can foster—creating the right mind-set going into every session and every game.

The visualisation exercises learned at Level 1 will become even more important when you start playing 9 v 9 on bigger pitches at Level 2. There will be new physical and technical demands to be met; a young player will need a more durable mind-set to help him meet those demands and continue to excel. At Level 2, a young player needs to start focusing on self-belief, being aware of what gives him the confidence to be really productive in sessions and games.

JOIN THE CONVERSATION!

Recovery, sleep, and nutrition are all important for your health and best performance on the field. For tips & techniques from coaches and professionals, download the **COMPLETE ATHLETE** app!

BUILDING CONFIDENCE

- Think about positive feedback you've had from coaches, team-mates and parents.
- Think about how you have made an impact on games in the past; with that in mind, there's no reason to believe you can't make that impact again. And again!
- Think about how well you have prepared and trained for this match. How ready you feel.
- Recognise mistakes are part of the game, but it only takes a split second—one good shot, one great assist, one brilliant tackle or save— to become the match winner.
- Be patient with yourself, focussing on what you're about to do not on what you just did.
- Realise the important people around you will always be proud of how you perform as long as you give your all in every moment of every game.

COACH >> As a coach, it's up to you to create the best learning environment for your players. You are there to help each individual player with his technical and athletic development. If there is a problem in a boy's game, which is leading to him making mistakes during games or sessions, it's your responsibility to make the necessary technical adjustments and help the player find a solution to the problem. Be aware, though, that mistakes can affect a player's mentality, as well as holding back the rest of his game.

How you react to a player making mistakes or bad decisions can have a huge impact on his confidence and self-belief. If the error or misjudgement is as a result of laziness or a bad attitude, then it's important you are very clear and direct in stressing the standards expected from your players. But if confidence is an issue for a young player, a very different approach may be called for. You need to let the player know you have complete belief in him. You don't care how many mistakes he makes, the only thing that matters is that he keeps trying to improve, keeps trying to express himself on the pitch.

Once you change the player's perspective, change in their game can begin to happen. He shouldn't be worried about pleasing you or letting you down: he should be trying as hard as he can to become the best he can be. Taking the pressure of avoiding mistakes away at this age will allow him to play with freedom. That's when you'll see the young player flourish.

PLAYER >> *When I was a boy, a lot of it came naturally to me but I've studied the mental side of the game since— the qualities of concentration, confidence, having a positive attitude. I used imagery. If I did something good in a game when I was a young keeper at QPR, I'd get a video clip of it, watch it, practice it, try and repeat it—a save, a catch, a kick, whatever it was.*

And the more you watch yourself doing good things and practice doing them, the sooner those good things become second nature. You have to learn toughness, too. In your career, you're going to have to deal with criticism from your manager, from your team-mates, from opponents, from their fans, from your own fans. You'll have to criticise yourself. Can you handle that? As a goalkeeper, mistakes come with the job. You have to deal with them. You can't crumple. You have to work out what happened, what you did wrong. And put it right.
—Tony Roberts

Every player has his own individual mentality. At this age, you'll just be starting to learn about how your mind works in and around games. What makes you feel confident and focused may be particular to you and very different to what works for a team-mate. Don't feel embarrassed to try different techniques until you find out what works for you:

- Listening to your favourite music before games.
- Watching videos of your favourite players before games.
- Closing your eyes and trying to visualise the moments when you've made a real impact in previous games.

- Try to imagine yourself doing the same in the game you're about to play.
- Going onto the pitch before the game and walking over specific areas of the pitch. Imagine how you'll be able to influence the game in those areas.
- Make good contact with your team-mates. Let them know they can rely on you. And you're happy to be relying on them, too.
- While you're physically warming up, try to focus so completely on each stretch and movement that you forget all about what's happened before the game and what might be going to happen after it.

2.3 FITNESS

It's simple: the fitter you are, the better you will perform. A footballer needs to develop strength and speed to play the game effectively and limit his chances of injury. One of the keys to maximising strength and speed is mobility. Mobility is the ability to move efficiently through a full range of motion. A **COMPLETE ATHLETE** always maintains a high level of:

LOWER-BODY STRENGTH

UPPER-BODY STRENGTH

FLEXIBILTY/MOBILITY

CORE STRENGTH

SPEED/EXPLOSIVENESS/AGILITY

ENDURANCE

At Level 1, we set out a number of drills and exercises to test and improve a young player's overall **FITNESS**. At Level 2, a young player should be able to perform all of these tests more effectively and over longer periods of time and distance. Along with some new additions to the young player's fitness programme, the exercises from Level 1 have evolved and been adapted to now challenge him at Level 2.

PARENT » *What you want is for boys to fall in love with the game. By the time a boy is 11, you want him to love the game just as much as he did when he first started playing: he can't imagine the rest of his life without football being part of it, at whatever level or in whatever way he's going to be involved later on.*

Physically, by then, you want him to be athletic: able to run, jump, change direction; be agile, balanced and co-ordinated. By then he can have worked on building speed. He can have started to work on power and core strength: I don't mean weight-training, but exercises using his own body-weight push-ups, sit-ups, squats, football-based exercises—the kind of things kids can do for themselves at home as well as them being part of training sessions.
—*John Folwell*

JOIN THE CONVERSATION!
For additional drills to improve speed, mobility, and agility, be sure to check out the **COMPLETE ATHLETE** app. New video content is continually updated!

LOWER-BODY STRENGTH

LOWER BODY STRENGTH will start to become a more important part of a player's game at Level 2. Putting more work into developing his lower-body strength, he will begin to see significant gains in speed over short and long distances and increases in the power of his explosive movements, his changes of direction, and his striking of the ball. If strengthening the lower body is neglected, on the other hand, it can undermine a player's balance when attempting technical elements such as dummying an opponent; it can weaken his ability to maintain control of the ball under pressure, especially if this means him fending off an opponent.

Exercises like **SINGLE-LEG SQUATS**, **WALL-SITS** and **BROAD-JUMPS** will all help young players to develop strength in the hamstrings, quadriceps and gluteal muscles, thus developing better balance and posture. Those elements are all crucial to the development of a player's all-round game.

SINGLE-LEG SQUATS »

• Balance on one slightly bent leg while your other leg is positioned slightly in front of your body.
• With your arms straightened out on each side to aid balance, start to bend the knee of your planted, balancing leg slowly, going as low as you can while still maintaining balance and control.

- Slowly straighten your knee again to return to the starting position. Repeat on your other leg.
- It's important to bear in mind that a player actually builds more strength on the way back up to his starting position than on the way down. Therefore, control and balance on the way back to the starting position are vital.

SINGLE-LEG WALL-SIT »

- Stand with feet shoulder-width apart against a smooth-surfaced wall.
- Slowly slide down the wall until both your knees and hips are at 90 degree angles.
- Slowly lift one foot off the ground until you can feel muscle tension in the planted leg.
- Keep the lifted foot raised for as long as possible before putting it back on the ground.
- Remain in the sitting position but rest for 30 seconds.
- Repeat the lift, using the other foot.
- Time how long you can hold on each foot off the ground.

Remember to be aware of any imbalance in strength between the dominant and non-dominant legs. Work towards being able to keep each foot off the ground for equal lengths of time. Any significant difference in strength can be lessened by increasing repetitions with the weaker planted leg.

BROAD-JUMP »

A controlled broad-jump is an excellent exercise for developing explosive strength, balance and coordination between upper and lower-body movements in young players.

- Stand behind a marked line on the ground with feet shoulder-width apart.
- Bend your knees and raise both arms forward in front of you.
- As you swing them back behind you, start to bend your knees. Swing your arms back out in front of you again and, as you do so, leap forward with both feet leaving the ground at the same time.
- Look to increase the power in your jump and measure it by how far your jump takes you.
- At the end of the jump, it's important to land as softly as possible with your knees bent and both feet alongside each other.
- Your knees should never be propelled ahead of your toes as this causes instability and the possibility of injury.

UPPER-BODY STRENGTH

At Level 1, **UPPER-BODY STRENGTH** was identified as an important but often-neglected aspect of a footballer's fitness regime. Upper-body strength helps a player hold off opponents. It is also an element in being able to sprint and balance efficiently with or without the ball. For goalkeepers, upper-body strength is not only essential for shot-stopping, but will also help improve capability across a range of goalkeeper-specific actions and movements. At Level 2, pull exercises like the bent-arm pull-up are used to increase upper back strength and mobility. Push exercises, like push-ups increase chest, shoulder, and arm strength.

BENT-ARM PULL-UP »

- Grip an overhead bar with an underhand grip, palms facing toward your body.
- Try and pull your body up slowly with the aim of getting your chin above the bar. The emphasis should be on using your arms and back to lift your body. (Don't try to use any momentum generated by your legs swinging backwards and forwards.)
- At the highest point, with your chin above the bar, your legs should be completely straight.
- Hold at the highest point for 2 seconds and then lower yourself slowly, maintaining control at all times.
- If necessary, a parent or team-mate can take partial weight in order to maintain good balance and form in the exercise.

PUSH-UPS >>

- Lie face-down with your palms under or slightly wide of your shoulders, fingers straight, legs straight and parallel.
- Straighten your arms, pushing your upper and lower body up together in one smooth movement, back and knees are straight throughout.
- Push up until your arms are straight then slowly lower again until your face, chest, and knees are an inch or two from the floor.
- Perform as many controlled repetitions as possible before resting.
- Be very careful not to let your back arch as this will put strain on your back muscles and risks injury.

FLEXIBILITY/ MOBILITY >>

Increased levels of flexibility and mobility will foster better technique and performance on the pitch and help prevent injury. Improving and then maintaining your flexibility will help sustain your endurance and level of play as you move onto larger pitches and 9 v 9 football.

The Sit and Reach Test is an effective exercise for improving a young footballer's hamstring and lower back flexibility. It can also be used as a marker to assess flexibility and gauge continuing improvement.

THE SIT AND REACH TEST >>

You'll need a box around 8 to 12 inches high. A shoe box is perfect. Use a ruler to mark out inch-divisions across the top of the box to measure your reach.

- Place the box against a wall with the top of the box facing upwards.

- Sit on the floor with the soles of your feet flat against the side of the box in front of you.
- Keeping your legs straight and flat on the floor, slowly stretch forward with straight arms and try to reach the box.
- Do this slowly and with control three times then, on the fourth stretch, reach as far as possible and hold for at least three seconds.
- Note the distance you reached using the inch-marks on the box. Work to increase the distance you are able to reach. If you cannot reach the box, ask someone to measure how close you are to the box. Monitor progress and increase flexibility until you can reach he marks on the box.

CORE STRENGTH AND BALANCE

The effective functioning of your core muscles is an essential component of fitness for football-specific strength, power, and explosive movement. The core is the base for transferring power into a player's football movements and actions—kicking, jumping, sprinting, and protecting the ball. Development of useable **CORE STRENGTH** is achieved by a much wider range of exercises than sit-ups and crunches, although those can have roles to play.

The core muscles wrap round the body, through the abdominal area, the lower back, and the glutes. Planks and functional planks are proven and straightforward ways of developing core strength and stability. Core strength at Level 2 is a vital part of becoming a better footballer, especially as your body continues to grow. At these ages, the increased physical demands made on your body can mean a young player is prone to injuries to his obliques, the side abdominal muscles which support the lower back.

Simple self-testing can identify any weakness in your core area. It may help to have someone with you who can check alignment of your hips and buttocks when you do the exercises. The exercises will help develop core muscles to increase strength and help prevent injury. We continue to use the Plank and Functional Plank exercises first used at Level 1. The Marching Hip-Raise introduced at Level 2 tests and develops lower back, glute and hamstring strength.

A PLANK >>

• Lie face-down on the floor. With elbows bent at a 90 degree angle, hands in a fist and shoulder-width apart, on the floor facing forwards, lift your body to balance on your arms and toes.

- Your body should be completely level and straight, at roughly shoulder height.
- No sagging or arched back as this puts concentrated strain on other areas.
- Think of the flat shape of a plank of wood.
- Now squeeze your stomach in and tighten while in plank position, keeping your body level.
- Hold this position for as long as you can.
- Bear in mind the aim is always to avoid rotation in the hips or lower back, taking the weight in your core muscles exclusively.
- As you become comfortable with the Plank, you can further challenge yourself. Once you've got into the plank position, raise one foot slowly off the ground, keeping your leg straight and aligned through the hip. Repeat with the other leg. You can also try lifting one arm at a time out straight in front of you.

A FUNCTIONAL PLANK >>

- Follow the same guidelines as above.
- Once in the plank position, slowly bend your left knee out beside you and move it up towards your left arm. The moving leg never goes above shoulder height.
- Slowly move back into plank position then repeat with your right knee moving towards your right arm.
- Repeat on both sides as many times as you can.

A MARCHING HIP-RAISE >>

- Lie flat on your back with your knees raised and bent at 90 degrees, feet flat on the floor.
- Keeping your back straight at all times, lift your hips as high as possible with only your feet and shoulders touching the ground.
- Now raise one knee toward your chest in a controlled marching movement.
- Repeat on alternate sides for as long as you can.

SPEED/EXPLOSIVENESS/AGILITY

As discussed in Level 1, the most relevant types of speed in football are straight line speed, explosive speed and lateral (side-to-side) speed. At Level 2, growth and development of the body should be matched by work designed specifically to improve all these elements.

The drills outlined here will also promote a young player's ability to stop/start and accelerate/decelerate in multiple directions of travel. The 30 Yard Sprint helps a young player improve straight line speed. The 5-10-5-5-10 shuttle runs help develop explosive speed and promotes agility.

STRAIGHT LINE SPEED is your ability to get from point A to B as fast as possible.

EXPLOSIVE SPEED is how quickly you can take off in the first 5 yards of a sprint (explosive speed in football is multi-directional).

AGILITY is your ability to get from point A to point B via multiple other points and moving in multiple directions.

STRAIGHT LINE SPEED: 30 YARD SPRINT »

- Place two cones 30 yards apart.
- Run from cone 1 to cone 2 as fast as you can.
- When doing sprint work, it's important to rest for 8 times as long as the action has taken (for example, after a 6 second sprint you should rest for 48 seconds before going again).
- Time your sprint or get a friend or parent to time it so you can chart improvement. The aim here is train your mind to tell your body to run faster. This will only happen by continually sprinting as fast as you can. As the body becomes used to moving at a speed, it'll then be possible to want to move faster.

This will only be effective with the appropriate rest times of 8 to 1. If you don't rest appropriately, you risk the sprints becoming just an endurance drill. This is counter-productive as your sprints will become slower the more you do. Our purpose is training the mind to recognise, get used to and then increase the body's maximum speed.

EXPLOSIVE SPEED: 8-10 YARD MULTI-DIRECTIONAL SPRINTS »

- Practice 8 to 10 yard sprints in different directions by placing cones 8 to 10 yards away from you at different angles.
- Start each sprint by getting your body low and gradually raising it toward the end of the sprint.
- Choose a spot in the distance and focus on this point while sprinting.
- Keep your body in line, arms pumping in a straight line faster than your legs (the faster your arms pump the faster your legs will move) and keep your head as still as possible.
- Don't let your arms and head flop side-to-side as this will reduce the efficiency of your explosive movements.

AGILITY: 5-10-5-5-10 SHUTTLE RUN

• Set up five cones or markers, each 5 yards apart, in a
  symmetrical shape as below

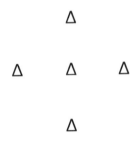

• Start in the centre and sprint 5 yards to the right cone.
• Then turn and sprint 10 yards to the furthest left cone
• Sprint 5 yards back to the middle and then 5 yards
  running backwards to the bottom cone.
• Then explode 10 yards through to the top cone
• Rest for six times longer than it takes you to complete
  the drill. Then repeat drill with your first sprint going
  to the left cone.
• When you get close to each cone in turn, try to start
  getting your body low to prepare it for a change of
  direction.

ENDURANCE

At Level 2, you will begin to play on bigger pitches,
up to 80 yards by 50 yards in size. Games will often
last longer, up to 4 x 20-minute quarters per game.
Training sessions will last longer proportionately as well.

Working on increasing **ENDURANCE** at Level 2 is
essential if a young player is going to be able to sustain

a high standard of performance for longer periods of time and over greater distances.

Endurance is a function of your heart/cardiovascular system working to supply your muscles with enough oxygen to keep you running without fatiguing or breaking down. Low levels of endurance will result in lower amounts of oxygen in your blood and an inability to sustain the levels of intense physical activity football demands.

The best tests of endurance for Level 2 players are the Beep Test and the 30 Second Run. They will also function as exercises to develop a young player's stamina.

THE BEEP TEST »

The **BEEP TEST** is an endurance test: a series of shuttle runs between markers 20 metres apart, each run starting on a beep. It begins at level 1 and ends at (an impossible!) level 20. There are around 8-10 runs per level with the gaps between beeps gradually getting shorter, giving you less time to make it to the 20 metre line before the next beep. For example, level 1 (not much more than a walk) has 10 runs and you have 8 seconds to complete each one between beeps.

At level 10, you have around 6 seconds between beeps in which to complete each 20 metre run. If you fail to complete the runs at any level in sync with the beeps, you will have failed that level. Note the last level you completed: that's the level you achieved in the test.

To provide your beeps, you'll need to download a Beep Test application to your phone or tablet. You'll also have to be able to measure, accurately, the 20 metres between lines for the runs.

- On a non-slip floor surface, place cones or simply mark lines 20 metres apart.
- After you press start on the Beep Test app, the recording will sound a beep for each twenty metre run and then sound a sequence of beeps to register you are moving up to the next level and your speed will need to increase.
- Make sure one foot touches the line before each turn. And do not start to run until the beep has sounded.
- You should stop when you fall short of the 20 metre line 2 beeps in a row.
- Remember to note your last completed level (not the one you failed to complete).

THE 30 SECOND RUN »

- You need five cones and a timer or watch with alarm function.
- Place the cones in a straight line, each 10 yards apart.
- Set the timer for 30 seconds and press start.
- Run to Cone 1 and then back the 10 yards to your start position. Then run to cone 2 and back the 20 yards to your start position. Keep working your way up the line of cones until you've reached cone 5 and run the 50 yards back to your start position.
- If you get to cone 5 before the 30 seconds are up, start from cone 1 again and continue your way back up until the 30 seconds have run out.
- Now rest for 1 minute before re-setting the timer to 30 seconds again and repeating the runs. Look to complete six 30-second sets.
- Keep track of how many yards you cover in each 30-second set in order both to monitor progress and challenge your endurance capacity.

LEVEL 2 PERFORMANCE TESTS

LOWER-BODY STRENGTH

• Single-leg squat held for 40 seconds on each leg.
• Series of four broad jumps of 70 inches or more.
• Single-leg wall-sit held for 40 seconds on each leg.

UPPER-BODY STRENGTH

• Bent-arm pull-up held for 20 seconds.
• 30 push-ups in 60 seconds.

FLEXIBILTY/MOBILITY

• Sit and reach test of at least 2.5 inches

CORE STRENGTH & BALANCE

• Plank for 2 + minutes
• Functional plank for 1 + minutes
• Single-Leg balance for 30 seconds with slightly bent knee
• Marching hip-raise for 90 seconds with no rotation in
  hips or back.

SPEED/QUICKNESS/AGILITY

• 30-yard sprint in less than 5 seconds.
• 8-yard multi-directional sprint in 1.3 seconds.
• 5-10-5-5-10 shuttle run in under 6.2 seconds.

ENDURANCE

• Beep Test: minimum score of level 10; aim for level 12.
• 30-second run: six sets, each set to be completed to
  50 yards + 10 yards.

 TECHNIQUE

At Level 2, a **COMPLETE ATHLETE** is playing 9 v 9 and can begin to be aware of team shape. With that comes starting to understand the roles and responsibilities of particular positions; he'll begin to recognise how different arrangements of positions combine to improve the team's structure and help a group of players achieve their goals.

It's important to remember, though, that continuing to improve individual technique is the most important thing to be concentrating on at this age.

At Level 2, everything gets bigger: the size of the pitch, the length of the games; even the size of the goals, which increase from 12 feet by 6 feet, to 16 feet by 7 feet. Working to keep improving ball mastery and technical skills continues but there will be some adaptations to take into account the changes which come in at ages 9 and above. Some examples of new skills which need to be learnt and practiced include:

- STRIKERS' CONTROL OF LONGER PASSES: more space in behind defences due to increase in the size of the pitch.

- STRIKERS/MIDFIELDERS SHOOTING FROM GREATER DISTANCES: increase in the height and width of the goal.

- MIDFIELDERS HAVING WIDER RANGE & TYPES OF PASSES AVAILABLE: a bigger pitch creates greater distances between players and thus more angles.

- WIDE PLAYERS HAVE MORE ROOM & GREATER DISTANCES ON CROSSES: more space to use in 1 v 1 situations but the final ball needing to travel further.

- GOALKEEPERS CHALLENGED WITH SAVES & DISTRI-BUTION: the goal being defended increases significantly in both height and width.

- DEFENDERS' LONGER PASSING RANGES & DEFENDING OPPOSITION GOAL KICKS: a bigger pitch will often invite more aerial passes and crosses.

PLAYER >> It's important to be aware of the new skills outlined above but these new techniques all still rely on the same fundamental elements of a footballer's all-round game:

BALL CONTROL

BALL MASTERY & DRIBBLING

PASSING

SHOOTING

HEADING

AWARENESS

I'm not sure what you can do, as a 10-year-old or an 11 -year-old, to prepare yourself for moving up to 11-a-side on full-sized pitches. If you're in at a club or getting good coaching, they'll be doing what they can. But, even on a smaller pitch, a boy can look up and play a longer pass. Even though that'll be 20 yards on a small pitch rather than 40 yards, it still means playing longer, away from the players who are immediately around you. And however big the pitch is, you've still got to do your running. Kids take different times to adapt to 11-a-side and full-sized pitches.

A lot of it's physical, just about how they grow and when. Your game just has to change. I remember when I was a kid. One day you'd be playing in the street, 1 v 1 or 2 v 2, or more boys would turn up and it'd be 7 v 7 or 8 v 8. The next day, you'd be playing 11 v 11 for your District team. You'd adapt. And, if you couldn't run as well as the bigger lads yet, or you couldn't kick the ball 50 yards, you'd just have to use your brain to work out how to play and still be effective. You're finding your way round the challenges. On a full-sized pitch, the bigger, stronger boy suddenly has an advantage but the smaller, cleverer player will find ways to adapt. —Terry Burton

BALL CONTROL

- First and second touches
- Controlling the ball with all surfaces of the foot
- Direction of touch
- On the ground
- Bouncing
- On the full
- Controlling under pressure (awareness/pre-scanning)

TECHNICAL TIPS »

- Lower your body and bend your knees slightly to encourage a soft and precise first touch.
- Do not lunge and stretch onto the ball as this will inhibit balance and quality of touch. Invite the ball onto your foot (or any other part of your body) rather than meeting it with a stiff approach.
- Always try and get your body behind the ball. This will help you to protect the ball, to stay balanced and to keep your body in line within the width of your hips.
- When making contact with the ball, don't have your foot raised too high or it will connect with the top of the ball, pushing it into the ground. Don't have your foot too low, either, or it will connect underneath the ball and lift it into the air without you controlling that.

Can you start to work on your awareness (pre-scanning) of what's happening around you before receiving the ball? Looking around the pitch and seeing where team-mates and opponents are positioned before you touch the ball will help you make the right decisions by decreasing the amount of guesswork involved in what you do when you receive the ball. This, in turn, will leave you free to focus on the quality of your first touch and then the pass or run you want to make. Top players have a picture of the other players on the pitch in their minds at all times. It cannot be stressed too often that your first touch, receiving the ball, is the starting point—the catalyst—for everything else you do afterward.

BALL MASTERY/DRIBBLING

- Try keeping the ball within 5 inches of your foot as you move with it. This will allow you to change direction quickly in tight spaces without surrendering control.
- Try dribbling with the ball at different speeds. Draw in your opponent then beat him!
- Dribble with your head up if you can so you can see what else is going on around you.
- When you have the ball under control, try to manipulate it by touching it with all the different areas of your foot.

TECHNICAL TIPS ≫

- Close control is paramount when you need to change direction quickly, under pressure or in a tight situation. Remember that 5-inch rule!
- Vary the speed and direction of your dribbling. This breaks up your opponent's stride pattern and under mines his balance. Those are the weaknesses you can capitalise on to beat him.
- Try and be aware of where you're taking the ball in order not to lose it and in order to use your skills most productively.
- Running too quickly with the ball can sometimes mean

you lose control of it. Focus on control first and build up your running speed as you develop.
- Dribbling with your head down can take you into a crowd of opponents or even off the pitch altogether!
- As you build confidence in ball mastery, start to use your imagination and develop your own personal sequences of movement.

The challenge is to complete these moves quickly but with efficiency and maintaining control.

START BY MASTERING »

- Cruyff turns
- Drag backs
- Drag back and push
- Step-overs
- Snakes
- Touch/fake step and push
- Touch/roll, drag, step-over and push
- Triple-pace multi-directional dribbling

Attacking players should be aware that, on a bigger pitch, you may have more space in behind your opponents' defensive line. You may have the option of a different kind of dribbling: pushing the ball further out in front of you to get you into the space 'in behind'.

To do this successfully, you may have to sprint 10, 20 or even 30 yards between touches, something which wasn't useful on 7 v 7 pitches. Focus on ensuring your second touch is precise and controlled. You'll be arriving at the ball at pace and with momentum. Retaining control with that second touch is vital if you're going to make sure the move is productive.

PASSING

Be aware that, at Level 2 and on the bigger 9 v 9 pitch, a player has more scope for varying the pace, direction, and trajectory of his passes. There's more space for playing the ball into 'passing lanes' and in behind midfield and defensive lines. You can begin to experiment with longer passes as you build up lower-body strength and become more familiar with the 9 v 9 environment.

Remember: being aware of what's happening on the rest of the pitch (pre-scanning) can help you make the right decision—and make it more quickly—once the ball arrives with you.

The fundamental range of passing which you worked on at Level-1 remains the same. You will discover for yourself (with help from your coach, if you need it) how best to exploit those basic passing techniques on the bigger pitch with more players on it.

INSIDE FOOT PASS

- Try to make a good, clean, firm connection with soft instep of the foot with your hips guided towards the target.
- For a low pass, keep your follow-through low. To play a pass through the air, raise your foot on your follow-through.
- To keep the pass controlled, try to strike the ball with the soft instep so it doesn't clip your heel or your toe.

DRIVEN PASS

- Connect with laces tight against the ball. Short, punched follow-through with your hips facing the target.
- If you chop underneath the ball, you'll find it slices off in another direction to the one you intended.

CURVED PASS

- Connect with the ball using the inside of your foot on the outside of the ball. Shape your follow-through to describe the shape you want the ball to make as it travels.

- Always lift your follow-through to lift the ball off the ground. Keep your follow-through low if you want your pass to travel along the ground.
- Twisting your hips too sharply will make your follow-through take the pass beyond your target.

HALF-VOLLEY PASS

- Connect with the ball when it's just off the ground, within 2 inches of it bouncing, to give you maximum control over the pass.
- If you mis-time the connection and the ball is too far off the ground when you strike it, you'll hit underneath the ball and the pass will either slice or go too high.

VOLLEY PASS

- Get your body over the ball and connect in the middle of the ball, your laces guiding it downward to keep the pass controlled. Standing foot and hips should be pointed towards the intended target.
- Let the ball come onto your foot. If you connect too early, you'll hit the bottom of the ball and slice it. If you connect too late and strike the top of the ball, you'll push it into the ground instead of towards your target.

SHOOTING

INSIDE FOOT

LACES STRIKE

CURVE

VOLLEY

HALF VOLLEY

'KNUCKLE' BALL

TECHNICAL TIP »

If you are taking a touch to set yourself up for a shot, pay special attention to the placement of that touch. If you can, get used to pushing the ball out from your shooting foot at a 45-degree angle.

This will allow you a more favourable approach to the ball and it will also take the ball away from an opponent facing you. The set-up touch is something which can be mastered by simple repetition.

INSIDE FOOT

- Body behind the ball and make a good strong connection with the inside of the foot. Transfer your weight through the ball with your hips angled towards the corner of the goal.
- Over-rotating your hips will tend to guide your shot towards the centre of the goal instead of the corner.

LACES STRIKE

- First point of contact with the ball should be your laces right against the centre of the ball. Keep your follow-through below knee height and guide it towards your target.
- If the ball's first point of contact is the front of your foot and not your laces, this will mean you don't get a clean strike away and the ball will usually rise over the crossbar.

CURVE

- Similar to the curve pass, for a curve shot you need to connect on the outside of the ball with the inside of your foot. Shape your follow-through to describe the same shape you want your shot to make on its way to the target.
- Over-rotation of your hips or a loose follow-through may cause you to guide the ball wide of the target.

VOLLEY

- If possible, let the ball drop to knee height before striking it and connect with laces tight against the centre of the ball. Follow through on a high-to-low arc to keep the shot under control.
- Connecting underneath the ball—as you often do if the ball doesn't drop to knee height or below—will mean your shot flies up over the bar.

HALF VOLLEY

- As with the half-volley pass, it helps to strike the ball when it's as near to the ground as possible to ensure a clean, controlled connection.
- Allowing the ball to rise more than a couple of inches before striking it makes the shot much more difficult to keep low and on target.

'KNUCKLE' BALL

- When connecting with the ball for this kind of shot, make contact with the knuckle of your foot striking the lower part of the ball. Aim for the least possible amount of follow-through as you 'punch' the ball towards goal, keeping the connecting foot flat and straight. The intention is to make the ball move laterally in the air and dip without warning by striking it with an uneven part of the foot, the 'knuckle'.

* The trick is to connect with the 'knuckle' of your foot. Striking with the inside of the foot will not give the ball swerve and dip in the same way.

COACH >> It goes without saying that goals are what win games for your team. It's a good idea to give your attacking players drills which are designed to give them specific repetitions on shooting technique in areas of the pitch which will help them with decision-making and efficient execution during games.

It's worth remembering the footballer has not yet been born who doesn't enjoy shooting practice: it's always looked forward to as an enjoyable part of any session. Practicing shooting skills will also benefit other areas of a young player's game because it focuses a player's attention on good first touch and clean striking of the ball.

As with any technical work, the more imaginatively you can structure the necessary repetitions, the longer your players will be able to commit full concentration to what they're being asked to do.

Away from work, I've managed a team all the way through: they'll be Under-12s this season. It's amazing to watch them develop. They go through growth spurts. Their lives change as they move through school. And that means what you can do with them as a coach changes, too. At 5 and 6, I used to tell them stories, 'Here's a swamp full of crocodiles and you've got to get the ball across the swamp without the crocodiles getting you.'

If I said that to a 9-year-old, he'd just look at me and go, 'What?!' Instead, at that age, you can explain a drill and explain what you're trying to achieve with it, too. You have to. As they get older, kids start asking, 'Why? Why are we doing this?' You need to be able to answer that question: we're working on touch, or on decision-making, or on what to do when we're out of possession.

You can start giving older boys responsibility to help develop their leadership skills: you're picking the team today or you're going to decide what formation we play. Kids want ownership of their game, and they respond to that in positive ways. —John Folwell

HEADING

NOTE >> It's very important not to spend too much time on heading repetitions at the age of Level 2 players. As with players at Level 1, there are health and safety and developmental issues which need to be respected as regards young footballers and frequent heading of the ball. Any heading drills, therefore, should be condensed so players are only heading short distances and focusing on timing and point of contact rather than power and distance.

The work outlined here will be similar to the work done at Level 1. The difference is that young players will now be able to generate extra spring when they jump and should be focusing on control and touch as their technical ability develops. In 9 v 9 games, it may well be that the ball will travel through the air more often and boys will be challenged to head the ball in more match situations at both ends of the pitch. Practice at Level 2 should focus on heading the ball better in terms of technique.

INTRODUCTION TO AGE APPROPRIATE HEADING TECHNIQUE >>

CUSHIONED PASS HEADERS

HEADING AT GOAL

DEFENSIVE CLEARANCE HEADERS

CUSHIONED PASS HEADER

- As you approach the ball (or the ball approaches you), try to keep your eye on it and concentrate on making contact with your forehead. This will help you to avoid mis-timing connection and making connection with the top of your head.
- Don't follow through with too much momentum. The intention is to cushion the ball in the direction of the intended area or target.

HEADER AT GOAL

- When moving towards the ball with the intention of heading it, it's important to arrive at the point of contact with some momentum if possible.
- Always keep your eye on the ball. Use your neck muscles as your forehead connects with the ball to push the ball downwards towards the corners of the goal.
- Try to keep your eyes on the ball as you travel towards it. This gives you the best chance of connecting with your forehead rather than the top of your head, which would mean the ball bouncing upwards and over the bar.

DEFENSIVE CLEARANCE HEADER

- Try and get a run up towards the ball to generate some momentum.
- Keep your eyes focused on the ball all times and lift one bent arm across the front of your chest to protect your face.
- Try to generate power from the waist and spine, putting your whole body weight through the ball when connecting. This will to guide the ball upwards and away from you.
- Practice the timing and control of your jumps. Try to make sure you don't close your eyes. This is very important if you're going to avoid the ball hitting either the bridge of your nose or the top of your head.

2.5 LIFESTYLE

As a young Level 2 footballer starts to mature and develop into the player he dreams of becoming, he will find the demands on his time increasing. Those demands will be around football—training, practicing, playing games—but also in other areas of his life. It's essential to find the right balance between his commitments to football and those he needs to make to school, family, and time spent with friends.

Even at these younger age groups, finding the right balance will involves making decisions about his schedule, establishing priorities, and managing the different demands on his attention. Secondary school is just around the corner and there may be an element of extra pressure that comes with that, notably his SATS tests in Year 6.

By now, of course, he may be playing for a team at school as well as for one outside. He'll need to develop organisational skills to find a way through the different challenges facing him now. He wants to be the best he can be, not just as a footballer, but in every other area of his life, too:

FAMILY

SCHOOLWORK

SOCIAL LIFE

ROLE MODEL

LIVING YOUR SPORT

FAMILY

As discussed at Level 1, parents will take on a fair amount of extra responsibility when their sons begin to play football. Parents will have to make sure they can get a boy to training and games and will want to find the time to be there themselves; they'll be financing a boy's progress by paying subs and buying boots, shinguards, goalie gloves and match kit; they'll be keeping an eye on a boy getting the right kind of food and the right amount of sleep. Parents love to support a son's enthusiasm, of course. But sometimes it can feel like a full-time job: as if the rest of life is wedged in around your son's football commitments!

PLAYER » Players who work on their organisational skills and learn to take their share of responsibility tend to have more positive family relationships. It starts with being aware that what happens to you impacts on parents and siblings, too.

Players who know when they expect to be training or playing in matches can let their parents know: talk about your schedule. Even write it down somewhere!

That way, kit will be washed and ready, food prepared and packed, and transport arranged in plenty of time. Announcing things at the last minute will force the rest of the family to change plans: you and everybody else will be rushed, stressed and annoyed. Worse still, if those plans can't be changed for whatever reason, you may end up missing a session or game.

There are simple ways of staying organised: have a special place in the cupboard or wardrobe where you keep all your kit; a shelf downstairs where you know your boots and astros belong. Think about taking on one or two of the jobs which need doing to get you ready for football: cleaning and looking after your boots, for example.

Or putting dirty kit in the washing machine or the laundry pile instead of kicking it under your bed where it'll still be the following Sunday morning. Taking some of the pressure off your parents will take pressure off you, too. Instead of chasing round to get ready, you can be relaxing and preparing properly for the game.

SCHOOLWORK

PARENT >> *I'm working at Portsmouth now. Our Head of Education always talks to parents at the start of every year. He's honest with them. Boys are embarking on a journey, hoping to become professional footballers, and the chances of them making it are very small.*

But if they're going to go on the journey at all, the boys and their parents are going to have to make sacrifices, even though they'll probably end up disappointed. It's why finding the time, somehow, to keep boys going with their education is so important.

If a boy's in an academy, he'll be taken out of school at times during the week. He'll be training in the evenings. He'll play at the weekends. And boys that age are easily distracted anyway. But you have to find some way of him keeping up with studying. Give him structure, try and put in a routine. Otherwise, without any qualifications, when the club turns rounds and says they're letting him go, what is he left with? Where does he go from there?
—*Mark Chamberlain*

It's not just about what a young player can and can't do on the pitch. Schoolwork is an absolutely fundamental part of the journey towards becoming a **COMPLETE ATHLETE**. Not every young footballer is also going to be an A+ student, of course, but it's important he's seen to try and improve and be the best he can be in the school environment, as well as out on the pitch.

It's a case of trying to be better at what he does every day: applying that work ethic—and those standards of behaviour—to school will have a positive effect on a boy's progress as a footballer, too. The ability to concentrate, take instruction and self-motivate are all qualities which will get a positive reaction from his schoolteachers, as well as his football coaches. They are qualities he'll need to move forward in football and in the rest of his life. A young player's chances of achieving his dreams in football will always be improved by working equally hard at his studies.

PLAYER >> Developing organisational skills as you move up through the year groups at primary school can make a huge difference to what you're able to achieve in your studies. More schoolwork on your plate at the same time as you're training more than ever: to squeeze the maximum into every day, keeping track of what you need to be doing is vital.

It may help to create a to-do list at the start of every school week which you can refer back to. Organising your time—getting schoolwork done on schedule rather than letting it pile up on you towards the end of the week—can only help you get better marks. Which will leave you more time to devote to football, family and friends.

SOCIAL LIFE

It's natural: if a young player spends a lot of his time training and playing, he'll start to develop friendships in connection with football. He and his mates share a passion, after all. And maybe they share the dream of making it as players as well. In any group of boys, though, spending a lot of time together means cliques can emerge.

With cliques come the possibilities of gossip, teasing, and bullying. Parents and coaches need to keep track of those problems if they happen, and do whatever they can to put a stop to them. In training and in games, that'll mean working to create new bonds between team-mates rather than just trying to break up those that already exist.

Despite the understandable focus on football in a young player's social life, it can only ever be a good thing if he finds ways to make and keep friends from other areas of his life: school, clubs, church or neighbours, for example. That **SOCIAL LIFE** away from football can foster a more rounded individual, one whose self-esteem and confidence aren't wholly dependent on his achievements as a player. Support and encouragement from those other friends can help create a sturdier sense of identity for a boy who's on the brink of becoming a teenager and about to face the challenges that brings.

As boys move towards the end of their primary school years, socialising online and via social media may well become an important part of their lives. Whether parents like it or not, an online social life has become the norm for a new generation of children.

It's important, though, for young people to remember an online life isn't a substitute for spending real time with friends face-to-face. This is, if anything, even more relevant for young footballers whose progress in the game will increasingly depend on good interpersonal and communication skills.

Face-to-face interaction is both more challenging and more rewarding, fostering the ability to understand other people, especially friends, and helping to build confidence in social situations, not least in the dressing room.

PLAYER » If you're communicating with friends and family online for longer periods than you're communicating face-to-face, you might want to think about ways of changing that balance. You can actually add up the minutes and hours you spend socialising online during a week and compare it to the amount of time you spend face-to-face with those people. If online is outweighing offline, you should start putting in the little bit of extra effort to catch up with your mates in person rather than just gaming or Facebooking together.

You may well have a phone of your own by now. Problems and challenges posed by social media can wait until Level 3, but you need to be thinking right now about when and where you use your phone.

You'd be in all sorts of trouble if your phone went off during school classes. Make sure it's switched off, as well, before every training session and every game. And perhaps afterwards, too: wouldn't it be better to talk to team-mates and your coach as you wind down and get ready to go home? Whatever you're rushing to check on your phone screen can definitely wait for another half hour.

When I was a teenager, I was practicing on my own or with a mate all the time, even if it was just kicking against a wall in the little yard at the back of where we lived. And I was around grown-ups, too: watching how they behaved, how they talked to each other, training and playing alongside them. I'm not sure it's like that for kids now—TVs everywhere, mobile phones and all that. When I first started coaching the young keepers at QPR, in the 90s, it coincided with the start of everybody having mobiles and playing computer games.

Now, it's just the way of the world. Rather than practising, they're on the phone! Players come in wearing headphones, in their own little worlds. They don't speak to each other. Maybe it helps them be focussed, in the zone or whatever.

But what about the camaraderie, the team spirit, that comes with being together in a dressing room? Have we lost some of that? Communicating—that's how we grow, not just as footballers but as young men. A goalkeeper's got to be confident, assertive. He won't learn that sitting in a corner on his own. —Tony Roberts

ROLE MODEL

We've defined a **ROLE MODEL** as someone who possesses qualities others admire, such as behaviour, and demonstrates respect for themselves and for other people. At Level 2, a young player can start being an effective role model for younger—or even older—siblings, friends, and team-mates by behaving in the right way in school, at home, and at football. Good behaviour often starts with knowing the rules and respecting them. That's true in the classroom, of course. It's also true when it comes to making progress as a player.

Listen to coaches and follow their instructions. Have a positive attitude even when things don't go your way.

Respect your team-mates and support them when they need it. Try to take responsibility when a game gets difficult. Treating others the way you'd want them to treat you is a good place to start. Learn to do the right thing, even in those moments when it might not be the easiest thing.

PLAYER >> *If people ask me now what was the most important thing when it came to making a success of becoming and being a professional footballer, I will always say it was that mental side of the game. How do you deal with being dropped? How do you deal with being injured? There are so many hurdles you have to get over. There might be a parent or a friend or a coach who can talk to you.*

But I used to have the conversations with myself, 'This is a bad situation right now but I'm going to get through it. I'm going to make it.' Every time you do that, you're learning. You're teaching yourself how to be mentally strong. It's the same in any walk of life: how do you deal with a problem? Are you going to find a way round it or are you just going to give up? —Paul Davis

LIVING YOUR SPORT

PLAYER » *It all starts with that passion, that love of kicking a ball. It's a pity now: boys can't just go out in the street the way we used to, to play with their mates and get their practice that way. There are clubs, of course. But, even at home, you can find a way. When I was at Wimbledon, we had a young player called Lionel Morgan: the best youth player I've ever seen.*

Unfortunately, injuries meant he had to retire when he was just 21. But Lionel was unbelievable, made his first team debut when he was 17: came on as a sub at Millwall in centre midfield and ran the game.

Anyway, when we signed Lionel, when he was about 14, we went round to his house. He grew up in Tottenham. His mum was there and said, 'Oh, this boy is driving me mad!' Lionel had a rolled up sock that he used as a ball and just played with constantly inside the house: keepy-uppys, headers, volleys, everything. He was non-stop. Maybe your mum wouldn't be happy if the sock hits something and breaks it. But, if she has a go at you, maybe that helps make you better at controlling it! —Terry Burton

Young footballers who are serious about turning professional—getting the best out of themselves at the highest possible level—will develop a lifestyle in which they live and breathe football.

At Level 1, a player will demonstrate that passion simply by playing for the love of the game. At Level 2, that love burns just as bright, but young players who live for their sport will now be ready and willing to spend more time practicing and mastering skills and techniques. They'll be the boys seen dribbling a ball whenever and wherever they can; the ones getting out of the car with a ball in their hand, ready to throw it down on the ground and start to play.

They'll also be watching as much professional football as they can, soaking up whatever lessons they can from their favourite players, studying how those players pass, move, think, and score goals.

Another less obvious thing young players at Level 2 should be doing in order to progress towards their ambitions is to learn and understand the Laws of the Game, which cover everything from the size of the pitch through to what constitutes a 'red card' offence during a game. The Laws of the Game have a history all of their own and understanding them is vital if you're going to understand football properly.

The 17 Laws are laid out by FIFA and cover all professional and international matches. Some slight modifications are made for grassroots and early-age football. To read the latest version of the laws of the game, go to FIFA'S website at www.FIFA.com. The Laws are amended from time to time. **COMPLETE ATHLETE** will always keep you updated on any changes.

PLAYER >> *The first house I can remember growing up in was in Green Walk in Whalley Range. That's South Manchester, not far from the city centre. It was a cul-de-sac so it was pretty quiet and, in the middle, there was a patch of green which the houses were around. That's where I first remember playing football. We'd either play* on the green, in between the trees, or on the road, and using driveways as goals. That's when I was maybe four years old. If there were more of us, there was a fence at the bottom of our garden. We could climb over into the primary school, Manley Park, which had a long patch of grass next to it, and we'd play 5 v 5 on there. It was football every day!

There were a couple of other boys my age but we used to play with my brother and his friends. They were five or six years older than me, and of course, it was difficult physically. There'd be tears sometimes and my brother would say, 'OK. Go inside. You're not playing any more.' But I'd insist. I had to keep playing. It was a bit of a struggle, but it meant that, when I went to play with boys my own age, it seemed easier for me.

I'm 6'4" now, but back then, playing with those bigger boys, I had to find different ways to get into the game, even to get a touch on the ball. I think it was really good for my development. I had to have the right mentality to cope with it, which maybe other boys my age didn't have. At my primary school, I had a friend whose dad ran a team, Chorlton Sports, and I went down and played with them even though I was a year younger than the friends I had playing there. That was the first coaching I ever had and, from there, I got invited into Manchester City's development centre at Parrs Wood High School.

I was 5 years old. Then they moved me up to sessions at Vida, which was an Astroturf pitch behind Whalley Range High School. The training there was mostly just playing 6- and 7-a-side. It was where younger boys went until they could sign for City, aged 9, and start going to the old training ground at Platt Lane.

Before I had to sign for a club, I could still play for a boys' team with my friends: Chorlton Sports; and then, when my coach moved and started up a new team, Hough End Griffins. City had seen me playing for Chorlton Sports but, at Hough End, there were scouts from United and Blackburn as well. I started training with all of them on different nights of the week. It was just more chances to play! I had different friends who were training at all those clubs so it was always a case of playing with mates; I used to travel to Blackburn with another boy who lived on Green Walk like me.

At 7 and 8 years old, it all took some organising: I think my mum had a lot on her plate, but she did incredibly well for me, getting me to all the different training sessions somehow. Sometimes it'd be in a car, if she could arrange for someone to pick us up; other times it'd be a bus ride or even a walk.

There was a scout who'd come and get me and my friend after school to take us up to Blackburn on a Friday night and drop us back home after the session. I would have played every single night of the week if I could! I just wanted to be playing football all the time.

At nine years old, you had to decide to play for one club and, for me, it came down to a choice between City and Blackburn. I remember clubs used to arrange days out for the boys they were hoping to sign. It got as far as me going up to Blackburn for the day: they took us to a game, we went bowling, for a meal and then the idea was I was going to sign for them afterwards.

But, right at the last minute, I decided not to. It was all my own decision. I realised City was nearer to where I lived. Even more important, there was a guy at City who had a huge influence on me and who I really looked up to: Billy Hughes, my first coach, who just retired this year. Looking back, I think he was the main reason I made the decision I did.

Billy was an incredible man. He was great with me. Great with my family. From the day I met him, he always believed in me, always supported me. And he gave me ambition: even when I was a young boy, he was telling me I could be a top player at City, that I could captain the club one day. I don't know what would have happened without Billy. I know God put him here to make sure I got to where I am today! The coaches were like that at City: setting you targets, like being a first team player in your teens, playing for England, captaining England. It just took the lid off my ambition: pushed me to aim as high as I can.

Once I'd signed as a schoolboy at City, the biggest thing that changed was that I couldn't play with my friends at Hough End Griffins any more. I could only play for City and I remember that annoyed me at the time. We went to training two or three nights during the week and then a game on Sunday. At that age, they introduced lots of passing drills, but those were things that I'd been doing at the younger age groups with Blackburn so it didn't seem so new to me. Before then, at City, training had really just been playing games, even at Under-9s.

Doing a lot of repetitions with our drills just seemed to me like the thing that was happening at the time. It wasn't till later, when I was 13 or 14, that I realised those repetitions were a really important part of learning to be a footballer. Generally, though, sessions were a lot less structured back then. I see the younger boys now at the Academy, and I don't remember doing any of those things at Platt Lane when I was their age. The passing drills, the movement, seem pretty much the same for the young ones now as they'll going to be doing when they're playing at Under-16 and Under-18.

I always thought respect was a very important thing. That's something I grew up with, something that started from home. So, when it came to training sessions, I'd *always make sure I did little things like shaking the coach's hand when I arrived and before I left. I spent so much time around older boys when I was young. That carried on when I was a schoolboy at City because, after Under-10s, I always played up a year or two above my own age group.*

A lot of it goes back to my parents, my mum in particular. Her values were pretty simple, and we could apply them to football. It was all about school, working hard, not misbehaving. And not causing her too many headaches! You know, it wasn't easy for my parents financially, and we could see the obstacles they had to overcome. But they were striving to make things better for us. I was the youngest but I still knew how to behave when I was away from home, at school or at the football club. I had good examples to follow. I knew what was tolerated at home and, however things were away from there, the example from home was the one I followed, being polite and respectful.

Both my older brothers, Gbolahan and Fisayo were a massive influence for me as well. Fisayo was also at the City Academy so I got an important insight into how older boys behaved, for good and for bad, and it meant I took that in naturally. It gave me a more mature mentality and I think maybe the City coaches picked up on that. Gbolahan is the oldest of us three—he's my agent now—and he really reinforced Mum's values.

He could relate to me, too, because he was nearer my own age. He was hard-headed and had a real knowledge of football from playing himself and having friends who played right up to the top levels in the game. It means he was able to guide me all the way through, to whatever successes I've achieved.

I was probably 12 or 13 when I realised that football could be something more than just a game I loved playing, that it could be a career. By then we were putting more hours in at training, and it was when I found out about academy scholarships. I was playing Under-15s at that stage and those lads were all thinking and talking about whether or not they would get scholarships the following year.

Right around then, as well, my older brother, Fisayo, was an Under-16 and he didn't get taken on at City, so he left and went to Birmingham City. The result of all that was, the older I got, the more I realised I had to work even harder if I was going to get where I wanted to go. When I was 13, 14, the Academy became almost a full-time thing. All of us boys were transferred from our own schools to a school called St. Bede's. From then on, we were training every day as well as doing school.

At that age, I was playing for the Under-16s but their training schedule didn't fit with my schooling so they moved me back to Under-14 for a couple of weeks. I remember my family talked to City because we realised—and City realised—that going back two years wasn't the right thing for my development.

The decision was made to push me on even more and I started training with the Under-18s, first and second year scholars, which fitted my schedule better. I was still only 14 but, a few months after that, I played for the Under-18s for the first time. It was pretty clear then that I would be getting a scholarship. I was already playing at that level and matching it.

My first secondary school was Chorlton High School, and I was just like any other boy there, even though I was training with City. I used to go onto the school playing fields in the evenings and play on the 11-a-side pitch with my brothers. That stopped when City put us into the private school, St Bede's, though. I was busy training every day. School was different, too, because we weren't really integrated with the other students. I think they just thought of us as 'the footballers' or 'the City players'. We had our own schedule and didn't really cross over with them.

Leaving Chorlton High School changed a few things for me. While I was growing up with City, I made 3 or 4 really close friends, a couple of whom had been with me when we were going to training at 5 years old. But some other friends—friends I had at my old school—I had to sort of cut off from when I was 13 or 14.

These were boys I'd known since kicking a ball around in Green Walk; I'd been to their houses, met their families. They'd always been nice to me. But, as their lives changed and some of them realised they maybe weren't going to make it as footballers, they started getting into stuff that I knew I couldn't be a part of.

Nonsense stuff. It got to a point where I knew—and my family knew—that I couldn't hang around with them and it be right for me as a young footballer. But it also meant I wasn't going out to play football with my mates in the evenings any more.

Because the Under-18s had one day out of school altogether, I did too. It meant I needed extra help with some subjects, like Maths and English, to try and keep up. It was hard for me—I was tired after school or I just wanted to go out and play football—and so I think it was hard for the tutor as well!

It wasn't the same as being in class but I knew I just had to get on with it. It was my mum who really insisted I keep studying hard. She still wasn't thinking about football as being a career. It's only very recently—the last few years, maybe, that my mum's realised where football could take me.

I think back to when I was young and so many of the other boys' parents were already talking about the future, talking about their boys playing for United and City. When they were 5 or 6 years old. It was never like that for my mum. She couldn't always get to my games because Fisayo was playing as well and our games were always at different venues.

Mum had all the family to look after so it was just a practical thing for her: My boys want to play football so I have to get them where they need to go; I need to feed them properly when they get home; I need to clean their kit for tomorrow. But I need to make sure they're doing their homework as well and not just getting carried away with football. —Tosin Adarabioyo

JOIN THE CONVERSATION!
Follow your favorite pros in the **COMPLETE ATHLETE** app.

IN LEVEL 3

As a young footballer steps up to Level 3, he will face entirely new challenges, on and off the pitch. So much is happening to him, physically and psychologically, during these early teenage years. It's a constant process of change, adaptation and having to learn from new experiences. Football is part of that. His love for the game and his ambitions to excel as a player may be a thread running through the rest of his world: social, domestic and academic.

At times, the game may be his only escape from the pressures every young man is subjected to. At other times, the extra demands placed on him by his parents, his coaches and his team-mates may seem like problems rather than solutions. Hardest of all to come to terms with may be the pressure he puts on himself, determined as he is to realise his potential.

At Level 3, a young player will move up to 11-a-side football on full-sized pitches. Training is now aimed at preparing for adult football. He may be playing for his school, for representative sides, for his team on a Saturday or Sunday, too.

Or he may have been picked up by a professional club and be trying to work his way through the academy system with the aim of securing an academy scholarship by the time he turns 16. He'll be learning constantly: technically and tactically, of course, but also about the psychological and social elements of the game. He'll need to become resilient, self-motivated, and brave, an effective team-mate as well as an outstanding individual player.

Football may feel like the most important thing in a teenage boy's life. But it can never be the only thing. Secondary school will be his chance to prepare for adulthood, to gain the qualifications and the life experiences which will in many ways define him as a young man, whatever the career path—inside or outside football—that lies ahead.

The young player will need to commit to his studies with the same energy and discipline as he does his training sessions and games. He'll need to play an increasingly active role in life at home, taking on responsibility for himself and for other family members. He'll be faced, as well, with navigating a teenager's social life; the emotional ups and downs that accompany adolescence; the temptations put in his path by a new-found sense of independence, on the one hand, and the straightjacket of peer pressure on the other.

Everything, it'll seem, is new and constantly changing. The young footballer with ambitions to realise, however, will need to remember that some things remain the same. As well as making whatever sacrifices he must on the way to achieving his potential as a player, a **COMPLETE ATHLETE** also commits full-time to the business of becoming the best student, the best friend, the best family member—the best person—he can possibly be.

PLAYER » *Maybe we do try and set everything out for young players: train, play, be here at this time, do this at this time. I don't mean just as academies. I mean as adults, as coaches. I'd say up until the age of 14, when things need to perhaps become more focused, it's good for boys to do other sports, to play for their schools, with their mates. To play in less structured environments. Go and play and train wherever and whenever you can.*

Don't miss out on having time with your mates, playing in games where you can just have fun and maybe try things you wouldn't in a more structured environment. Of course, it's good to get coached, to get advice on the 'right' way to play but, especially for younger boys, it's important to have those other experiences as well.

—Terry Burton

COACH » *Whatever level a boy's playing at, between 12 and 16 years old, a coach becomes a very important person in a boy's life. The challenge for the coach is to recognise what his young players need from football and deliver that. At a Sunday League club, the boys are there because they want to be with their friends. They want to win and they want to enjoy themselves. A coach needs to foster that. At a professional academy, the boys are probably there for a different reason. They've got a target they're aiming at: playing for that club's first team. The coach still needs to make sure they're enjoying themselves; he wants them to win games, but he's also got to recognise there's that target ahead of each individual player.*

To get to 16, to get an academy scholarship and a first professional contract. Recognise it but not add to the pressure that comes with it. What a young player needs from a coach at grassroots level and what he needs from a coach at a top academy are very different things.

You know, I sometimes wonder whether 'coach' is a good word for what's needed. As soon as someone's identified as a coach, they're automatically expected to tell people what to do and how to do it. But, with young players especially, that's not the coach's role. Just as much, he has to support the players' own development. Maybe 'supporter' would be as good a word as 'coach'!

At academy level, certainly, it's about finding the right balance between offering a boy leadership and structure, on the one hand, and fostering the spontaneity and the freedom he's still got in his game, on the other. You can't put percentages on it. The balance will vary from player to player and from group to group and finding it is the real skill in coaching, I think. —Paul Davis

PARENT » *I don't know where my love of football came from. It certainly wasn't from home. My older brother liked football but not the way I did: for me, it was everything. I collected stickers and cards. I'd lay them out and imagine games. I'd be commentating out loud. When Andros was growing up, I could hear him through the bedroom door, doing the same thing.*

It's just being consumed by football. Some people might say it's too much, too single-minded a focus. But if the aim is to be a professional footballer, it's got to start somewhere.

I think the right attitude can make a huge difference. Skills that matter in life can matter in football, too. I know for sure that boys who perhaps don't have outstanding talent get a chance because they're polite, respectful, hard-working; they do all they're asked to and then go out on the training pitch and do more. If clubs see that in a boy, they may take a punt on him, giving him time to develop. Whereas the boy who perhaps has more natural talent but who gives them grief day in and day out doesn't get that chance. —Troy Townsend

3.1 ATTITUDE

A **POSITIVE ATTITUDE** is essential to the success of a **COMPLETE ATHLETE**. That's the case throughout a player's growth and development, but never more so than at Level 3. The player is now competing 11 v 11 and attending secondary school—two significant steps forward which will challenge him in very new ways.

A positive attitude will be key to negotiating those next steps. At this age, scouts and coaches are looking not only at footballing ability but also judging a player's demeanour, body language, and character when considering recruitment decisions.

A positive attitude is something that can be developed and improved with training, just like any other skill.

As a player, you'll be developing physically, technically, and tactically. At the same time, you will need to be learning to train your brain and handle emotions as you encounter new challenges, new situations, and new environments at Level 3. A **COMPLETE ATHLETE** continues to make a habit of recognising and demonstrating the importance of five attributes:

RESPECT

SPORTSMANSHIP

TEAMWORK

PROFESSIONALISM

LEADERSHIP

RESPECT

RESPECT means treating people in ways which show you recognise that they have worth and value. At Levels 1 and 2, the stress was on ways to make sure you were treating coaches and team-mates with respect. At Level 3, a young footballer needs to build on this. As you find your way through adolescence, it's very important for you to recognise the importance of respecting yourself. That will be key to dealing with your own personal issues and will also reinforce the positive way you deal with other people, on the pitch and off it.

Thinking about those 12 to 16 age groups, I think respect is an important part of what the young player needs to bring to his work. I will talk to a 16-year-old as a young adult, not as a child. He needs to talk to me as his coach. That's something I learnt as a gymnast: that respect for your coach. The boy needs to buy into what we're doing at the club; he needs a willingness to learn. I've had to explain to boys that they're un-coachable at a particular time because they don't want to listen.

But if you're 15 or 16 and you already know everything about football, why aren't you playing for our first team? Why aren't you playing for Chelsea or Real Madrid? At that age, you only know a tiny part of what you're going to need to know. Respect your coach, respect the club, respect the environment and then you've got a chance of making progress in the game. —Rossi Eames

One of the most important ways of developing self-respect is to pay attention at all times to your fitness, nutrition, and recovery. You're now becoming responsible for your own health and well-being. It's no longer enough to assume that your parents or coaches will be there 24/7 to make sure you're doing what you need to do. As a young player, you need to nourish, hydrate, and exercise your body. That will give you the best chance of playing at your maximum on a consistent basis. It will also help you avoid injury. Just as important, it'll keep you in good condition for staying healthy in the rest of your life, too.

You'll be aware that you're being given more room for personal independence. You might also find you're feeling peer pressure, around football, around school or around your social life. Some of that freedom and some of that pressure can very easily become a serious threat to your progress towards becoming a **COMPLETE ATHLETE**.

As well as keeping at arm's length the temptation to try drinking alcohol or using recreational drugs, it cannot be stressed enough that you should, in all circumstances, and whatever anybody else says or does—avoid experimenting with any kind of performance-enhancing drugs. These substances can have a very bad effect on both body and mind in the short-term. In the long-term, they can cripple your ambitions as a sportsman. They're more likely to end your career than help it in any way.

An important element of developing self-respect is learning to forgive yourself. Your shot may fly off your foot and balloon wide of the target. You might miss that vital challenge or block, and the other team scores. You'll have training sessions and games in which, for whatever reason, you don't perform at your best. You need to learn that those moments of coming up short are part of football. The world's very best players miss simple chances and fail with interceptions. Be like those top players: don't dwell on your mistakes. Learn from them and work to constantly improve. It's the way you'll build resilience, a quality which will serve you well in life as well as in the game.

SPORTSMANSHIP

Good **SPORTSMANSHIP** starts with respect for your team-mates, opponents, coaches, and match officials. It's also about respecting the game and its rules, playing football with integrity at all times. That includes acknowledging any foul play immediately and accepting the judgement of match officials without argument.

Accepting and taking responsibility for your mistakes can be demonstrated in relation to your team-mates, too. Bound up with good sportsmanship is a willingness to maintain a positive attitude in adversity and being accountable for your actions and decisions rather than looking to put the blame on others. If you make the wrong run or shoot when you should have passed, acknowledge the mistake and don't look for excuses.

PLAYER » If you make an error of judgement during a game-or even in training—the most effective way of dealing with it is to raise a hand or call out to say you acknowledge the mistake and then get on with the game. This will keep the situation from escalating or hanging over you and the team; it'll also earn you respect from team-mates, coaches, and opponents.

What you're looking to avoid at all costs is the mistake being made worse by it undermining your focus on the game.

The game, even at the highest level, is littered with mistakes. And everybody makes them. Blaming other people for yours will betray insecurity on your part and can damage the balance in your team.

COACH » Mistakes are made by even the very best players every other minute in training and constantly during games. Knowing that, it's vital a coach encourages honesty, accountability, and good sportsmanship in the group. This isn't just to do with what goes on between your players; it's also about your relationship with them,

individually and collectively. Be honest with every player about your decisions and why you've made them.

If you've made a wrong one, acknowledge it. If, in the middle of a session, you realise a particular drill isn't working in the way you'd planned, stop. Recognise what's wrong with what you've set up and do whatever you need to do to adjust it. You being accountable will always provoke a better reaction in the group than you watching a drill not working and letting your players continue with something they're unlikely to learn from.

TEAMWORK

TEAMWORK depends on individuals working as a group to achieve a common goal. A balance of talents and personalities, along with a willingness to work hard collectively, will help any group to fulfil their potential. And more: the mark of good teamwork is when the whole is equal to more than the sum of its parts.

In football, teamwork doesn't rely on everybody liking each other. It relies on honesty, commitment, and mutual respect. At Level 3, the ability to function as a member of a team is a quality looked for by coaches, scouts, and potential new team-mates.

PLAYER >> As a Level 3 player, you may be playing for your school and hoping to be called up to a representative side; you may be playing for a Sunday club and hoping to be spotted by a professional scout; you may be playing in a professional academy and hoping to be kept on the following year. Of course, it's important to express yourself as an individual and to make plain what's unique in terms of your natural abilities.

In every case, though, anyone watching you play will want to see you working hard for the group, intelligently combining with team-mates, and thus making the most effective use of your talents. Humility is the hallmark of every great player. That allows him the chance to be part of a great team. Teamwork is founded on the understanding that football is less about 'Me' at the top level. And more about 'We.'

I think English academies are now probably the most professional anywhere. Youngsters are almost part-time players. They train four or five times a week, clubs are taking more responsibility than ever for boys' educations. So English boys are ahead in that respect, although sometimes I wonder if we're too professional, perhaps, too strict.

The most important thing as a teenage player is that you love what you're doing, after all. But to succeed a boy needs to be able to work within a structure, needs to show he's willing to make sacrifices and, most important of all, he has to show that he's able to learn. That he's coachable.

The game has become more and more tactical. Players are more intelligent. There are fewer 'mavericks'. From one to eleven, every player has to be responsible tactically. Teams can't carry anyone any more, however talented they may be. You can't have weak links.

Everyone's got to be able to do their job at whatever level they're playing at. Football's not an individual sport. A player has to fit into a team structure. You want to do the best for yourself but you always have to remember you're part of a team. —Paul Clement

JOIN THE CONVERSATION!

Teamwork, respect, and community are all important parts of becoming a **COMPLETE ATHLETE**. Check out the app to learn more!

COACH >> *One secret of being a great youth coach is having the ability to put your own emotions and your ego to one side in the interest of developing individual players and the team that they're a part of. Your technical work, of course, needs to be of the highest standard possible and enormous personal satisfaction is a natural response to exceptional performances by your players.*

But your responsibility to creating an environment in which players can learn and grow is paramount. Think twice before shouting at individual players: are you just trying to reinforce your sense of authority? Or before making a short-term decision in the interests of winning a particular game: is that a decision which may actually hinder your players finding their own solution to a problem and learning to think for themselves? Decisions you make with your own—rather than your players'—interests in mind may cost them in terms of their development and may cost you in terms of losing their respect.

My association with West Ham as a coach lasted 43 years. Most of that was working with younger players. I think I was drawn to that because of the amount of detail that went into it. Things have changed now but, back in the day, first team football was about coming in, doing a session, bit of five-a-side and then some finishing and that was it.

Obviously it's much more complex now. With young players, though, I think development work always meant being very clear about what you wanted to achieve with each session, recognising what individual lads needed to work on and thinking up ways to help them improve.

I think it's all about developing the right environment for kids. I don't mean a glitzy training ground. I mean the human environment. Every training night, we'd always do our best to make parents feel welcome. There'd be a cup of tea, a smile, time for a chat. We tried to make sure that every member of staff knew the name of every boy we had with us. Families felt welcome and felt they could express themselves. We did our best not to add to the pressure that was naturally there.

And really important: at West Ham they could see a pathway for their boys. They saw Frank Lampard and Rio Ferdinand in the first team, Michael Carrick and Joe Cole: there was a route all the way through. —Tony Carr

PROFESSIONALISM

A young player at Level 3 isn't a **PROFESSIONAL** in the sense of him being paid to play football. However, he should be developing the mentality, good habits, and work rate of a professional footballer to help him progress in the game. At Level 2, a young player was starting to take responsibility for arriving at training sessions and games on time, physically and mentally ready to go to work. At Level 3, being properly prepared becomes even more important, especially if there's the possibility of scouts and coaches from the professional game being there to watch you. First impressions can count for a lot.

PLAYER » *Generally speaking, gymnastics and football are different in that, as a young gymnast, you're given the apparatus to work on but everything else has to come from you. At top football clubs, boys are provided with*

everything in terms of kit and facilities: the very best. Here at Barnet, though, we only give the boys what they're actually going to need. We tell them that their talent has got them in through the door, but it's hard work that'll keep them here. And that goes for their whole careers. You can get your first pro contract, but then, if you take your foot off the gas, you won't get another one and will find yourself out of the game. —Rossi Eames

LEADERSHIP

A leader has the ability to inspire, motivate, and breed confidence in others, helping those around him to perform at higher levels. As a player at Level 3 gets involved with 11-a-side football on the pitch and the secondary school environment off it, natural leaders will continue to develop their skills as they interact with team-mates and coaches, teachers, and classmates.

Even in his early teens, a young player may stand out as a natural choice as a captain or group leader. His success in that role, though, will depend on him having earned the trust and respect of those around him. The most effective leaders share a common trait: integrity. You can't con your way as a skipper. There are different ways, though, for **LEADERSHIP** quality to express itself. In the football context, a player may be the type to lead by example: quiet vocally, perhaps, but consistently setting standards for team-mates to follow.

On the other hand, a player may find that he can motivate those around him by talking and spurring his team-mates on. A player, at this age, may not even be particularly aware that he functions as a leader.

His team-mates, though, and his coach, are already looking towards him as an example in terms of his dedication, work-rate and consistency.

3.2 PREPARATION

PLAYER >> *I worry about sometimes being the first person to stand up in front of boys and say, 'This might not work out for you. In fact, only 2 or 3 percent of you will end up making a living in the game. There may be another player, in your position, waiting just down the line.' It can be harsh: football's a very selfish industry.*

Of course it's a team game but, ultimately, you have to look out for yourself. Your goal is a contract and the team can't get you that. You'll only achieve it by being the best individual you can be within the team structure. It might come down to you or your best mate for the last pro contract offer or the last scholarship place at a club. Well, you have to outdo him. You have to work as hard as you can to make sure you're the one who gets asked to sign. —Troy Townsend

PREPARATION is about practicing your technical skills, studying top players, eating well, continually staying hydrated, getting enough rest and sleep to allow you to properly prepare for training and games. Preparing properly gives you confidence and assurance that you can perform at an elite level with complete focus.

A **COMPLETE ATHLETE** prepares to perform at his best by consistently working and improving on the following:

TRAINING

NUTRITION

HYDRATION

RECOVERY

MENTALITY

TRAINING

A footballer at Level 3 already considers football a huge part of his life. He'll have his dreams and ambitions but, at the same time, he'll be starting to understand the realities of the game. For a start, he'll know now the areas of his game that need to be worked on technically and which elements of his physical and mental performance he needs to improve on.

COACH ›› *As a coach, watching a young player developing through his teens, it's always important to keep an open mind. You don't need to fix a boy in a single position too early. Instead, watch how he grows and develops. Look at Glen Johnson: he was a striker, then a central midfielder, then a right winger and then a right back.*

That's where he ended up playing for us and for England. There's a boy at West Ham now who I brought to the club: Declan Rice. Declan was a really neat and tidy midfield player until he was 15 or 16, but he wasn't ever going to get around the pitch enough, wasn't going to get forward and score goals. He had to become a holding player and he was a good one. But then he suddenly grew a few inches and we thought that maybe he could play at the back. Everybody wants a ball-playing centre back. He's 18 now and a centre half: he's made his first-team debut for West Ham and he's been in Republic of Ireland squads already.

It's not only the coaches. The player needs to be open-minded as well, not to see a change in position as representing some kind of failure step backwards. That's where coaches need to think carefully about introducing the idea of a lad moving to a different position.

Rio Ferdinand was a striker at first and then a central midfield player but I remember, in the '90s, going to a conference where the subject was how Germany played: they shifted their best midfield player into the middle of a back three, let him drop off a little and then bring the ball into midfield. I thought, 'Rio could do that!'

At first, Rio didn't like the idea of moving back into central defence but we talked and I explained to him about bringing the ball out from the back, starting attacks, creating overloads in midfield. He understood the idea, 'Yeah. Yeah. I'll have a go at that.' And we all know what happened from there! —Tony Carr

With the move up to 11-a-side football, a player may now recognise that there are particular positions on the pitch in which he feels most comfortable. It may be, though, that it's only over the course of the next few years that he'll find the position he'll specialise in for the rest of his career. There's certainly no rush: it's something a player can experiment with and take guidance on from his coaches as he grows and matures. Either way, it's absolutely essential that a player continues to develop his all-round game, becoming as proficient as possible in the skills that are fundamental to playing the game at any level—and in any position—in the future:

• Receiving with left and right foot and receiving angles
• 1st and 2nd touches with both feet, thigh, chest and head
• Short and long passing with both feet
• Crossing with both feet
• Shooting with both feet
• Awareness before receiving the ball
  (shoulder checks/pre-scanning)
• Positioning

PLAYER ›› Self-development will always be key to whatever success you achieve as a player. As well as committing fully to every training session at your school, club, or academy, you can look for ways to put in more work elsewhere. Think for a moment about a technical session with just you and a team-mate or you and a coach. Think about the sheer number of touches, the number of repetitions you'll have in those environments: 600, perhaps? 700?

Compare that to the number of touches or repetitions you're likely to get in the context of a team session: of course the work is of a high standard but the actual time you spend in contact with the ball is bound to be far less. Team sessions offer tempo and intensity, but you should take any opportunity you can to train outside those sessions, making the number of touches a priority. Repetition is how technical skills become absorbed by the subconscious mind; how mastery of the important parts of your game becomes instinctive.

LEVEL 2 SAMPLE TRAINING SESSION »

- Warm up
- Drill 1 - Position specific
- Drill 2 - Position specific
- Drill 3 - Position specific
- Warm down

NUTRITION

At Level 3, football's played 11 v 11 on bigger pitches: 90 x 55 yards at Under-13 and Under-14, rising to 100 x 60 yards at Under-15 and Under-16. Games will last longer: 70 minutes at Under-13 and Under-14, 80 minutes at Under-15 and Under-16. The length and intensity of training sessions will increase proportionately. That in itself tells you that the physical demands made on a player will become greater, too.

Nutrition at Level 3 plays an even more vital role in a player's ability to function and perform effectively. Young footballers' bodies are trying to build muscle, burning calories, and lurching between growth spurts. Growing teenagers need to take on the right kind of fuel and to properly hydrate at the right times, especially in relation to football. They need to replace calories and fluids lost during training and games as well as during general exercise at school and in their free time.

A structured and conscious approach to diet is essential. An active Level 3 footballer needs to consume healthy foods and beverages in order to:

- Replenish his energy supply.
- Maintain hydration.
- Obtain the vitamins and minerals needed to support metabolism, tissue growth and repair.
- Help avoid injuries and or/illness.
- Perform at his best both on and off the pitch.

NOTE » *All of the* **COMPLETE ATHLETE***'s sports nutrition guidelines have been developed and set out by Courtney M. Sullivan, founder of "NUTRITION FOR BODY AND MIND". Sullivan is a Registered Dietician certified by the Academy of Nutrition and Dietetics, and a Certified Personal Trainer recognised by the National Academy of Sports Medicine. APPENDIX 2 provides more detailed guidelines as well as suggested meals and recipes developed by Sullivan specifically for optimal health and football performance.*

FOOTBALL-SPECIFIC NUTRITION GUIDELINES »

- All athletes should consume up to five balanced meals spread across the day, every 3 to 4 hours.
- Pre-match and pre-training meals should be eaten 2 to 3 hours before activity and snacks eaten 1 to 1.5 hours before activity.
- Eat when you're hungry to prevent lean-muscle breakdown. Stop eating when you're full to prevent feeling sluggish.
- Eat breakfast within 30 minutes of waking up to prevent lean-muscle breakdown, increase energy and concentration, and maintain good blood sugar control.

- Choose whole grains, fresh fruit and lean protein for breakfast.
- Eat well-balanced meals and snacks, consisting of carbohydrates, lean proteins and heart-healthy fats.
- Drink a protein shake or eat a snack or meal that has the right balance of protein and carbohydrates within 30 minutes of completing training or games.
- Choose fresh whole foods when possible (instead of processed foods which have been packaged or refined) to increase nutritional value. Avoid foods that are high in sugar and either saturated or hydrogenated fats.

LEVEL 3 PLAYER NUTRITIONAL GUIDELINES »

Each young player will have his own specific nutritional requirements depending on age, height, weight, activity level, metabolic rate and genetic background. Therefore, the following suggestions for daily nutritional proportions are guidelines based on the average age and activity level of a Level 3 player:

- 50 percent carbohydrate
- 25 percent protein
- 25 percent fat
- No more than 7% saturated fat
- No trans fat
- Approximately 38 grams of fibre per day
- No more than 150 calories per day from sugar (37.5 grams or 9 teaspoons)

Effective **NUTRITION** is about achieving the balance outlined above. The sources of a player's nutrition, though, are equally important in keeping his body fuelled and replenished:

CARBOHYDRATES: High-fibre foods such as whole-grain bread, brown rice, whole-grain pasta, beans, starchy vegetables such as corn, peas and potatoes, quinoa and cereals.

PROTEINS: Chicken, turkey or fish, especially wild salmon, tuna, trout, mackerel and sardines, which are all high in heart-healthy omega-3 fatty acids.

FATS: Low-fat cheese, nuts and nut butters (preferably without added sugar or salt), avocado, seeds and heart-healthy oils such as extra-virgin olive oil, rapeseed oil, sunflower oil and peanut oil.

VEGETABLES: any and all (leafy green vegetables are of particular value). Raw vegetables and fruit are highly recommended.

PLAYER >> At Level 3, games last longer, anything up to 80 minutes. Training sessions are more physically demanding, too. Your games will be played on longer, wider pitches. As the demands on your body increase, so does the amount of fuel you'll need to maintain good levels of focus and performance. Nutrition is more important than ever. You need to plan what you eat and when you eat it; how much you drink and how often you drink it, especially in the build-up to training and games.

Elite players may have support staff who ensure that what each individual needs is available. But those elite players also take charge of their diet for themselves away from the training ground. That's what you need to be doing now. It's time to establish good habits.

When you think about food, you should be thinking, too, about preparation, performance, and recovery, and then organising the nutrition you'll need if your body's going to rise to new challenges.

Your parents and your coaches should be re-enforcing the message about how important it is to eat and drink properly. Over the course of Level 3, though, you'll need to look after yourself in all sorts of new ways. Nutrition is one thing you can already be taking responsibility for, until making the right decisions day-by-day evolve into good habits that'll be with you forever.

HYDRATION

Up to 60 percent of the human adult body is water. The brain and heart are composed of 73 percent water and the lungs are about 83 percent water. A vital nutrient, water also regulates our internal body temperature through sweating and respiration. Carbohydrates and proteins are metabolized and transported by water in the bloodstream. Water acts as a shock absorber for the brain and spinal cord, and allows us to flush waste out of our systems. It forms saliva and lubricates every joint in the body. Drinking water, therefore, needs to be part of a player's daily routine and not just something that's thought about before, during, and after games. Regularity is the key: staying hydrated at all times empowers muscles and vital organs, keeping them healthy and working efficiently full-time.

PLAYER >> Everywhere you go you should have a bottle of water with you. A bottle of tap water is just as good as a bottle of expensive mineral water. Sipping regularly will be more effective than glugging a bottle at a time without drinking in between. Particular attention should be paid to hydration, of course, in and around games and training sessions. At Level 3, you should be aware that a fluid loss of 5 percent of your body weight can result in a performance drop of 30 percent. You may now be travelling further to games and be less able to count on Mum or Dad being around to remind you. Your coach will mention it from time to time, perhaps, but may have other things on his mind on a match day. It's your responsibility now to hydrate properly before, during, and after games.

MAINTAINING HYDRATION AROUND GAMES »

- Drink 16 to 20 fluid ounces (450 to 550 millilitres) within a 2 hour period before exercise.
- During exercise, drink 4 to 6 fluid ounces (120 to 170 millitres) and perhaps extra at half-time.
- After exercise, you'll need to replace 24 fluid ounces for every 1 pound (0.5 kilos) of body weight lost during exercise.
- 5 fluid ounces equal half a cup, 20 fluid ounces therefore equal a couple of cups.

NOTE » These figures are approximate. If you feel thirsty, you may already be dehydrated. Drink!

* Adapted from guidelines provided by the American College of Sports Medicine (ACSM)

JOIN THE CONVERSATION!
Don't miss out on additional tips about recovery and proper hydration from coaches and professionals in the **COMPLETE ATHLETE** app!

RECOVERY

Young footballers—all footballers—need to eat and drink within 30 minutes of finishing a training session or game in order to replace the calories they've burnt and the fluids they've lost during those intense bursts of physical activity. Replenishing calories and fluids will also help muscle **RECOVERY** and repair.

HOW TO REPLENISH CALORIES AND FLUIDS »

- Drink 24 ounces of fluid (not sugary drinks) for every pound of body weight lost within a 2 hour period of training or a game. As a guide: 20 fluid ounces is about one pint. Look to drink that amount (or more) after your session or match.
- Consume around 20 to 25 grams of protein plus an equal amount of carbohydrates within the 30 minute recovery window. As a guide: 20 grams of protein is equivalent to about a single chicken breast or a can of tuna. Twenty grams of carbohydrate is equivalent to a slice of bread.

COACH » Now that your players are needing to use greater amounts of energy during games, it's important to remind them how important nutrition and hydration are in helping their bodies to recover. You'll already be developing post-match recovery exercises: loose jogging (or swimming) and stretching major muscle groups are vital in helping to stabilise the heart rate and disperse lactic acid from players' muscles.

Those exercises aid recovery and prepare players for training or the next game. Asking your players to eat and drink properly is just as important as taking them through those warm-downs. They'll take nutrition and hydration seriously if you do.

SLEEP

The extra physical demands put on a young player's body at Level 3 increase the need for adequate nutrition and hydration. They also increase a young player's need for **SLEEP**, allowing his body to rest and heal after the intense activity of training and games.

According to the National Sleep Foundation, a Level 3 footballer should get between 9 and 10 hours of sleep each night to ensure necessary growth and development. If that's not possible, or if a young footballer needs additional recovery time, he can take short naps (no longer than 30 minutes), or enjoy quiet rest periods (lying down, watching football on TV, or reading).

PLAYER >> At Level 3, more is being asked of you physically, technically, and tactically. It may well be that you're starting to feel new kinds of pressure associated with playing football, too. Whether it's a Cup semi-final, a trial at an academy or a match against your biggest rivals, the extra importance of some games will be starting to sink in.

This can sometimes make it difficult to sleep the night before a match. You may feel anxious about the possibility of making mistakes; you may be excited by the prospect of your team coming out on top. Either way, it can hinder relaxing and winding down enough to get off to sleep.

First of all: you'd probably better get used to it! Elite players, with years of experience behind them, often suffer from exactly the same problem. It may be that they've worked out ways to help them nod off and you can try to develop your own routine: a bath before bed-time; taped music or a relaxation soundtrack in your bedroom; counting backwards down from 50. If any of that stuff works, great. If not, don't be anxious about it.

You may not have had the best night just before a game, but it's been proven that your sleep two nights previously is actually what accounts for a large percentage of your energy and focus on the day itself.

MENTALITY

COACH ›› *You could say we put a sort of line in the sand at 11 or 12 years old. Boys will move up to 11-a-side football. There'll be formal competition, published results and league tables and so on. I think coaches need to be very aware that boys will be maturing at different rates and so you need to adjust what you do with individual players. But I think you can say that once boys start at secondary school winning becomes more important.*

That shouldn't be at the expense of individual development but I do think work starts going in at this stage with a focus on how to win games of football. You can start practising scenarios in training. You're 2-1 up with five minutes to go: how are you going to make sure you win the game? What are you going to do out of possession? Will you drop deep? That kind of tactical information wasn't relevant for younger boys but in the youth development phase it becomes important. —John Folwell

218

174-196

PLAYER >> Becoming a **COMPLETE ATHLETE** doesn't simply demand that a young player trains for harder or for longer. As well as making sure his body's ready to cope with the workload of training and games, learning and practicing the right kind of **MENTAL PREPARATION** is also important in ensuring he performs consistently at the upper limits of his ability. To be successful in football, players must apply 100 percent of their concentration and focus to every match or training session. As they say: Your head needs to be in the game. At Level 3, a player should be practicing techniques which will help make sure that's always the case.

HOW TO IMPROVE YOUR FOCUS >>

The following suggestions are adapted from the work of sports psychologists and best-selling authors Leif H. Smith and Todd M. Kays.

KNOW WHAT YOU NEED TO FOCUS ON. The clearer you can be about what it is you need to focus on, the more likely you'll be to stay focused on the factors that contribute to your success.

FOCUS ON WHAT YOU CAN CONTROL. You have control over yourself and your own actions and attitudes. And that's all. Keep your focus on those and don't waste time thinking about the rest. If you start to dwell on outcomes (things which you can have no control over), you'll inhibit yourself by creating unnecessary anxiety. Focusing on the process—what you can do and how you can do it—is the only way to affect a possible outcome. It'll definitely increase the likelihood of positive results.

STAY RELAXED UNDER PRESSURE. When you're stressed and anxious, your focus drops. Find ways to stay calm in high pressure situations: taking deep breaths, stretching muscles to relax them, or developing an effective pre-game routine designed to keep your focus where it needs to be.

USE CUE WORDS. Cue words are simple words and phrases that remind you of your key focal points. Repeating words and phrases such as, *'Keep shots low; Get my body open when defending crosses; Be aware when receiving the ball; At any moment, I can be a match-winner.'* Repeating phrases which describe what you need to concentrate on will actually remind you to focus on specific things you need to do. Focus your mind on your cue words and your body will follow.

Two other things, briefly. 1: if someone tells you they don't think you're good enough, remember that's just an opinion. It's not a fact. Recognise that's how life is: people are often negative. Deal with it however you need to, and move on. And 2: Look for inspiration wherever you can find it. I'm not a great reader but I pick up books by people who've achieved things, who've been successful not just in football but in life. Take what will help your own development. Inspiration's always out there. And, with the internet and modern life, it's accessible. You just have to go and look for it. And decide what you need.
—*Paul Davis*

3.3 FITNESS

PLAYER >> *Small-sided games are good for development but they're not really effective as a guide to future potential. Boys really start to grow, I believe, when they start playing eleven versus eleven. It's between 12 and 14 that you start to see them take shape as players, as they go through adolescence. So you mustn't be fooled by early success when boys are younger. I remember a boy who came through with Mark Noble, a lad named Tony Stokes. Between 9 and 12, he was untouchable, scoring 30 or 40 goals a season, a terrific finisher.*

But then, on a big pitch, with bigger, stronger boys, it became clear he just lacked a little bit of pace that he needed to get to the very top. He made pro at West Ham and became a very decent player. He's had a great career in non-league. But Tony is an example of what I'm talking about: the changes that happen between 12 and 14 when boys start playing 11-a-side on full-sized pitches. That's the age you start to get an idea. Then 14 to 16 is when you really start being able to judge how far a boy's going to progress. —Tony Carr

FITNESS matters. Strength and speed are required to play football effectively. Flexibility and mobility are, too, and will also help a player avoid injury. At Level 3, a young player will be able to set himself apart from his peers by being dedicated to his personal fitness. On the one hand, he will establish a foundation of athleticism for his game.

On the other, the discipline required will help both mind and body develop resilience and a work ethic. On both counts, dedication to personal fitness will stand a young player in good stead as he moves into open-age football or up to the elite levels of the game, where power, pace and tempo become key.

PLAYER » Fitness will enable you to meet the physical challenges you'll face playing football at Level 3 and will also prepare you for whatever level of senior football you want to play at in future. Players who don't find the time or the will to work on the different elements of fitness outlined here (and at previous Levels) will find themselves at a real disadvantage if they get offered the chance to play football at a higher standard. They'll struggle, physically, to keep up. They'll also risk injury in games played in a quicker, more athletic, environment. Fitness work can be demanding, physically and mentally, but it gives you the chance to perform at your best whatever the circumstances.

That one vital game or academy trial, that invitation to move up an age group or from 2nd XI to 1st XI: you may only get one chance to prove yourself. Making sure you're physically prepared may be the difference between you taking that chance or it passing you by.

LOWER-BODY STRENGTH

UPPER-BODY STRENGTH

FLEXIBILTY/MOBILITY

CORE STRENGTH

SPEED/EXPLOSIVENESS

ENDURANCE

LOWER-BODY STRENGTH

At Level 3, every player will discover, if he hasn't already, that many of the physical demands of football rely on good **LOWER-BODY STRENGTH**. Stronger leg muscles will make you quicker between points A and B. They'll give you explosiveness when you take off in sprints. They'll offer you extra spring when you have to challenge an opponent in the air. Just as importantly, lower body strength is a foundation when it comes to avoiding injuries and absorbing physical contact. That resilience will allow you to shrug off crunching tackles and run those extra yards in training.

At Level 3, you should be showing significant improvement with the squats and jumps you were working on at Levels 1 and 2. We've repeated them here so you can check you're performing the exercises correctly without referring back to previous pages. We are also adding the Vertical Leap Test, which will measure the power in your legs when you explode from the ground and jump as high as you can.

Of course the test also functions as an exercise for developing that power. The Vertical Leap Test is performed during every professional pre-season and is monitored as a way of measuring a physical attribute seen as key in the modern game.

SINGLE-LEG SQUATS »

- Balance on one slightly bent leg while your other leg is positioned slightly in front of your body.
- With your arms straightened out on each side to aid balance, start to bend the knee of your planted, balancing leg slowly, going as low as you can while still maintaining balance and control.
- Slowly straighten your knee again to return to the starting position. Repeat on your other leg.
- It's important to bear in mind that a player actually builds more strength on the way back up to his starting position than on the way down. Therefore, control and balance on the way back to the starting position are vital.

SINGLE-LEG WALL-SIT »

- Stand with feet shoulder-width apart against a smooth-surfaced wall.
- Slowly slide down the wall until both your knees and hips are at 90 degree angles.
- Slowly lift one foot off the ground until you can feel muscle tension in the planted leg.
- Keep the lifted foot raised for as long as possible before putting it back on the ground.
- Remain in the sitting position but rest for 30 seconds.
- Repeat the lift, using the other foot.
- Time how long you can hold on each foot off the ground.

NOTE >> Remember to be aware of any imbalance in strength between the dominant and non-dominant legs. Work towards being able to keep each foot off the ground for equal lengths of time. Any significant difference in strength can be lessened by increasing repetitions with the weaker planted leg.

BROAD-JUMP >>

A controlled broad-jump is an excellent exercise for developing explosive strength, balance and coordination between upper and lower-body movements in young players.

- Stand behind a marked line on the ground with feet shoulder-width apart.
- Bend your knees and raise both arms forward in front of you.
- As you swing them back behind you, start to bend your knees. Swing your arms back out in front of you again and, as you do so, leap forward with both feet leaving the ground at the same time.
- Look to increase the power in your jump and measure it by how far your jump takes you.
- At the end of the jump, it's important to land as softly as possible with your knees bent and both feet alongside each other.
- Your knees should never be propelled ahead of your toes as this causes instability and the possibility of injury.

VERTICAL LEAP TEST »

If you're training at an Academy or a well-funded club, you may have access to the technology which measures both the velocity and reach of your vertical leap, giving you and your coaches an idea of the explosive power you're able to generate in your legs and lower body. It's not necessary to have access to that technology, however, for the Vertical Leap Test to be useful both as a measure and a way of improving your lower body strength.

- Stand next to any wall and, with your feet completely flat. Reach up with the hand closest to the wall and measure the highest point you can touch, ideally with a piece of chalk. Otherwise, you'll need to have someone with you who can do the necessary measurements.
- Keep the piece of chalk in the hand nearest the wall. Now, let your knees bend and then jump upwards, using both your legs to generate power and your arms to help balance and propel. At the highest point of your leap, try to mark the wall with the chalk again.
- Measure the distance between the two chalk marks. That distance is your result.
- Repeat the test a few times, each time trying to leap higher and leave a fresh chalk mark on the wall.
- Repeat the test on a regular basis and compare measurements to chart progress.
- Repetitions of all other lower-body exercises will help to gradually improve your Vertical Leap Test scores.
- The Vertical Leap Test can be done off one leg if you want to isolate muscles in just one side of the lower body.

INJURY PREVENTION

At Level 3, with tackles becoming harder, player contacts happening with more force, and extra strain being put on muscles and joints by you having to cover more ground during games, it's advisable to start introducing an injury prevention element into your fitness work. Becoming a **COMPLETE ATHLETE** demands constant re-enforcing of a self-improvement mind-set: you'll do whatever it takes.

At this stage of your development, you can ill-afford to miss games and training sessions due to injuries. Progress and opportunities for advancement can depend on you playing as often as possible. Of course, injuries happen. They happen to every player. But the very best players do all they can to lessen their impact.

Most contact injuries are suffered in the lower half of a footballer's body, particularly around important joints like the knee and ankle and within surrounding ligaments and tendons. Fitness work can help in two ways: protecting and strengthening those areas to make injury less likely in the first place, and speeding up recovery from an injury if you're unlucky enough to suffer one.

A good starting point for a planned injury prevention programme is with simple balance exercises. These will strengthen and protect areas of contact during games, such as ankles, knees, and hips, and also develop resilience in the connective tissues and muscle groups around them.

THE BALANCE DISK >>

- You will need a balance (or stability) disk which can be bought for less than £5 online or on the High Street.
- Place one foot on the very centre of the disk.
- Now slightly bend your knee and raise your arms out straight beside you, to make a T-shape.
- Try to remain as still as possible, balancing for at least 30 seconds.
- You will start to feel the muscles and ligaments around your planted ankle start to burn/fatigue. This is exactly what you want: improving overall balance and, at the same time, strengthening muscles and ligaments surrounding the joints, making your body more resilient when the next tackle comes in.
- Now change feet. Repeat six times on each foot.

BALANCE DISK PROGRESSION: 1 »

- Once you've mastered the static balance disk hold for a minimum of 30 seconds on each foot, progress using the same piece of equipment.
- Place one foot in the centre of the disk and step onto it as before. This time, though, once you're set, try to bend your knee, raising yourself 3" to 6" each time. The movement is similar to the Single-leg squat. Repeat the movement six times, slowly enough to retain stability in the upper half of your body throughout.
- This will strengthen your hamstrings and quadriceps as well as building resilience into hip, knee, and ankle
- Repeat six times on the other foot.

BALANCE DISK PROGRESSION: 2 »

- Once you are comfortable with that sequence, put one foot onto the centre of the disk and assume the static position. Then ask a friend or team-mate to throw a ball to you, gently enough for you to catch it without losing your balance.
- Throw the ball back and then lower yourself slowly on your planted knee as you would for a Single-Leg Squat.
- Aim for ten repetitions of this sequence on each leg.

JOIN THE CONVERSATION!

Fitness is essential to becoming a **COMPLETE ATHLETE**. Learn more by downloading the app and checking out the tips & techniques videos!

UPPER-BODY STRENGTH

At Level 3, physical strength becomes a very important part of any young player's game, giving him the ability to shield the ball, ride tackles, and win 1 v 1 battles, even against bigger and more powerful opponents.

At these ages, there can often be a more aggressive edge to the game. Some of the lads playing will appear to already be fully grown men. One way or another, a young player will have to find ways to remain competitive. Part of the knack is balance and coordination, learning how to time challenges. He'll need to be stronger himself too, though, particularly in his upper-body.

There's no shortcut: it's gym work and adding new exercises to those practised at Levels 1 and 2. At Level 3, a teenager may not be ready to use weights or resistance machines: he's still growing into his own body and shouldn't put more pressure on that process than necessary. He can, though, commit time to upper-body strength work, which uses his own body weight for its impact in exercises known as calisthenics. They will help him compete physically, build confidence, absorb contact more readily, and retain his balance when challenged in possession.

Much of a young player's work on his upper-body strength at Level 3 will already be familiar. At this stage, he'll be building on what he already knows.

A FULL PULL-UP »

- Grip an overhead bar with underhand grip with palms facing toward your body.
- Your arms should be fully extended. Ideally, you'll be high enough off the ground for legs to be hanging straight down.
- Try and pull your body up slowly with the aim of getting your chin above the bar. The emphasis should be on using your arms and back to lift your body (don't try to use any momentum generated by your legs swinging backwards and forwards).
- At the highest point, with your chin above the bar, your legs should be completely straight.
- Hold at the highest point for 5 seconds and then lower yourself slowly, maintaining control at all times.

PUSH-UP »

- Lie face-down with your palms under or slightly wide of your shoulders: fingers straight, legs straight and parallel.
- Straighten your arms, pushing your upper and lower-body up together in one smooth movement, back and knees straight throughout.
- Push up until your arms are straight then slowly lower again until your face, chest and knees are an inch or two from the floor.
- Perform as many controlled repetitions as possible before resting.
- Be very careful not to let your back arch as this will put strain on your back muscles and risks injury.

FUNCTIONAL (CLOCK) PUSH-UP »

- Start by positioning yourself on the floor as you would for a basic push-up.
- Perform a basic push-up.
- At the highest point of the push-up, with your arms straight and locked, move your right hand one shoulder width to the right, bringing your left hand cross and adjusting your feet to balance in the new position. Then return your body to the floor to complete the push-up.
- Perform another push-up and repeat the sequence movements at the push-up's highest point, again moving to the right. This time, though, edge to the right and up slightly as well as out so that your body will move like the minute hand on a clock face.
- Repeat the sequence 10 times so that you arrive back in your original starting position, at 12 o'clock.
- Rest for 30 seconds before repeating the 12 push-ups, his time moving anti-clockwise by moving your left hand first at the highest point of each push-up.
- Just as in the basic push-up, form and technique are paramount. Don't arch your back or allow your bottom to stick up in the air.

DIPS »

- Use either a dip machine or two parallel bars set just wider than shoulder-width apart.
- Raise yourself onto the bars. Once in position, grip a bar in each hand, lift your upper body and lock your arms straight. Your legs can be straight out beneath you or bent at 90 degrees.
- Lower your body through the bars until your arms create right angles either side. Keep your back straight.

at all times and look at a point on the wall opposite to make sure your head and chin are level.

- Lift yourself back up through the bars until your arms lock straight again.
- Repeat the sequence as many times as you can without having to use twists of the legs or torso to help your lifts.
- Be conscious of all the power you generate coming from the arms and upper back. Your legs and lower body move as little as possible throughout.

FLEXIBILITY/MOBILITY

Increased levels of flexibility and mobility will improve a young player's technique and performance in training and during games. Flexibility also helps to prevent injury.

Any improvement in this area of fitness will also have less obvious benefits, especially in helping to sustain endurance and consistency on larger pitches and in the 11-a-side games the young player will be introduced to at Level 3.

The Sit and Reach Test is an effective exercise for improving a young footballer's hamstring and lower back flexibility. It can also be used as a marker to assess flexibility and gauge continuing improvement.

THE SIT AND REACH TEST >>

You'll need a box around 8 to 12 inches high. A shoe box is perfect. Use a ruler to mark out inch-divisions across the top of the box to measure your reach:

- Place the box against a wall with the top of the box facing upwards.
- Sit on the floor with the soles of your feet flat against the side of the box in front of you.
- Keeping your legs straight and flat on the floor, slowly stretch forward with straight arms and try to reach the box.
- Do this slowly and with control three times then, on the fourth stretch, reach as far as possible and hold for at least three seconds.
- Note the distance you reached using the inch-marks on the box. Work to increase the distance you are able to reach.
- If you cannot reach the box, ask someone to measure how close you are to the box. Monitor progress and increase flexibility until you can reach the marks on the box.

YOGA

The Sit and Reach Test focuses attention on the flexibility of the hamstrings and lower back. At Level 3, you will see massive benefits from any extra work you can do in terms of improving your mobility. Yoga is a proven method of working on those elements of fitness, benefiting muscles and joints all over the body.

Yoga can also significantly improve your body's durability and its capacity for swift recovery after the intense exertion of training and games. The discipline, for some, can build mental resilience as well, as you focus on patient, careful movements very different from most physical work associated with football.

Over the past 20 years, yoga has been introduced into the fitness and conditioning schedules of the overwhelming majority of elite clubs worldwide. Every leisure centre and every gym in the country now runs yoga classes at Beginners and Advanced standards. Finding one near you to join won't be difficult or expensive. If you prefer, there are online courses and TV shows which will be able to guide you through the basics and allow you to learn and practise yoga at home.

CORE STRENGTH AND BALANCE

The effective functioning of your core muscles is an essential component of fitness for strength, power, and explosive movement. The core is the firm base from which larger muscles do their work of converting energy into a player's football-specific movements and actions: kicking, jumping, sprinting, and protecting the ball. Development of useable core strength is achieved by a much wider range of exercises than sit-ups and crunches, although those can have roles to play.

Simple self-testing can identify any weakness in your core area. It may help to have someone with you who can check alignment of your hips and buttocks when you do the exercises.

The exercises will help develop core muscles to increase strength and prevent injury. We continue to use the Plank and Functional Plank exercises first used at Level 1. The Marching Hip-Raise introduced at Level 2 tests and develops lower back, glute, and hamstring strength. We are now adding the functional side plank at Level 3.

A PLANK >>

- Lie face-down on the floor. With elbows bent at a 90 degree angle, hands in a fist and shoulder-width apart, on the floor facing forwards, lift your body to balance on your arms and toes.
- Your body should be completely level and straight, at roughly shoulder height.
- No sagging or arched back as this puts concentrated strain on other areas.
- Think of the flat shape of a plank of wood.
- Now squeeze your stomach in and tighten while in plank position, keeping your body level.
- Hold this position for as long as you can.
- As you become comfortable with the plank, you can further challenge yourself. Once you've got into the Plank position, raise one foot slowly off the ground, keeping your leg straight and aligned through the hip. Repeat with the other leg. You can also try lifting one arm at a time out straight in front of you.
- Bear in mind that the aim is always to avoid rotation in the hips or lower back, taking the weight in your core muscles exclusively.

A FUNCTIONAL PLANK >>

- Follow the same guidelines as above.
- Once in the plank position, slowly bend your left knee out beside you and move it up towards your left arm. (The moving leg never goes above shoulder height)
- Slowly move back into plank position then repeat with your right knee moving towards your right arm.
- Repeat on both sides as many times as you can.

A FUNCTIONAL SIDE PLANK »

- Lie on your side with your legs straight.
- Now slightly raise your body up onto your right forearm and elbow.
- Activate your core by contracting your abdominal muscles.
- Raise your hips until your body forms a straight line from your ankles to your shoulders. This is your hold position.
- Breathe deeply while holding this position.
- Now, keeping your legs together and parallel, slowly lower your right hip until the outer surface of your right thigh touches the floor.

- Slowly raise your hip to return to your hold position.
- Repeat as many times as you can.
- Repeat, raising yourself on your left forearm and elbow.

A MARCHING HIP-RAISE »

- Lie flat on your back with your knees raised and bent at 90 degrees, feet flat on the floor.
- Keeping your back straight at all times, lift your hips as high as possible with only your feet and shoulders touching the ground.
- Now raise one knee toward your chest in a controlled marching movement.
- Repeat on alternate sides for as long as you can.

SPEED/EXPLOSIVENESS/AGILITY

Every Level 3 player will need to be working hard on the three types of speed relevant in football: straight line speed, explosive speed, and lateral (side-to-side) speed. These are the years during which real development can take place as regards a player's pace and running power.

Once his body settles into adulthood, improvement will only be possible in ever-decreasing small increments. Between 12 and 16, though, real and visible change is still possible. As with all his fitness work at Level 3, a young player should remind himself constantly that he's equipping himself now with the tools he's going to need in the 20 + years of elite footballer he hopes are ahead of him.

The drills outlined here aim to develop speed over the ground for the young player. They will also promote his ability to stop/start and accelerate/decelerate in multiple directions of travel. The 30 Yard Sprint helps a young player improve straight line speed. The 5-10-5-5-10 shuttle runs help develop explosive speed and promote agility. At Level 3, the Fast Feet drill will help a player make quicker and sharper adjustments of his feet, enabling him to explode more powerfully into his sprints.

STRAIGHT LINE SPEED is your ability to get from point A to B as fast as possible.

EXPLOSIVE SPEED is how quickly you can take off in the first 5 yards of a sprint (explosive speed in football is multi-directional).

AGILITY is your ability to get from point A to point B via multiple other points and moving in multiple directions.

STRAIGHT LINE SPEED: 30 YARD SPRINT »

• Place two cones 30 yards apart.
• Run from cone 1 to cone 2 as fast as you can.
• When doing sprint work, it's important to rest for 8 times as long as the action has taken (for example, after a 6 second sprint you should rest for 48 seconds before going again).
• Time your sprint or get a friend or parent to time it so you can chart improvement.
• The aim here is train your mind to tell your body to run faster. This will only happen by continually sprinting as fast as you can. As the body becomes used to moving at a speed, it'll then be possible to want to move faster.

This will only be effective with the appropriate rest times of 8-1. If you don't rest appropriately, you risk the sprints becoming just an endurance drill. This is counter-productive as your sprints will become slower the more you do. Our purpose is training the mind to recognise, get used to, and then increase the body's maximum speed.

EXPLOSIVE SPEED: 8 TO 10 YARD MULTI-DIRECTIONAL SPRINTS »

• Practice 8 to 10 yard sprints in different directions by placing cones 8 to 10 yards away from you at different angles.
• Before each separate sprint, turn slightly away from the intended direction of travel (away from the next cone you're going to sprint to) so that each sprint begins with a turn in towards the cone you're heading for.
• Keep your body low at the start of each sprint and gradually come upright as you approach each cone in turn.
• Choose a spot in the distance and focus on this point while sprinting.

- Keep your body in line, arms pumping in a straight line faster than your legs (the faster your arms pump the faster your legs will move) and keep your head as still as possible.
- Don't let your arms and head flop side-to-side as this will reduce the efficiency of your explosive movements.

AGILITY: 5-10-5-5-10 SHUTTLE RUN »

- Set up five cones or markers, each 5 yards from the centre, in a symmetrical shape as below.

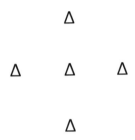

- Start in the centre and sprint 5 yards to the right cone.
- Then turn and sprint 10 yards to the furthest left cone.
- Sprint 5 yards back to the middle and then 5 yards running backwards to the bottom cone.
- Then explode 10 yards through to the top cone.
- Rest for six times longer than it takes you to complete the drill. Then repeat drill with your first sprint going to the left cone.
- When you get close to each cone in turn, try to start getting your body low to prepare it for a change of direction.

FAST FEET (3 POINTS OF CONTACT) »

- Place a single cone a couple of feet to your right and another the same distance to your left.
- Stand between these cones lifted onto your toes, jogging lightly from foot to foot, ready to move.
- Keep your body facing forward through the drill. Only your feet move to the sides.
- Starting on your left side. Three positions: 6 inches to your left, 1 foot to your left, and next to the cone.
- While still jogging lightly, touch your left foot gently and quickly to each point in turn and back.
- Repeat the sequence on your right side.
- Repeat the sequence twice more on each side.
- At the end, explode into a straight or angled ten yard sprint.
- It's important that your standing foot remains light and mobile while the reaching foot is active because it will be making small adjustments to help the other foot and then be ready to jump off into the sprint.

ENDURANCE

You're playing on full-sized pitches. Games are lasting up to 80 minutes and beyond. Training sessions are longer and carry a heavier workload, too. Working on increasing levels of endurance at Level 3 is essential if a player is going to be able to sustain a high standard of performance in this more demanding environment.

ENDURANCE is a function of your heart/cardiovascular system working to supply your muscles with enough oxygen to keep you running without fatiguing or breaking down. Low levels of endurance will result in lower amounts of oxygen in your blood and an inability to sustain the levels of intense physical activity football demands. The best tests of endurance for Level 3 players are the Beep Test and the 30 Second Run. At Level 3, a multi-directional 30-yard Run drill will be really useful, too. All function as exercises to develop a young player's stamina.

THE BEEP TEST »

The Beep Test is an endurance test: a series of shuttle runs between markers 20 metres apart, each run starting on a beep. It begins at level 1 and ends at (an impossible!) level 20. There are around 8 to 10 runs per level with the gaps between beeps gradually getting shorter, giving you less time to make it to the 20 metre line before the next beep.

For example, level 1 (not much more than a walk) has 10 runs and you have 8 seconds to complete each one between beeps. At level 10, you have around 6 seconds between beeps in which to complete each 20 metre run. If you fail to complete the runs at any level in sync with the beeps, you will have failed that level. Note the last level you completed: that's the level you achieved in the test.

To provide your beeps, you'll need to download a Beep Test application to your phone or tablet. You'll also have to be able to measure—accurately—the 20 metres between lines for the runs.

- On a non-slip floor surface, place cones or simply mark lines 20 metres apart.
- After you press start on the Beep Test app, the recording will sound a beep for each 20 yard run and then sound a sequence of beeps to advise that you are moving up to the next level and that your speed will need to increase.
- Make sure one foot touches the line before each turn. And do not start to run until the beep has sounded.
- You should stop when you fall short of the 20 metre line 2 beeps in a row.
- Remember to note your last completed level (not the one you failed to complete).

THE 30 SECOND RUN »

- You need five cones and a timer, watch, or phone with an alarm function.
- Place the cones in a straight line, each 10 yards apart.
- Set the timer for 30 seconds and press start.
- Run to Cone 1 and then back the ten yards to your start position. Then run to Cone 2 and back the 20 yards to your start position. Keep working your way up the line of cones until you've reached Cone 5 and run the 50 yards back to your start position.
- If you get to Cone 5 before the 30 seconds are up, start from Cone 1 again and continue your way back up until the 30 seconds have run out.
- Now rest for 1 minute before re-setting the timer to 30 seconds again and repeating the runs. Look to complete six 30-second sets.
- Keep track of how many yards you cover in each 30-second set in order both to monitor progress and challenge your endurance capacity.

MULTI-DIRECTIONAL 30 SECOND RUN »

- Set out five cones in an "X" pattern as shown. You'll need to time each repetition of the drill at 30 seconds.
- Spacing between cones 1, 2 and 3 is 10 yards between each cone. Likewise between cones 3, 4 and 5.
- Start the drill at cone 1.
- Sprint from cone 1 to cone 2 then sprint backwards to cone 1.
- Now sprint diagonally to cone 3, then backward to 1, then sprint all the way to 4.
- Sprint from 4 to 5, then backwards from 5 to 4.
- Now sprint diagonally from 4 to 3, then backward to 4 and finally sprint all the way back to 1.
- Start the sequence again from cone 1 and continue until 30 seconds are up.

LEVEL 3 PERFORMANCE TESTS

LOWER-BODY STRENGTH

- 8 full-range Single-leg squats on each leg
- Series of four Broad-jumps of 78 inches or more
- Single-leg wall-sit held for 60 seconds on each leg

INJURY PREVENTION

- The Balance disk: Progression 1, 20 dips on each leg

UPPER-BODY STRENGTH

- Bent-arm pull-up held for 25 seconds
- 40–45 push-ups in 60 seconds
- 1 full clock Push-up set
  (1 clockwise, then 1 anti-clockwise)

FLEXIBILITY/MOBILITY

• Sit and Reach Test of at least 3 inches

CORE STRENGTH & BALANCE

• Plank for 2.5 minutes
• Functional Plank for 1.5 minutes
• Side functional plank 30 reps, 15 per side, no rests
• Single-leg balance for 30 seconds with slightly
  bent knee
• Marching hip-raise for 2 mins with no rotation in hips
  or back

SPEED/QUICKNESS/AGILITY

• 30 yard sprint in under 4.6 seconds
• 8 yard multi-directional sprint in 1.2 seconds
• 5-10-5-5-10 shuttle run in under 6 seconds

ENDURANCE

• Beep Test: minimum score of level 13. Aim for level 15
  and above
• 30 Second Run: six sets, each set to be completed to
  50 yards + 10 yards
• Multi-directional 30 Second Run: complete over 2 sets
  in 30 seconds

JOIN THE CONVERSATION!

For level-by-level tips & techniques,
advice and conversation, please be sure
to download the **COMPLETE ATHLETE**
app today.

 TECHNIQUE

PLAYER >> *Our philosophy at Southampton at the time Alexander joined the club was to bring in boys who were technical, could do something with the ball and make things happen. Alexander was always small but he was technically good so his size wasn't an issue. But things can happen at a club: a new guy came in at Southampton and suddenly it was all about how tall players were. They were after the bigger boys, the boys born earlier in the year group.*

Lads would come on trial and get signed because they were 6-footers, never mind whether they could play or not. By the time Alex was 15, he was being played down an age group because he was smaller. Every now and again he'd play up with his own age group.

I remember him saying, 'They're all giants! But when I pass them the ball, when I go for a 1-2, they don't pass it back to me.' I just said, 'That's because they can't. They're not good enough!' It was hard for him for a while, bigger boys getting picked in front of him. Especially at that age, it's easy for the boy and his parents to feel negative about being played down an age group. I just tried to be positive with Alex, getting him to keep giving it his best. And wait till he grew! —Mark Chamberlain

I think if you look at the professional game, especially at the top end, I think you'll find that most of the players have been attached to a professional academy somewhere since they were quite young. There are other routes but they're more difficult to follow now. If a boy's not in an academy by the time he's 10 or 11, it's getting harder to make the jump into that environment later on. It gets harder the older you get, I think, to go from grassroots football into the professional game. If you take an academy at the top end of football, the football the kids are playing at 13 or 14 years of age is kind of unique.

It's a particular style developed through the academy. If a boy steps into that from grassroots football or schools football, I think it'd be rare to find a lad who'd be able to 'get' it straight away, understand what he was being asked to do and adapt to the pace of the game at that level. And how many chances would a boy get? Would a six week trial really give him time to adjust? —Paul Davis

At Level 3, a **COMPLETE ATHLETE** starts to play 11 v 11 football and can begin to be aware of team shape. With that comes starting to understand the roles and responsibilities of particular positions; he'll begin to recognise how different arrangements of positions combine to improve the team's structure and help a group of players achieve their goals.

It's important to remember that the continual push to improve your individual technical game is vital. At Level 3, that can be tied in to the ways in which what you do best impacts on matches most effectively. How and where do you make life difficult for opponents?

You may well be starting to think of yourself identifying with a particular position (although you should be open to that changing, more than once, possibly).

Work on improving ball mastery, your first touch, and other fundamental technical skills continues at Level 3. Adaptation and further development is needed, though, to take account of the changes in the football environment a young player now inhabits: not least as regards playing in a particular position.

Position-specific skills need to be learned and practised as the young player adapts to 11 v 11 football. Every player should be as familiar as possible with the skills relevant to different areas and positions all over the pitch.

This is in the interest of demonstrating the highest-possible level of all-round technical ability. It also allows any transition between positions to be easier and more effective if you or your coach want to experiment with changes in the team's shape or your place in it.

POSITION-SPECIFIC TECHNICAL SKILLS

STRIKERS: CONTROL OF LONGER AND AERIAL PASSES UNDER PRESSURE >> There is more space in behind defenses due to the increased size of the pitch. Some teams will compensate for this by defending deeper to limit the space behind their defensive line. In these situations, a striker will need to receive the ball more often in front of opposing defenders, either turning and shooting or protecting the ball until team-mates are well-placed to join in the move.

STRIKERS/MIDFIELDERS: SHOOTING FROM GREATER DISTANCES >> The increase in the height and width of the goal at Level 3 (21 feet by 7 feet at Under-13, rising to 24 feet by 8 feet at Under-15) is matched by an increase in the size of the goalkeepers defending them. Goalkeepers' individual fitness and technical work will also have improved their spring, reaction times and judgement of angles. Attacking players must work on accuracy and make a habit of hitting the corners of the goal when shooting, especially when shooting from distance.

MIDFIELDERS: WIDER RANGE & TYPES OF PASSES >> A bigger pitch will tend to create bigger distances between players. This can open up spaces from an attacking point of view. Penetrating passes played in between defenders or at angles which leave a defensive line unbalanced are part of the skill-set of a top midfielder. To execute these passes at the right time, you will need to have a picture in your head: 'pre-scanning', looking around the pitch and being aware of where your team-mates and opponents are and adjusting your own position accordingly, is vital before you receive the ball.

WIDE PLAYERS: MORE SPACE/GREATER DISTANCES ON CROSSES >> Wide players now have more room in which to execute 1 v 1 skills, but their final ball will need to travel further on bigger pitches. A lot of work needs to go into hitting specific areas of the 18-yard box with crosses: near post, far post, penalty spot, and so on. The trajectory of your crosses will need to be adjusted accordingly. Practice receiving the ball with the touchline behind you and one or two opponents in front of you. But also challenge yourself to receive and play the ball when you're inside and may find yourself surrounded by opponents.

GOALKEEPERS: SAVES/DISTRIBUTION >> The goal being defended increases significantly in both height and width at Level 3. A goalkeeper may be taller and stronger to compensate, but to excel it will be necessary to train as often as possible, ideally with a goalkeeping coach, focusing on drills designed to improve agility, footwork, and judgement of angles.

The larger size of the penalty area will also demand more from a young keeper: when and where to come for crosses, how to cope with 1 v 1 situations against attackers, whether a keeper's technical ability and pace will allow him to play as a last defender. The bigger pitch will mean technical and physical work will be necessary to ensure distribution, short and long and from both foot and hand, are effective.

DEFENDERS: PASSING RANGE/DEFENDING GOAL KICKS/1 V 1 >> A bigger pitch will often invite more aerial passes and crosses for a team to defend. Positioning (and pre-scanning) are key. So is decision-making. Because a defender may now find himself with more pitch around him to defend, his ability in 1 v 1 situations is even more vital.

Centre-backs are often only one mis-timed challenge away from disaster. Tackling is a technique like any other and must be practiced if it's to be mastered. 1 v 1 defensive situations should be worked on at every session, just as a striker will work on his finishing. Being able to defend and then, once the ball's been won, to begin your team's next attack is now expected of every top defender. This might mean a full-back getting forward—into space left behind by an opponent-and acting as a wide player.

To make effective use of that space, the full-back will need to have taken part in drills designed for midfielders and wingers. A centre-back may be asked to step forward into midfield, creating an overload in a key area. His awareness and passing technique will need to be strong enough to take advantage.

It's important to be aware of the new elements outlined above, but every development in your game is based around the fundamentals of technique you've been working on for many years now. Those fundamentals remain the basis for everything you do as a player and need to be worked on both as part of your formal schedule and outside it:

BALL CONTROL

BALL MASTERY & DRIBBLING

PASSING

SHOOTING

HEADING

AWARENESS

BALL CONTROL

- First and second touches
- Controlling the ball with all surfaces of the foot
- Direction of touch
- On the ground, bouncing, spinning, and on the full
- Controlling while being pressured by opponent (awareness/pre-scanning)
- Controlling in confined and congested space (awareness/pre-scanning)
- Controlling to move forward with momentum

TECHNICAL TIPS »

- Lower your body and bend your knees slightly to encourage a soft and precise first touch.
- Do not lunge and stretch onto the ball as this will inhibit balance and quality of touch. Invite the ball onto your foot (or any other part of your body). rather than meeting it with a stiff approach.
- Always try and get your body behind the ball. This will help you to protect the ball, to stay balanced and to keep your body in line within the width of your hips.
- When making contact with the ball, don't have your foot raised too high or it will connect with the top of the ball, pushing it into the ground. Don't have your foot too low, either, or it will connect underneath the ball and lift it into the air without you controlling that.
- Work on your awareness (pre-scanning) of what's happening around you before receiving the ball. Looking around the pitch and seeing where team-mates and opponents are positioned before you touch the ball will help you make the right decisions by decreasing the amount of guesswork involved in what you do once you receive the ball. This, in turn, will leave you free to focus on the quality of your first touch and then the pass or run you want to make. Top players have a picture of the other players on the pitch in their minds at all times.

PLAYER » The consistent quality of your first touch, your ability to control the ball with any part of your body on any part of the pitch, is the foundation for everything you do. The quality of a player's first touch is probably the single most significant measure in setting the great player apart from the rest. You need to train and challenge yourself every time you play—in a game, a training session, or a kick-around with your mates to improve how comfortable you are receiving the ball in every situation on the pitch.

BALL MASTERY/DRIBBLING

- Try keeping the ball within 5 inches of your foot as you move with it. This will allow you to change direction quickly in tight spaces without surrendering control.
- Try dribbling with the ball at different speeds. Draw in your opponent then beat him!
- Dribble with your head up if you can so you can see what else is going on around you.
- When you have the ball under control, try to manipulate it by touching it with all the different areas of your foot.
- Dribbling at full speed over larger distances, using both light and heavier touches on the ball.
- Being able to lift/scoop the ball over an opponent's foot while dribbling at high speed.
- Direct dribbling: recognising the shortest route to goal and dribbling with that destination in mind. Every successful direct dribble should finish with an attempt on goal.

TECHNICAL TIPS »

- Close control is paramount when you need to change direction quickly, under pressure or in a tight situation. Remember that 5 inch rule!
- Vary the speed and direction of your dribbling. This breaks up your opponent's stride pattern and under mines his balance. Those are the weaknesses you can capitalise on to beat him.
- Try and be aware of where you're taking the ball in order not to lose it and in order to use your skills most productively.
- Running too quickly with the ball can sometimes mean you lose control of it. Focus on control first and build up your running speed as you develop.
- Dribbling with your head down can take you into a crowd of opponents or even off the pitch altogether.

As you build confidence in ball mastery, start to use your imagination and develop your own personal sequences of movement. The challenge is to complete these moves quickly but with efficiency and maintaining control.

AT LEVEL 3, YOU SHOULD HAVE MASTERED »

CRUYFF TURNS

DRAG BACKS

DRAG BACK AND PUSH

STEP-OVERS

SNAKES

TOUCH/FAKE STEP AND PUSH

TOUCH/ROLL, DRAG, STEP-OVER AND PUSH

TRIPLE-PACE MULTI-DIRECTIONAL DRIBBLING

PASSING

At Level 3, on bigger pitches and playing 11 v 11, a player has more scope for varying the pace, direction, and trajectory of his passes. There's more space for playing the ball into passing lanes and in behind midfield and defensive lines. Practice your range of longer passing. Work at varying distance, pace, and trajectory. Remember that being aware of what's happening on the rest of the pitch (pre-scanning) can help you make the right decision—and make it more quickly—once the ball arrives with you. The fundamental range of passing which you worked on at previous Levels remains the same.

• Inside foot pass
• Driven pass, high and low
• Curved pass, high and low
• Feathered penetrating pass
• Low-threaded penetrating pass, between the lines pass
• Half-volley pass, inside foot, high and low
• Half-volley pass, driven with laces, low
• Volley pass, high and low
• Sharp link passes (one-twos and wall passes)

INSIDE FOOT PASS

- Try to make a good, clean, firm connection with soft instep of the foot with your hips guided towards the target.
- For a low pass, keep your follow-through low. To play a pass through the air, raise your foot on your follow-through.
- To keep the pass controlled, try to strike the ball with the soft instep so it doesn't clip your heel or your toe.

DRIVEN PASS

- Connect with laces tight against the ball. Short, punched follow-through with your hips facing the target.
- If you chop underneath the ball, you'll find it slices off in another direction to the one you intended.

CURVED PASS

- Connect with the ball using the inside of your foot on the outside of the ball. Shape your follow-through to describe the shape you want the ball to make as it travels.
- Always lift your follow-through to lift the ball off the ground. Keep your follow-through low if you want your pass to travel along the ground.
- Twisting your hips too sharply will make your follow-through take the pass beyond your target.

LOW PASS BETWEEN THE LINES

- Passes between the lines are struck firmly enough to ensure they break the defensive lines, but must also take into account the pace and direction of travel of the team-mate arriving at the ball.

FEATHERED PASS

- A feathered pass is achieved by striking the ball a little less heavily so that it arrives at the target just as it loses pace and momentum.

HALF-VOLLEY PASS

- Connect with the ball when it's just off the ground, within 2 inches of it bouncing, to give you maximum control over the pass.

* *If you mis-time the connection and the ball is too far off the ground when you strike it, you'll hit underneath the ball and the pass will either slice or go too high.*

VOLLEY PASS

- Get your body over the ball and connect in the middle of the ball, your laces guiding it downward to keep the pass controlled.
- Standing foot and hips should be pointed towards the intended target.
- Let the ball come onto your foot. If you connect too early, you'll hit the bottom of the ball and slice it. If you connect too late and strike the top of the ball, you'll push it into the ground instead of towards your target.

SHARP LINK PASS
(ONE-TWOS/WALL PASSES)

As well as relying on very accurate judgement of distance and pace, it's important to be balanced, with your body behind the ball, when making short, sharp link passes. This will help ensure you make the cleanest contact possible with the ball and also allow you to move onto a return ball with real explosive speed. Balance also helps you adjust quickly if the pass to you lacks precision or your team-mate takes up an unexpected position.

218-240

SHOOTING

INSIDE FOOT

LACES STRIKE

CURVE

VOLLEY

HALF VOLLEY

KNUCKLE BALL

As well as mastering the basics of the full range of shots, it's very important that you practice being able to perform them in the full range of situations that may present during the course of a game:

- Opposed, where decision-making and keeping your balance are all challenged
- Unopposed, where your focus is on technical discipline and developing consistency
- First-time
- Touch and finish
- Touch—set—finish
- Touch—set—fake— finish
- Inside the box
- From angles
- Outside the box

JOIN THE CONVERSATION!
Improve your technique with more tips in the **COMPLETE ATHLETE** app!

TECHNICAL TIP >>

When shooting, it's important that your hips are square to the target whenever possible as you follow through. Over-rotation of your hips on your follow-through will tend to push the ball wide of its intended target.

INSIDE FOOT

- Body behind the ball and make a good strong connection with the inside of the foot. Transfer your weight through the ball with your hips angled towards the corner of the goal.
- Over-rotating your hips will tend to guide your shot towards the centre of the goal instead of the corner.

LACES STRIKE

- First point of contact with the ball should be your laces right against the centre of the ball. Keep your follow-through below knee height and guide it towards your target.
- If the ball's first point of contact is the front of your foot and not your laces, this will mean you don't get a clean strike away and the ball will usually rise over the crossbar.

CURVE

- Similar to the curve pass, for a curve shot you need to connect on the outside of the ball with the inside of your foot. Shape your follow-through to describe the same shape you want your shot to make on its way to the target.
- Over-rotation of your hips or a loose follow-through may cause you to guide the ball wide of the target.

VOLLEY

- If possible, let the ball drop to knee height before striking it and connect with laces tight against the centre of the ball. Follow through on a high-to-low arc to keep the shot under control.
- Connecting underneath the ball—as you often do if the ball doesn't drop to knee height or below—will mean your shot flies up over the bar.

HALF VOLLEY

- As with the half-volley pass, it helps to strike the ball when it's as near to the ground as possible to ensure a clean, controlled connection.

* Allowing the ball to rise more than a couple of inches before striking it makes the shot much more difficult to keep low and on target.

KNUCKLE BALL

- When striking with the ball for this kind of shot, connect with the knuckle of your foot making contact the lower part of the ball. Aim for the least possible amount of follow-through as you 'punch' the ball towards goal, keeping the connecting foot flat and straight. The intention is to make the ball move laterally in the air and dip without warning by striking it with an uneven part of the foot, the 'knuckle'.
- The trick is to connect with the 'knuckle' of your foot. Striking with the inside of the foot will not give the ball swerve and dip in the same way.

HEADING

It's very important not to spend too much time on heading repetitions as a Level 3 player. The health and safety and developmental issues which we were aware of at previous levels are still relevant.

Between 12 and 16, boys' bodies (and brains) continue to grow and change. It's very important not to run the risk of compromising this developmental phase in any way by frequent heading of the ball. Heading drills should be condensed so that players are focused, above all, on the technical elements of heading rather than repetition to increase power and distance.

That said, work on heading the ball correctly will need to be done as this element of the game presents itself more and more often during 11-a-side matches on full-sized pitches. Young players can begin to take advantage of the extra spring and power they're now generating thanks to work on fitness elements such as lower-body strength. In training sessions, however, it's worth remembering that improving technique is much more useful than simple repetition.

CUSHIONED PASS HEADER

• As you approach the ball (or the ball approaches you), try to keep your eye on it and concentrate on making contact with your forehead. This will help you to avoid mis-timing connection and making connection with the top of your head.
• Don't follow through with too much momentum. The intention is to cushion the ball in the direction of the intended area or target.

HEADER AT GOAL

- When moving towards the ball with the intention of heading it, it's important to arrive at the point of contact with some momentum if possible.
- Always keep your eye on the ball. Use your neck muscles as your forehead connects with the ball to push the ball downwards towards the corners of the goal.
- Try to keep your eyes on the ball as you travel towards it. This gives you the best chance of connecting with your forehead rather than the top of your head, which would mean the ball bouncing upwards and over the bar.

DEFENSIVE CLEARANCE HEADER

- Try and get a run up towards the ball to generate some momentum.
- Keep your eyes focused on the ball all times and lift one bent arm across the front of your chest to protect your face.
- Try to generate power from the waist and spine, putting your whole body weight through the ball when connecting. This will to guide the ball upwards and away from you.
- Practice the timing and control of your jumps. Try to make sure you don't close your eyes. This is very important if you're going to avoid the ball hitting either the bridge of your nose or the top of your head.

3.5 LIFESTYLE

Between 12 and 16, we probably experience more profound changes—physical, emotional, intellectual—than we do over the course of any other comparable length of time in our lives. A boy becomes a young man, his identity gradually becoming clear to himself as much as to those around him.

By the end of Level 3, we can already start to pick out the kind of player this teenager will become when he steps up to senior football: he and his coaches will know his strengths and weaknesses by now, what he can and can't do.

If, at 16, the young player still loves the game with the same passion as he did when he first discovered football, he'll know what his next steps are likely to be and how far his passion is going to be able to take him. He'll have an idea as to where football's going to fit into the rest of his life.

Or he may believe he's got a chance of it becoming his life: the chance of a professional career may be on his horizons. At 16, there'll be some big choices to make and those choices will be at the forefront of the player's mind all through Level 3. Parents, extended family, teachers, coaches, friends, and mentors—they'll all have their own ideas and will want to have their say. Those big choices will be looming throughout Level 3.

Every boy's journey in the game will be unique to the player and his circumstances. By the time you're 15, you may already have a scholarship offer in place from a professional club. You may have been connected to an academy for several years and be waiting to find out if they want to take the next step with you.

You might be looking forward to A Levels as a way to secure a college place in the UK or abroad on a football programme. You may already have decided that your future isn't going to be as a professional player, but that you want to carry on playing football at the highest level possible, whatever else you end up doing.

For certain, life will be running at full capacity: the ever-increasing demands on your time as a footballer—training, practicing, playing—will be matched by the demands being made on you in other areas of your life. It's probably dawned on you by now that, one way or another, this is when it comes down to making the most of your opportunities and your resources.

JOIN THE CONVERSATION!

Striking, shooting, heading tips & techniques and much more can be found in the **COMPLETE ATHLETE** app.

What happens next will be up to you in terms of being independent, self-sufficient, and self-motivated. Wherever football fits into all this, a **COMPLETE ATHLETE** needs to take care of his own business now, which means pushing on as a player and pushing on, too, in the rest of his life:

FAMILY

SCHOOLWORK

SOCIAL LIFE

ROLE MODEL

LIVING YOUR SPORT

FAMILY

PLAYER >> For you to chase your dream as a footballer, at least one person in your family—and maybe the whole family—has had to commit an enormous amount in terms of time, energy, and resources to making sure it's been possible for you to work at becoming the best you can be. They've been there for you, taking the strain in ways you probably weren't even aware of at the time. They've not done all that for you as a favour. They've done it because they love you and believe in you.

At Level 3, you've reached a point in your life where you can start to give something back, perhaps. All it needs is you to take responsibility for your own life and your own decisions in ways you never have before. Your coaches will have been telling you it's time you started really thinking for yourself out on the pitch.

Same goes for the rest of your life—independence and self-sufficiency are the keys:

- Always remember what your parents and family do to support you. Being grateful for that doesn't mean saying thanks every day. It does, though, mean never taking them or what they do for granted.
- Try to be a positive influence around the house. Take on your share of the workload, whether that's keeping your room tidy, cooking a meal, or washing up now and again, or taking younger siblings outside to play football or go to the cinema, for example.
- Take ownership of everything around you and football. You might still need lifts. You might still need help paying for things. But getting yourself organised for training and games, thinking about your diet, about getting enough sleep, and about fitting in your school work: those are all things you can be taking responsibility for now. Think about them so your parents don't have to.
- If you're exhausted after training or a game, take care of your own recovery rather than insist on other people waiting on you hand and foot. Take a bath, take a nap, whatever you need. But don't expect anybody else to run around after you in the meantime.
- If you've had a bad game or a poor day at training, don't ruin everyone else's life over it. Feeling sorry for yourself won't move you forward, after all: identify for yourself what went wrong and do whatever is necessary to fix it.

PARENT >> *We need to remember that, between the ages of 12 and 16, there's a huge amount of change going on in young people's lives. There are the growth spurts that come with early puberty. They're moving towards GCSEs. Energy levels and motivation levels will go up and down. They're becoming young men.*

They'll be bringing lots of new emotions to training sessions and coaches at grassroots clubs need to be aware of all that going on. We need to be able to use football to help boys deal with what may be going on at school and in the rest of their lives.

Around 14 and 15, too, we see a drop-off in the level of parental support. In the Foundation phase, lots of parents are involved but, in the boys' teenage years, coaches at grassroots clubs find they have to pick up more and more players to get them to training and games. Maybe it's just a natural part of young people growing up: they're probably having to get themselves to school now, after all.

They're becoming more independent. But I'd like to know why it happens from the parents' perspective: has the dream of professional football started to slip away? Is it younger brothers or sisters who need looking after? Or is it just having other things they want to do with their weekends?

There's a dropping out of players around the same age, too. It probably happens for a number of reasons, but my thinking is that it's often boys who'd thought they had a chance of 'making it' but who now realise they won't who are lost to football at this age. Boys who are around the academy system—dropping out of clubs, going into development centres, looking to get back in—keep playing.

There's a purpose for them. There are other boys who have never really thought about careers in football but just love the game. They'll keep playing for life. Maybe it's those ones in between who fall away. They think it's not going to happen for them and they look for other things—video games, a part-time job, extra homework—to do instead. —John Folwell

SCHOOLWORK

It's not just about what a young player can and can't do on the pitch. At Level 3, **SCHOOLWORK** is an absolutely fundamental part of the journey towards becoming a **COMPLETE ATHLETE**. If you're one of the few who'll go on to have a career in the game, the discipline and application that you demonstrate in football should be reflected in your attitude to your schoolwork. No player was ever the worse for passing exams and learning to study. Self-motivation, diligence, a work ethic: qualities that help you achieve at school will also help you achieve as a player.

If football's going to be a big part in your life—at semi-pro or amateur level—the importance of committing to your schoolwork can't be over-emphasised. Your chances of getting onto an academy programme, here or elsewhere—the US, for example—can depend on your exam results at GCSE and beyond.

School will set you up for a life, a life that football can remain a big part of even if it's not how you pay the bills. If you've had your brushes with the professional game and want to leave a door open on a possible return via a less obvious route than Academy/Scholarship/Pro, taking education as far as you can will be a huge plus. Lessons learnt in class can help you develop into a young man coaches, scouts, and managers are interested in, now and in the future.

PLAYER >> *I went to an all-boys school in Epsom, in Surrey, which had a great tradition in sport and sports teams, both within the school and playing against other schools. I was involved in everything: I was a keen footballer, a keen sportsman. By the time I was 13 or 14, I had a group of good mates. We played football together.*

As we went for District trials and County trials, some of them were getting the chance to trial with professional clubs. But I wasn't getting those opportunities and I realised then that I probably wasn't going to be a professional footballer, however much I might love to be.

I think dealing with the disappointment of not becoming a footballer was helped by the fact that I was actually better at a different sport: basketball. I was as good as anyone, both at school and at the club I joined, so I understood what you needed to excel at a particular sport. In basketball, I could hold my own but, as a footballer, I couldn't. It's not a great feeling: other people are stronger than you, more physical. Playing the game isn't so enjoyable. Whereas if you're the best at something, or close to it, that's very exciting.

So I started trying to work out what I might do instead. My PE teachers were an inspiration to me. I looked at them, saw that they were involved in lots of different sports, that they were running teams at the weekends, and thought that perhaps that was something I'd be interested in doing in the future. I asked them about what I needed and they sketched it out: GCSEs, A levels, University. I set my mind on doing that. I kept playing football but it was at a level that was right for me, and that wasn't at the elite level. —Paul Clement

JOIN THE CONVERSATION!

Live your sport & join the **COMPLETE ATHLETE** community of athletes, parents, and coaches by downloading the app today!

SOCIAL LIFE

At Level 3, a player is growing up as a footballer. He's also growing up as a young man. Between the ages of 12 and 16, **SOCIAL LIFE** can come under pressure: on the one hand, commitments to football and school life mean time is squeezed short. But there are also elements of a social life that are only now becoming part of the picture, such as social media, fashion, and getting invited out to parties and gigs. A player can get advice from parents, coaches, mentors, and peers, but, in the end, he'll have to learn how to handle those pressures for himself. What's certain is that he'll need the right kind of people around him and he'll need to handle his relationships with those people in the right way.

It's natural that players will tend to establish friendships with other players. They work to the same schedules, they share experiences, and they may be chasing the same dreams. But those friendships shouldn't be at the expense of time spent with mates who've already been around for the long haul and may turn out to be friends who can be counted on in the future as well. Who a young man spends his time with can define how other people see him and how he sees himself. Friends made outside football can bring values and perspective that are too important to be lost just by not bothering to make the effort. It's worth thinking about what makes a true friend. And about how to be one, too:

- BE TRUSTWORTHY. True friends earn trust by always having each other's backs and never sharing anything that's been said in confidence.
- SHARE VALUES. Sharing the same values is a bond whether it relates to football, school or family.
- BE EMPATHETIC. Good friends are happy when good things happen for each other. They're there with support when things are more difficult to handle.

- AGREE TO DISAGREE. Friendships are tested when disagreements occur. True friends will usually find ways past those conflicts. However, if one friend is risking the future or reputation of the other by engaging in illegal or anti-social behaviour, the other needs to be strong enough to walk away from that friendship, in the short term or even for ever.

PARENT >> *It's hard at 14 or 15. There's a lot going on: growing, hormones, finding out about life. Of course, focus is important. But we want boys to grow up as rounded individuals. We want them to have time with their mates, time discovering other things in life.*

But, ideally, football's right there in front of them: the most important thing. It's about finding the right balance. At the elite level, it's almost full-time down to 14 years old: training three or four times a week. Games at the weekend. But you still want a boy to have a laugh with his mates, don't you? Talk about girls, go out to the cinema, play their music together. You want him to enjoy growing up. —Terry Burton

COACH >> *Teenage years are obviously a complicated time. I can say that as a coach working with young players and I can say that as a parent, too: I've learnt a lot watching my own sons grow up. On and off the pitch, boys that age are going to be demanding some freedom. They want a feeling of independence. And, as a coach or as a parent, you have to give them that. But, at the same time, they're going to be finding themselves in more challenging situations and may be looking for guidance in dealing with those. Out on the pitch, moving up to 11-a-side football, they'll need some structure, some help with adapting. It's an age, as well, where boys will start to find their level in the game. They'll be judging themselves against the other boys in a team or in a squad.*

It's important that parents and coaches make sure every boy gets a chance to stay involved. If you're left on the sidelines all the time while your mates play, it can get disheartening. You don't want boys to fall out of love with the game because they're not being included. But it's tricky: you could say that if a boy's not getting enough time on the pitch at one club then he can move to another. But that might mean breaking up friendship groups he's a part of, moving to a club where he doesn't know anybody. Will a boy want to do that or will he want to stay with his friends even though the football side of it isn't really working? He can be torn. Do I stay with my friends or do I go somewhere I'll play? That's a big decision for a boy at that age. —Paul Davis

PLAYER >> Andros wasn't great at school. He was bright enough. But behaviour? He missed out on playing for England Schoolboys against Scotland one time because the school felt that was a way to punish him. Presented with the choice between education and football, he went with football every time. And, of course, there are lots of boys like that. I was like that!

I think, nowadays especially, a lot of boys are seeing the end goal—a professional career—from very young. As soon as they're in an academy setting, look what happens: while their classmates are going home and watching telly, doing homework or putting their feet up, young players are training three nights a week and there's a game on Sunday, too.

Can you be surprised they start looking towards the future almost at once? If a boy has the talent and the determination, that can be an amazing journey. But, because of all that time spent in the academy, if it ends in disappointment, the impact is so much greater: you've been doing it all your life and, suddenly, they're saying, 'No. He's not for us.' —Troy Townsend

ROLE MODEL

PLAYER >> You're still young and experiencing new freedoms. If you're serious about your football, though, don't for a moment imagine that, at Level 3, there's nothing much at stake. Of course, you're going to need to prove yourself, again and again, in every game and every training session. The same goes for the way you behave away from your club. One mistake can cost you your dream even at this early stage, when it feels as if a career hasn't even begun.

Coaches and scouts do their work on the touchline, of course. But, for them, analysing a young player's potential and making decisions on his future don't just happen in the course of watching a game. Increasingly, attention is paid to a young man's character: he may have the ability, but does he have the personality, the attitude, and the standards of behaviour which he'll also need to reach the top? When coaches and scouts look at a player, they're not just judging potential.

They're also evaluating risk. One mistake on your part can mean they decide not to bother investing time and attention if they suspect you will let them down somewhere along the line. Think about leadership qualities in relation to yourself and your friendships.

Demonstrate the highest standards of behaviour and value those standards in the people you spend time with. Don't give in to peer pressure and get involved with illegal drugs, alcohol, or performance-enhancing substances. Don't get caught out by social media. Respect the law and your social responsibilities. Making it in football is about giving yourself the best chance, on and off the pitch.

PARENT » *In relation to criminal law and me going into academies to talk to young players, it's usually ages 14 and upwards. But, of course, I've had to be involved in situations with much younger people. And younger footballers: as young as 12 years old; the sort of thing which will usually be about having been in the wrong place at the wrong time.*

It often amounts to no more than a slapped wrist but that, in itself, can be a real eye-opener for a boy. The more serious issues have tended to happen as boys got older. The push now, as regards education, is towards talking to boys under the age of 16 because of the laws relating to sexual activity and to the exchange of sexual images. —Kyle Phillips

PLAYER » *With young goalkeepers, I'll show them the first team keeper in action and then all their work is about learning to do what the senior guy can already do. Physically they might not be strong enough, might not be able to reach the top corners yet, but we break down all the different processes, work on all the details.*

The first team is where they all want to be isn't it, even though very few of them will ever make it to that level? But it's good to show them what you want. In that way, the internet can be a great tool. I use it myself: if I want to find an example of a particular technique or if I want to get an idea to work on in a session, I'm straight on YouTube!

A kid can do that, too. He can have his heroes but he needs to find his own character as a keeper: he can look at what the greats do—how they take off for crosses, how they kick the ball, how they set themselves for one-on-ones-and take bits from all of them. —Tony Roberts

By the time you reach Level 3, you probably can't imagine a life without football. In that sense, you're already living the game. Loving football has meant you've spent years mastering ball skills, listening to coaches, bonding with team-mates and feeling the joys and disappointments that come with competition.

At Level 3, your relationship with game will have to deepen as the lessons you learn get more complex: tactical play, positional skills, 11-a-side football on bigger pitches. You're wondering how far this can take you and, as part of that, you're thinking about stars of the professional game who you can learn from as you start to carve out an identity as a player. Like anything else related to football, you can let your imagination run while, at the same time, you try to structure your learning and analysis:

• Watch full matches and not just the highlights. Better still, if you can, go the game. This will let you take in the detail of how your role model performs from first minute to last.
• Study the players that relate to your position. How do they deal with the technical challenges set by their direct opponents? How do they win their one-on-ones?
• Try and analyse where on the pitch they're able to make the difference. And which team-mates/positions they combine with most often.
• Watch what they do out of possession as well as in possession.
• Study how they react to adversity and mistakes.
• Gauge their attitude to work-rate and their desire to win games.
• Watch their confidence and composure, even under pressure.
• If you could ask that player five questions about their game, what would they be?

PLAYER » *I grew up in Wolverhampton but, when I was a boy, I played for a Sunday League club called Meir K.A., in Stoke-on-Trent. My nan and granddad lived in Stoke and I used to go and stay with them every weekend, Friday till Sunday. My grandad knew someone at the club—that's how I got introduced to them—and he used to take me to every game.*

Grandad was a huge influence for me. He wasn't a player, didn't tell me what to do or anything, but he and my nan would make sure I was eating right, looking after myself, and—the most important thing—he'd always take me to my game. My nan and my mum were important as well, but it was my grandad who really pushed me and believed in me.

I don't know how old I was—9 or 10, maybe—but I remember a PE teacher at my primary school introduced me to a scout from Wolves. They invited me down for trials. I went along for about six weeks and then they signed me. I was too young to be thinking much about the future. It was just one of those things: football was something I loved doing and I got the chance.

It was very different, of course: all the nice kit, playing against the best teams around, playing alongside some of the best players in the Midlands at the time, lads like Kyle Bennett, who's at Portsmouth now. Kyle and I are still good friends.

Life in the academy was stricter in many ways. Certainly compared to Sunday League. At Meir K.A., if a boy's parents couldn't get him to a game then that was OK. You know: you could just not turn up. At Wolves, though, you had to find a way to make sure you never missed a session. Home from school, get changed and then straight up the road to training. And that was a couple of times a week as well as games.

One big change was that, instead of me going up to Stoke, my grandad started coming to watch me play for the academy down in Wolverhampton. My nan, too: I can still picture her, sitting by the side of the pitch in a little deck chair. One afternoon she got hit by the ball and knocked out!

Seriously, though, it made a real difference for me, having them there. And I took it quite hard when my grandad passed away when I was 13.

To be honest, I think I came off the rails a bit after that, getting in to trouble at school. I was so used to him being around, being at games, talking to me afterwards. I still miss him now. It's a bit of a blur, but I know I got released by Wolves at right around the same time and I seem to remember them actually feeling quite bad about having to do it because they knew what else was going on in my life. For me, though, at the time, being released was just one of those things that happen.

I was upset at first but my mum took me to another Sunday League club, Deansfield Young Boys, which was run by the father of Connor Goldson, who's now at Brighton. I was straight back in really, and played for them for a couple of years.

Getting released hadn't stopped me wanting to play football. I got back to loving the game with Deansfield, to be honest: I played as a striker on Sundays whereas, at Wolves, they'd been playing me at right back. I really enjoyed it.

Football wasn't about a career back then. It was just what I loved doing. My attitude has always been to get on with whatever's in front of me, anyway, rather than worrying about things in the future which might never happen. So much can change so quickly in football, after all.

I was so young when I got released by Wolves and I don't really know if there were things I could have done that would have meant they kept me on. Maybe it was a blessing in disguise that it happened when I was young. You see so many kids who do all the right things and then, at 16, they don't get a scholarship and it's really difficult for them. Anyway, I was at secondary school by then and we had a PE teacher, Mr Stobart, who used to push us on. We had a good team and some very good players. I rediscovered my hunger for football around that time.

Me and my best friend, Leon, used to go to the estate near school. It was in Eastfield, right next door to the boxing club that we went to as well. They had a big metal cage for playing football: me and Leon used to go there every evening after school, just the two of us, playing for hours, whatever the weather. Trying to score against each other in these little goals. It was working hard at the game, I suppose. Both me and Leon had the ambition of getting back into a club in mind by then.

Those months with Deansfield Young Boys were good for me, I think. It was tough: men's football, really. I was playing up two or three years, one of the youngest players in that league. It's why I say to lads now that, if you get the chance to go out on loan, into lower league football or non-league, then take it. Go and prove yourself. That's how it was for me: I needed to prove myself at Deansfield. Prove that I was good enough to go back in and get a chance at an academy.

Our teacher, Mr Stobart, had a connection with Shrewsbury Town and, when I was 15, he got Leon and I trials up there. It worked out and we got scholarships. I think those couple of years were maybe the best time of my life. It seemed like it then, anyway! The academy was at North Shropshire College and there was a block we all stayed in together.

The coaches went home at 5 in the afternoon and then it was just us, the scholars. We got to know other students who were at the college: we kept ourselves entertained; got up to a bit of mischief! Trained every morning, college in the afternoon. It was a brilliant time.

We had a great coach at Shrewsbury, Nigel Vaughan, a former Welsh international. He was unbelievable with us, worked with us the whole time: trying to make us better players, trying to make sure we got our pro contracts. The first year was a lot of fun; the second was much harder, focussed on getting that deal at the end of it. It was good to be working for something, fighting for something, having the goal of a first contract in front of us. It was during those couple of years that I really started scoring lots of goals for the first time.

It wasn't just the football. I remember, when I got the scholarship, it was quite a scary thing as well as being exciting. You know, it meant moving out, leaving my mum. But I think it was the best thing that could have happened. I was getting myself into little bits of trouble back in Wolverhampton and getting away from all that was just what I needed. I was away all week and then went back to see Mum at the weekends. She was pleased to see me, of course, but I think she was happy I was away from stuff that was going on in Wolverhampton, too.

I was lucky, too, that I was at Shrewsbury with Leon, my best mate. We roomed together and, in a new environment, it's good to know you've got a mate there to watch your back. And he knows you'll watch his. It's daunting, going into a new club like that. It still is, going into a new club today! My only regret is that Leon got a bad injury in our second year and didn't get a pro contract, which he would have done if he hadn't been injured. Leon never really got back into football: makes you think how the game can go, what can happen to a career.

I got my pro contract eventually and maybe people would assume that was it, job done, I'm on my way. But it didn't work out like that. My first year as a pro I went off the rails again: not focussed, not concentrating, letting myself go and getting caught up in trouble away from football. It was all my own fault. It was a bad year for me and I had no one to blame but myself.

I dropped down into non-league and I was lucky: my chance came again. And that's what you have to remember: you have to keep working. You can't give up. Life can change in one game. Playing for Hinkley against Luton in the FA Trophy, that's what happened to me. Luton signed me and everything in my career has gone on from there.

—Andre Gray

IN LEVEL 4

Whatever pathways are open to a young player at Level 4, he will feel he's reached some kind of crossroads. He may have been offered an academy scholarship at a professional club. He may have secured a place at college where he can combine playing with furthering his education. He may be staying on to do A Levels at school and turning out for the First XI. He may be taking a different career path altogether but continuing to play the game he loves with a local club, experiencing "open age" football for the first time.

The young player is now a young man, responsible for making decisions that can affect the rest of his life. In a full-time academy, of course, the dream of becoming a professional footballer will feel very much within reach. It's important, though, that the young scholar heads into the next two or three years fully aware that his chances of "making it" remain incredibly slim. On the other hand, outside the academy environment, young players can commit to the world of study or work knowing that it's still not completely impossible to find a less conventional route into the professional game in the future.

What every young player should bear in mind is that the future is now in his hands. His passion for football has already brought him this far. No one can be sure what lies ahead, but what is certain is that his chances of success won't depend only on his footballing talent. Inside and outside the football environment, now more than ever, the Level 4 player will only move forward if he also works hard to become a mature, well-rounded individual who takes his education and his other responsibilities seriously.

At age 16 and older, scouts, coaches, and managers are looking at a young man's character as well as his natural ability when it comes to making their decisions. To be the best you can be on the pitch, you'll do what you're asked to do and then be the player who makes sure he does even more. You need to be ready to take on the rest of your life, too, in that same frame of mind. For a **COMPLETE ATHLETE**, the crossroads that's been reached at Level 4 doesn't represent the end of a journey. This is just the beginning.

It was a series of hurdles. A series of goals, all the way along. Of course, the first big one was getting a scholarship at age 16. That was a huge thing for both

Alexander and for his brother, Christian. I think we threw a party for each of them when it happened. With Alexander, it was more touch and go. By the time he was 16, Mark was at Portsmouth, working with his age group, the Under-16s. So, we had a fall back: he knew Portsmouth would take Alex because he was better than what they had. But we didn't want that. Southampton's was the better academy. But the guys there weren't sure, they said.

Mark couldn't believe it, really. He'd watched him train, watched him play. He was convinced Alexander was good enough. But it was only at the last minute that they said, 'Yes. We're going to offer him a Scholarship.' We were relieved, really. Even though we knew, deep down, that they were lucky that they'd made the right decision. But it was a massive thing for Alexander. He was so happy. He loved playing football, but I know that boys, even at that age, are feeling the pressure, as well.

—Wendie Oxlade Chamberlain

If you get to 16 or 17 and then get released, having got that close to a scholarship, to a first pro contract, it can be devastating if you don't. Especially if a kid's been associated with a club from 8 or 9 years old. To get rejected after you've spent half your life in that environment, as part of that club? That's really hard to take. I think clubs have a duty of care: Everybody at an academy should be reminding young players, whenever they can, that the chances of making it at a top club—even just the chances of earning a living from the game—are really slim.

JOIN THE CONVERSATION!
Take your game to the next level with the **COMPLETE ATHLETE** app!

People might perceive that as being negative. I think it's just being realistic. Families need to be aware of the bigger picture even if they're convinced their boy's going to do well. Do clubs do enough to make sure parents and boys don't get led along, convinced that a professional career's going to happen? If they knew where they stood from the start—and knew all along—I think families would go with it. After all, being in an academy can still be an amazing experience for a teenager even if it doesn't go anywhere at the end of it. —Paul Davis

The idea that you have to be involved at an academy by the time you're 9 or 10 if you're going to have a career in the game is absolute rubbish. And it worries me that a boy who's let go at 10 or 11 can think he's failed and start to fall out of love with the game. It's not that long ago that clubs could only sign players as schoolboys when they were 14.

So players like John Terry and Frank Lampard and Tony Adams just played all the time: school, district, Sunday League, sometimes even Saturday League, as well. Did them no harm. They all had stellar careers. At 17, 18, they were ready to play against grown men. They all had that resilience. —Tony Carr

If I was advising a boy, I'd always say play where you're going to get a game. Here at Ridgeway Rovers, that might mean being flexible about your position on the pitch. If there are a dozen midfielders and only a couple of defenders in your group, then go and play at the back. You'll get more time on the pitch, and you'll be a better player for the experience.

If a boy's been scouted by a professional club, I'd say the same but I'd mean something different.

Unless he's a truly exceptional player, I'd always say go to a Colchester or a Barnet or a Leyton Orient. That's where you'll get a game. The bigger the club is that you sign for, the bigger the chance is that you'll just get lost in the system and end up frustrated and disappointed. Or released. —Ian Marshall

4.1 POSITIVE ATTITUDE

At Level 4, the young player will feel as if he's facing new tests every day: of his ability, of his intelligence, and of his character. He will find himself in situations, off the pitch as well as on it, which demand resilience, a willingness to face adversity and a readiness to constantly challenge himself to improve. In this new environment—be it at an academy, at college, or out in the world of work—a **POSITIVE ATTITUDE** is essential if he's to make the most of his opportunities. And not be undermined by his disappointments.

At 16, a young man's character is well on the way to being fully-formed. But a positive attitude is still something which can be worked on as part of any young player's development. It can be reinforced by making sure that self-reflection is part of every success and every setback. A **COMPLETE ATHLETE** continues to grow by recognising and demonstrating the attributes that together represent a positive attitude:

RESPECT

SPORTSMANSHIP

TEAMWORK

PROFESSIONALISM

LEADERSHIP

RESPECT

At Level 4, a youth player may have become a full-time scholar at a pro club or be embarking on a full-time course at college. Or he may be still at school or out at work, but facing the very real challenges—physical and mental—presented by the move up into open-age football. In whichever environment he's playing the game, the Level 4 footballer knows that real progress will only be possible if he continues to show respect for coaches, match officials, team-mates, opponents, and himself. Now more than ever, showing **RESPECT**—and earning it in return—will be about making the right choices. He'll need to be mentally strong in his decision-making and committed to becoming his own man, behaving with integrity and focus at all times.

PLAYER » *I'm Education Manager for Kick It Out. I deliver education into Premier and Football League clubs. That education is based around equality and inclusion, talking about challenges that are out there in society as a whole and how they impact on football. But I talk about life skills, too. The focus nowadays is far more on the individual than it was when I was growing up and wanting to be a professional player.*

Back in the day, if you could kick the ball, left foot, right foot, and head it, that was all that mattered. Young professionals now are scrutinised from the moment they leave the training ground until the moment they drop off to sleep at night. The challenge is to help shape a rounded individual: someone you could take out of the football environment and put into everyday life without his way of behaving having to change.

We go into Premier League clubs as part of the Equality Inspires programme and talk to boys from 11 years of age right through to U23s, to their parents and coaches, too. The Football League work is focussed on the scholars, boys between 16 and 18, who are within touching distance of professional contracts but who also face the possibility of not being taken on.

That can mean a pro career over before it's begun and lads having to drop down into non-League to keep playing football and, at the same time, going out and finding a job and getting on with their lives. We try to provide a safe space in which to discuss issues like racism, homophobia and sexism. But we try not to talk at the boys: no player likes that! For me, a football man from year dot, it's a privilege to go in and help young players any way I can.

Let's be honest: if you mess around, if you're unruly, if you have a bad attitude, it'll come out in public sooner or later. People have all sorts of preconceptions about professional footballers: they're all paid enormous amounts of money, drive fast cars and have women hanging off them. Well, what if you break through in the game and all you want to do is play football? How are you going to deal with that baggage? Your privacy's gone. Who have you got around you then to help and advise you? Will you listen to an agent and ignore your family? Do you have parents who want to support your football career or parents who have been swept along by the money?

I'm talking to young players. They're young people but the game takes that away from them in the sense that, to get on in football, they'll need to stop doing a lot of the things young people do. If you're in an academy and you're doing the wrong things, the chances are football will find out and, because you're young, a club will turn round and say, 'Sorry. You're not for us.' So I'm just trying to get them to think about the way they behave.
—Troy Townsend

SPORTSMANSHIP

Good **SPORTSMANSHIP** should be instinctive for the Level 4 player if he's been committed to it since he began playing football. Good sportsmanship evolves organically out of a respect for yourself, for others, and for the game. It means playing and behaving with integrity at all times, especially when emotions are challenged in moments of triumph and despair. Of course, at Level 4, the stakes are higher—from day to day and game to game—and the pressure to perform and to win is greater too. As well as giving everything physically, the young player will be asked to commit every last bit of his emotional energy to the cause. That can have a profound effect on his decision-making and his self-control. To be sure of his ability to make the right decisions and to behave properly, even in the heat of the moment, the young player can train habits of good sportsmanship until they become second nature.

PLAYER » In regard to good sportsmanship, it's worth remembering that coaches, scouts, and managers are always judging your character as well as judging your ability. Don't justify unsporting behaviour by connecting it with the idea of demonstrating a will to win.

Good sportsmanship doesn't have to undermine your competitive edge in any way. Your true character is shown when you're most under pressure. Demonstrating good sportsmanship in those moments will create the most significant impression on anyone watching.

JOIN THE CONVERSATION!

For more stories and conversations with athletes and coaches, download the **COMPLETE ATHLETE** app!

And that could be the manager, coach, or scout who's making a crucial decision about you that day. Learn to do the right thing:

- Don't insult or belittle opponents before or after a game, either in person or online.
- Shake hands with opponents before and after games in a sporting manner.
- Around opponents—and even amongst your own team-mates—avoid gloating when you win or behaving resentfully when you lose.
- Behave professionally and responsibly at all times during games.
- Play football in a manner that demonstrates your respect for the game: accept the decisions of match officials without question; never cheat; recognise that you have a duty of care toward an opponent.

PARENT ›› *By and large, you find that with the young players who get into trouble—who lose the plot—it's a matter of education or the lack of it. And education begins at home. That's where you learn how to treat people, how to listen; it's where you find your values and the way to conduct yourself. A lot of that will have happened before a club gets anywhere near a player. Clubs can tell young players—on the pitch, off the pitch—but it's about how willing a young boy is to listen and to learn.*

And it carries on: how a player's parents react to him making progress, becoming a professional player perhaps, can have a big impact on a young man. You've got a problem when parents are living vicariously through their son. It's not just the boy. The whole family needs to stay grounded. The club and the parents need to be working together, and I'm not sure how often that happens. —Kyle Phillips

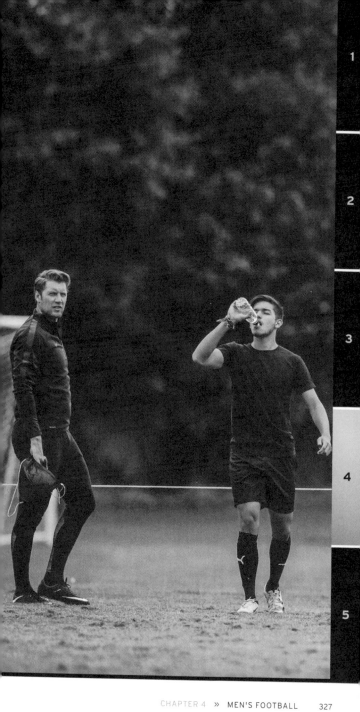

TEAMWORK

Effective **TEAMWORK** is the result of a group of individuals pooling their resources to achieve a common goal. As far as football's concerned, that's talented players co-operating in order to win games. Much of the work you put in to become a **COMPLETE ATHLETE** has, of course, been about developing your own physical and technical abilities in order to give yourself the best chance possible of success as an individual. Football, though, is a team game and, in order to achieve your full potential, you will have to learn how to contribute in a team environment, in games and in training, as well as away from your life as a player.

At Level 4, you will already have dedicated a great deal of time and effort to becoming the best player you can be. That may have helped to make you stand out as an individual at every stage of your development.

At this point, however, you'll discover that all the academy scholars, college players or adults you're lining up against are themselves capable of excelling at the level you've reached. You're facing a battle every time you cross the white line against opponents who want to win just as much as you do. To give yourself the edge and to make sure you come out on top, you need to know and trust your team-mates. And they need to know and trust you. Chances are you'll succeed together or not all.

There's a famous line from one of America's greatest Presidents, Abraham Lincoln: 'I don't like that man. I must get to know him better.' In every dressing room, there are different personalities and clashes between them. Not everybody is going to be everybody else's friend. Becoming an effective member of a team means recognising what others have to offer and understanding that the truth about another guy's character isn't necessarily what's obvious. Just because someone's loud and confrontational doesn't necessarily mean he's strong or confident as a young man. Because someone's quiet and reserved off the pitch doesn't mean he's going to be weak or unassertive on it. Take time to find out about your team-mates as people. You won't like every player who takes the field alongside you. But understanding him and trusting a team-mate will give you both a better chance of winning the battles that you're going to face together.

PLAYER >> *As a young player—and then through a career—you're going to come across all sorts of different coaches. And you've got to be able to handle that. It won't ever be enough to be able to get along with just one type of coach. You have to have that mentality that allows you to get on with all your coaches.*

You might not agree with everything he says or does, but you have to recognise that coaching is his role: I'm a player. I want to develop. I'm going to take as much as I can from this. You know, you may think you don't like him—can't like him!—and don't think he's any good. But you have to find a way to make that relationship work. That effort will ultimately be a benefit to you.

You can't go around saying, 'I don't get on with the coach. I can't play for this team,' because you'll end up not playing for anybody, and it's the same with your team-mates. You might be playing alongside someone you really don't like. But you have to find a way of making the relationship work: for you, for the other guy and for the team. And that's not something a coach can organise for you. It's a skill you have to develop for yourself. And it's hard sometimes. Harder maybe than dribbling through a defence and scoring a goal! And it matters just as much whatever level you're playing at, including at the top of the professional game. —Paul Davis

COACH >> You encourage teamwork and unity by doing everything you can to ensure your players feel comfortable and respected in the team environment. You can foster team spirit by helping them to understand and trust each other.

Some people, by nature, are more reserved in group situations and have to be prompted to speak out or engage in group activity, whether that's on the bus on the way to a game or in a lecture hall discussing video analysis. Talking about games, challenging every player to contribute to discussions, can be useful from a tactical point of view. It can also play a positive part in establishing trust and respect amongst the group. Your responsibility is to ensure those discussions remain respectful and constructive.

Any effort you make to discourage the development of cliques within the group and to break up those that exist will benefit the team going forward. Team-bonding games can play a useful role, especially if they're based around small groups and those groups are changed around each time the games are played. In the smaller group situations, more introverted characters find it easier to contribute and extroverts are encouraged to make room for the ideas and personalities of others.

TEAM BUILDING ACTIVITY: 2 TRUTHS, 1 LIE >>

- Split the squad into smaller groups of three or four.
- In those small groups, the game asks that each player tells the rest three things about himself, two of those things being true and one being a lie.
- The other members of the group have to guess (or work out) which statement is the lie. After every one has tried to guess the lie, the player tells his team-mates which statement was the actual lie.

- Like any game, 2 Truths, 1 Lie may feel awkward at first but the result, invariably, is better understanding of each other's characters and development of mutual trust and respect within the larger group.
- For this and other team-bonding games to work, it is essential that every member of the squad takes part.
- If there are cliques within the larger group, ensure that these are broken up in the smaller group exercises.

As a teacher, I was trying to give every boy an opportunity. And you have to remember that all of us want to feel good about what we're doing. I remember a player at Real Madrid who I talked to once about his relationship with the previous manager. It had been strained, he said. And when I asked why, he told me that, however well he played and however many goals he scored, that coach never once told him, 'well done.'

Whether you're a schoolboy or a successful professional player, you want to feel valued, feel appreciated. Back then as a teacher—and just as much now as a manager—I try to praise when I can, be positive rather than negative. I know other managers have different approaches: scolding, being aggressive, ruling by fear, even. But my philosophy is to be positive, to encourage as much as I can. I think it's often underestimated, what a pat on the back can mean to a player. To say, 'great job.' That can really mean a lot, you know. —Paul Clement

JOIN THE CONVERSATION!
Sportsmanship, leadership, and professionalism are all core aspects of becoming a **COMPLETE ATHLETE**.
Learn more by downloading the app!

PROFESSIONALISM

Whether it's an academy Under-17 team, a school First XI, or a local Sunday League side, at Level 4, **PROFESSIONALISM** is part of what's expected from a **COMPLETE ATHLETE**. It's a frame of mind without which he's unlikely to take the next step. Behaving like a professional amounts to a lot more than keeping your boots clean and getting to training on time. It's about your appearance and your attitude at every training session and during every game. It's about good manners, taking care of your diet, and monitoring your recovery time. It's about putting in extra training sessions, building good relationships with team-mates and staff, and keeping your online presence uncontroversial. In short, it's about working tirelessly to improve every day.

At Level 4, you need to realise that you don't just have decisions to make about football. Every other decision in your life impacts on football, as well. Ask yourself: Is that impact going to be positive or negative? The more professional you are in your approach to the game, the better you'll feel in terms of preparation for your future. The more professional you are, the more your coaches and peers will respect you and take you seriously as a player.

There are plenty of players—and ex-players—out there who feel they 'could have' or 'should have' but didn't. Not because they lacked ability but because they didn't have a professional attitude to football when it really mattered.

PLAYER » *I didn't really notice a change in Alexander's attitude until he got taken on as a Scholar at 16. He moved into digs in Southampton and was mixing with all the other lads. I suppose our attitude was quite strict with him.*

The other boys would be going out at the weekend, coming in Monday and saying, 'we did this and we did that. What did you do? Why didn't you come out with us?' We were quite close by, and he'd come home. We'd do family things together. But he was quite torn for a while, wanting to be out with his mates. I suppose I was tough in a way. I told him that if he wanted to be better than the rest, if he wanted to reach the top, he needed to make the commitment: eat well, sleep well, look after himself. No parties! We always had fun together, though. It was just he wasn't going out drinking and having late nights.
—Mark Chamberlain

For a while at Barnet, I was lead coach for the U12s to U16s and coached the U16s. That first Under-16 team I took was probably the most challenging group of personalities I've ever had to work with.

We played 45 games that season, against some really good clubs including Arsenal and Spurs, and we won just once: at Brighton, where we were 2+ hours late for the fixture because the coach broke down on the way there! But it wasn't about winning. The aim was to develop these players and get them scholarships at Barnet. The club ended up taking on 9 of the 12, our best ever success rate.

They had talent, and they worked hard but maybe didn't yet understand the game. A year later, I moved up to Under-18 coach, so I was working with that first group of lads I'd had as Under-16s. It was the most enjoyable year I'd ever had in football. The boys had matured. We had targets and so did they: to get offered professional contracts. I remember, at a presentation evening at the start of the season when we sat them down to talk about our goals, one of the lads stood up and said, 'We won one game all season as Under-16s. If we're serious about football and making pro, we need to stop talking about it and deliver.'

It was an amazing moment, really. I think I realised that the penny had dropped for these boys: they realised it was up to them. They took ownership of what was going on in their careers. We ended up winning our league by six points and nine of the team got offered professional contracts at the club. Six of them are in the first team squad now. —Rossi Eames

LEADERSHIP

A young player may already have experience of being a captain, in school, at his academy or playing for a grassroots team. At Level 4, he may want to continue in that role. On the other hand, it may be only now that a player feels confident or assured enough to take on that responsibility. The obvious demands placed on a captain aren't restricted to fulfilling the role during games. They include:

- Communicating effectively and expressing expectations clearly.
- Listening patiently and always keeping an open mind.
- Being loyal and treating all team-mates equally and with respect.
- Leading by example with your performances on the pitch.
- Encouraging and bringing the best out in others.
- Being clear and decisive with players who are letting the team down in any way, be that lack of work rate, loss of focus or obvious indiscipline.
- Being the voice of and for the team when communicating with coaches and staff.

At elite level, every player will be expected to embody leadership qualities of his own. Those attributes may have to be hard-earned and begin with the ability to take responsibility for your own actions and decisions, behaving with integrity at all times. Every individual will have his own way of expressing those **LEADERSHIP** qualities, but every individual will need to find them in himself if he's going to progress in the game.

PLAYER >> *Christian had a different kind of journey. He played at Southampton's development centre when I worked there and was doing alright but they had a trials day for the academy and he was just a bundle of nerves. Had a terrible day and didn't get in. So, we left football alone for a while.*

He kept playing at school, though, and was having a great time. He said he wanted to play for a team. This is when he was maybe 10 or 11. I worked Sundays, so Wendie had to take him. He joined a grassroots club in Portsmouth, but it got very competitive and very physical: Go on. Kick him! Parents shouting, fighting on the touchline. Christian even got racially abused at one point. These were 10- and 11-year-old kids! So, we had to get him out of there.

Luckily, we got to hear about another club in a Saturday league. Not so competitive, not so rough and tumble. The boys could express themselves a little bit more. Christian's team played against teams a year older but he really enjoyed the football. He got his passion for the game back. And he ended up being scouted by Southampton. He went for a week's trial and did ok but they decided not to take him on. Again!

Well, I was working for Portsmouth's Community Department at the time. So, Christian started coming along to our sessions. He worked with Paul Hardyman, a very good coach who also worked with Portsmouth's first team, and enjoyed it a lot. They set up a game between the academy and a team representing the Community Department. It was just a friendly, but Christian played really well, and the club took him straight in to the academy afterwards.

Christian, coming through at Portsmouth, had a tougher journey than Alexander in many ways. It was a different kind of environment, and it was hard for him sometimes, but we thought: If he can cope with this, he'll be able to cope with anything that might turn up later on. And Christian was strong. Never tried to change who he was. Kept working hard. He was very professional about things— happy not to be going out. Focussed on improving, on eating well, on getting his rest. Christian isn't as gifted technically as Alexander.

Coming into an academy later than his team-mates wasn't an advantage. They'd been working on a way of playing, getting technical coaching. They'd already forged friendships. It sometimes seemed as if they gave him grief every time he made a mistake. He had to earn their respect. And he did that. By the time he was 16, 17, Christian had proved he deserved to be there. You've got to admire him. It would have been easy to walk away. But he just got his head down and worked at his football.

Alex would probably have struggled in that situation. I know I would have. Christian's probably got more guts than the rest of us, to fight his way past all that and come through the other side. I've got so much respect for him. He's 19 now and signed pro last year.

—Mark Chamberlain

JOIN THE CONVERSATION!
Step up your mental game with more tips in the **COMPLETE ATHLETE** app!

4.2 PREPARATION

Level 4 represents a big step up for any young player: physically, technically, psychologically, and socially. It shouldn't come as a surprise, then, that **PREPARATION** is of prime importance at this stage of a career. As at previous levels, personal discipline with regards to training, diet, rest and mentality should remain at the front of your mind. But now, for perhaps the first time, other elements need attention too, not least you learning how to analyse games and your own performances in detail and with clarity.

Players who prepare properly and maintain focus for every game and training session will always emerge as leaders within the group. They're the players, too, who'll earn the trust of coaches and team-mates. They'll start more games than their less focussed peers and, as a result, get the minutes on the pitch to take in game experience and develop more quickly. Good preparation becomes a good habit and will also improve your opportunities and results off the pitch, at school, work, or college.

A **COMPLETE ATHLETE** prepares to perform at the highest level of his potential by continually working to improve in the following areas:

PRACTICE

NUTRITION

HYDRATION

RECOVERY

MENTALITY

PRACTICE

At Level 4, a player may now be training full-time in a professional environment, every session scheduled and supervised by club or college staff. Or a player may be working as hard as he can to improve outside the professional game, training with coaches who, like him, have to fit football in around the rest of their busy lives.

These are very different situations but, either way, time for one-on-one work is limited: in the professional environment by a coach having to work with an entire squad; outside the full-time environment by a coach only being available part-time to work with his players. If you want to stand the best possible chance of playing the game at the highest level of your potential, you will need to work every day on your own: increasing your strength and fitness levels, sharpening the technical elements of your game know you can improve on, analysing the matches you play and making the effort to watch elite players at work.

In a professional environment, sports scientists will be using state-of-the-art GPS and heart-rate technology to measure your every movement in every game and every session. If you still aspire to play at the elite level, you may want to use similar technology, which you can buy over the counter or online. When it comes to putting in extra work, tracking your fitness levels in training is very important. It gives you a standard to reach and then to surpass. But it can also serve as early warning if you're over-training: exertion for the sake of it won't necessarily improve you as a player. Over-training can lead to fatigue, sluggish performance, impaired decision-making, and an increased risk of injury.

It's worth remembering that an important part of **PRACTICE** at this age is about analysing your game, watching it back on video, or discussing it with a parent, mentor, or coach.When all's said and done, the ultimate responsibility rests with you now. Coaches, staff, and team-mates can help push you on, but the commitment to daily improvement must start with you. Just because there isn't a coach by your side doesn't mean you stop working on your game:

- Develop your own specific training program that allows you to keep improving technically, then spend time every day working on it. Daily intelligent repetition is key even if, on some days, that entails only 10 or 15 minutes of quality practice.
- Make sure you constantly assess and revise your programme of work, perhaps in consultation with a coach or personal trainer.
- Make sure you're continually working to develop physically as an athlete. Aim not just to cope with the demands of your position. Push yourself to excel, both in your specific position and also as an all-round player.
- Learn to listen to and respect your own body. Practice with that in mind, to ensure you don't run the risk of muscle strains or other injuries. Think very carefully before you play football or other sports outside your club's and your own schedule. Avoiding injury is ultimately your responsibility.
- Improving individually doesn't always mean working on your own. You can work on important elements of your game by playing head tennis or doing extra shooting or passing practice with team-mates after training.
- Be aware of how this work impacts on your own game specifically.

Time spent studying your game is vital. Most games (and many training sessions) at pro clubs or sports colleges are recorded on camera. Reviewing that footage is a useful tool. If your matches aren't on video, you can still discuss and think about them. Learn from mistakes; recognise where you can improve, on and off the ball.

With young goalkeepers, I'll always do cross-training: basketball, table tennis, badminton, whatever. I don't need to explain why to the boys but the skills they need—like footwork, body shape, movement—are there in those other games, too.

Wojciech Szczęsny, who I worked with at Arsenal, told me that Polish goalkeepers who work at their dedicated national goalkeeping academy do a lot of gymnastics while they're growing up. It's that same attitude to cross-training. Did you know there are now 80 Polish goal-keepers playing up and down the leagues in England? My own experience tells me that's no coincidence.

Down at Swansea, I still play basketball with Łukasz Fabiański all the time. He loves the game. It's a break from football but it's still working on things he needs to practice, like his footwork and taking off for crosses. I see a lot of boys now, though, whose parents or coaches just want them to concentrate on football.

They won't play other sports bcause they're afraid of getting injured, but I think they're missing out on something. For me, at their age, even rugby was good— it got me used to taking the physical knocks you face as a goalkeeper. —Tony Roberts

NUTRITION

At Level 4, a young player is probably playing and training harder than he ever has before. For longer, too. **NUTRITION** is a vital consideration if he wants to do everything he can to make the most of his ability. What a young player eats has a direct impact on his capacity to train and play at optimum levels. Given the importance of time spent on the pitch at this stage of his development, it's important that nutrition also helps maintain general good health, building resistance to infections and viruses which might mean missing out on days and even weeks out on the pitch.

NOTE >> *All of **COMPLETE ATHLETE**'s sports nutrition guidelines have been developed and set out by Courtney M. Sullivan, founder of NUTRITION FOR BODY AND MIND. Sullivan is a Registered Dietician certified by the Academy of Nutrition and Dietetics, and a Certified Personal Trainer recognised by the National Academy of Sports Medicine. APPENDIX 2 provides more detailed guidelines as well as suggested meals and recipes developed by Sullivan specifically for optimal health and football performance.*

JOIN THE CONVERSATION!
Recovery, sleep, and nutrition are all important for your health and best performance on the field. For tips and techniques from coaches and professionals, please download the **COMPLETE ATHLETE** app!

LEVEL 4 ATHLETE NUTRITIONAL GUIDELINES >>

Each individual has different macro-nutrient needs, based on height, weight, age, activity level, metabolic rate and genetic background. The following daily nutritional proportions are guidelines based on average age and estimated activity level for a Level 4 athlete:

- 45 percent carbohydrate
- 30 percent protein
- 25 percent fat
- No more the 7 percent saturated fat
- No trans-fat
- 38 grams of fibre per day
- No more than 150 calories per day from sugar
  (37.5 grams or 9 teaspoons)

One of the advantages of being a full-time scholar or college player is that you may have access to a professional nutritionist. If that's the case, make sure you develop a good and open relationship with him or her. The nutritionist can offer guidance on what to eat to encourage peak performance and general good health.

He or she can answer any questions you may have about what to eat when recovering from heavier training days, the quantities you should be eating on days when training is relatively light, and on days off. A nutritionist may be able to offer you supplements to support your metabolism's loss of vitamins and minerals during periods of peak exertion.

If you don't have access to a professional nutritionist, there's plenty of reliable and coherent advice available in books and online. If you're studying the subject for yourself, however, make sure you double-check information and don't rely on advice from only one source.

HYDRATION

At Level 4, a player is training at high intensity up to five days a week, sometimes twice a day, and spending time in the gym building strength, dynamic power, and resistance to injury. The speed and physicality of the games he's playing in has increased, especially as he may now be up against players a year or two older than he is; that age gap will be even greater out in grassroots, open-age football.

Keeping hydrated at all times empowers muscles and vital organs, keeping them healthy and working efficiently on a daily basis. In order to maintain peak levels of fitness and performance, **HYDRATION** is crucial and should be a conscious part of his preparation and recovery phases.

Players should have water with them at all times. It's particularly important to plan hydration in and around training sessions and games:

- Drink 16 to 20 fluid ounces (450 to 550 millilitres) within a 2-hour period before exercise.
- During exercise, drink 4 to 6 fluid ounces (120 to 170 millilitres) and perhaps extra at half-time.
- After exercise, you'll need to replace 24 fluid ounces for every 1 pound (0.5 kilos) of body weight lost during exercise.
- 5 fluid ounces equal half a cup, 20 fluid ounces therefore equal a couple of cups.
- These figures are approximate. If you feel thirsty, you may already be dehydrated. Drink!

* *Adapted from guidelines provided by the American College of Sports Medicine (ACSM).*

RECOVERY

Young footballers—all footballers—need to eat and drink within 30 minutes of finishing a training session or game in order to replace the calories they've burnt and the fluids they've lost during those intense bursts of physical activity. Replenishing calories and fluids will also help muscle **RECOVERY** and repair:

• Drink 24 ounces of fluid (not sugary drinks) for every pound of body weight lost within a 2-hour period of training or a game. As a guide: 20 fluid ounces is about one pint. Look to drink that amount (or more) after your session or match.

• Consume around 20 to 25 grams of protein plus an equal amount of carbohydrates within the 30-minute recovery window. As a guide: 20 grams of protein is equivalent to about a single chicken breast or a can of tuna and 20 grams of carbohydrate is equivalent to a slice of bread.

SLEEP

Whether he's a full-time scholar facing the demands of daily training or out in the world of work, competing in adult football and squeezing training into a busy schedule, the young player at Level 4 is expending more energy than he ever has. And it'll only get tougher from here. The extra workload demands adequate nutrition and hydration. It also means that getting sufficient **SLEEP** is important in giving the body time to rest and heal after the intense activity of training and games.

According to the National Sleep Foundation, a Level 4 footballer should get between 8 and 10 hours of sleep each night to ensure necessary growth and development. Regularly getting less than six hours of sleep a night will hinder any young player's progress. He'll suffer from fatigue, which can impact every area of his game—stamina, concentration, physical power, and resistance to injury. The body can't perform at its best without time to recuperate after exertion. Sleep deprivation can also affect hormone regulation, making the body crave more sugar and refined carbohydrates for quick energy, the opposite of the kind of fuel a player's body needs.

Being able to get off to sleep may need conscious effort and the development of good bed-time habits:

• Avoid stimulants such as coffee and energy drinks. If you do drink them, do so earlier in the day and try to cut yourself off by noon or early afternoon.
• Your body needs time to wind down before it's ready to shift into sleep mode. Spend the last hour before you sleep doing something calming and relaxing. Avoid using any electronic devices, such as a tablet or phone. The light emanating from the screens of electronic devices stimulates the brain and can hinder sleep.

- Think about establishing a relaxing bed-time routine just before you're ready for sleep, conducted away from bright lights and loud noises. This will help separate your time for sleep from the rest of your day and activities which cause excitement, stress, or anxiety. The idea is to fall asleep more easily and avoid any interruptions to your sleep patterns.

* Adapted from the National Sleep Foundation guidelines

MENTALITY

Becoming a **COMPLETE ATHLETE** doesn't simply demand that a young player trains harder or longer. As well as making sure his body is ready to cope with the workload of training and games, learning and practicing the right kind of mental preparation is also important if he's to perform consistently at the upper limits of his ability.

At Level 4, one focus should be on learning to use mental imagery. Mental imagery is simply imagining yourself performing successfully before you step onto the field of play. Athletes who can successfully envision themselves performing well actually perform better. Don't wait for your coach to deliver positive outcomes—imagine them for yourself.

Effective mental imagery takes a great deal of concentration but is a process which can be learnt and practiced. The key is to imagine, using all your senses: the smell of the grass as you move across the field of play, hearing and feeling your foot make perfect contact with the ball, seeing yourself deliver the perfect pass or finish.

In a professional environment, there may well be a full-time sports psychologist on hand to advise but there are several excellent books and online resources available which cover sports psychology generally and mental imagery in particular. Yoga, so useful as a means to relax and strengthen the body, is also something else to explore as a way of focussing the mind.

PLAYER » Mental imagery builds on the player's own drive and determination, complements his hours of hard work and self-improvement, and prepares him, finally, to make it all count when it matters—out on the pitch, in the game. It's one small part of the **MENTALITY** that great players develop to get them to the top in football.

I've worked with young players in academies at Chelsea and at Fulham. I've had the chance to work with some of the world's very best players at some of Europe's great clubs. And I'm pretty sure about what it is that sets successful players apart. It's desire. It's never being satisfied with whatever point it is they've got to in their careers. The most elite players—at Bayern, at Chelsea, at Paris St Germain, at Real Madrid—are all very similar in that respect.

Whatever they've done is never enough for them. They win a major trophy and all they want to do is win it again. And again. And again. There's never a moment of: Whew! We did it! Every small-sided game in training: got to win it. Every match on a Saturday: got to win it. Even when he wins: didn't play well enough, didn't score. Got to be better, got to train harder. That's what the real elite are like.

I wouldn't be surprised, if you went back, you'd find those elite players were the same when they were boys. I remember a young Swedish player I worked with at Chelsea. He was about 16, you know—that age when it's supposed to be all about being cool and fitting in, not being different from your peers.

But this lad, whenever he scored a goal in training, he used to cheer himself, 'Yes! Come on!' And the other boys would just look at him. Who is this guy? We're only training here, aren't we? I even thought that myself. But then I ended up at Real Madrid and saw Ronaldo doing the exact same thing in training. I thought, 'Who's the fool now, eh?' Not that the Swedish lad went on to have a big career or anything, but he had that desire. Ronaldo's all about scoring goals. That's his position. That's what he's measured on. So when he does it, he wants to feel happy about it!

I think most teenagers, particularly now with social media, are very concerned with how they're perceived by others. I think that drive and determination, that single-mindedness and not caring about what other people think of you, are very rare qualities.

Those kids are outliers. There are very few of them. Whether it's something that's just in someone, or whether it's something that can be developed and nurtured, is difficult to say.

I think about my own life and, like everyone, there are things that happen to you which can make you more or less determined. But, fundamentally, drive and determination are things that have to come from within you. Coaches, managers, support staff can all look to find that extra 10 percent or 15 percent in a player. But the sacrifices that have to be made to have a chance of getting to the very top, those can only be made by the person himself.
—Paul Clement

4.3 FITNESS

If I've got a young goalkeeper at the club, 16 or 17 years old, who I believe in and who's ready physically, I'll look to get him out on loan into men's football straight away. Being in a dressing room with guys who need that £40 win bonus to pay their mortgage, it's a different kind of pressure. If you make a mistake, they'll have a go at you. If they make a mistake, you've got to be able to help them deal with that.

You'll need to take the physical knocks, too. A young keeper will make mistakes but the only way you'll find out if he's got the inner strength to push through those and improve is by getting him out there. Otherwise, you'll never know, will you? —Tony Roberts

At Level 4, if a player is working in a professional environment, he will probably be able to draw on the experience of a strength and conditioning coach who supervises fitness and gym sessions. That said, much of what he or she delivers will be generalised: the coach is responsible for getting the best out of a squad of 20 or more players.

Level 4 players who want to approach elite levels of fitness will be prepared to do the extra work to make it happen. There are no short cuts. If a player is outside the full-time environment at this stage, he'll have to do almost all his fitness work alone or with team-mates and friends, outside whatever training sessions he has scheduled.

Either way, a structured programme, reinforced by constant assessment and development, creates a better fitness foundation. It also trains the mind, establishing the good habits and consistency of application needed for success at the elite levels of football.

There are fundamental elements of any fitness programme, which should already be part of a player's routine as he's grown through the levels towards becoming a **COMPLETE ATHLETE**:

LOWER-BODY STRENGTH

UPPER-BODY STRENGTH

FLEXIBILTY/MOBILITY

CORE STRENGTH

SPEED/EXPLOSIVENESS/AGILITY

ENDURANCE

LOWER-BODY STRENGTH

Level 4 builds on the work you've done in prior levels while your body has been growing and developing. You should now be aware of the football-specific advantages which follow on from each element of a fitness programme. At this stage, the work you've already done means you have achieved real progress: you're stronger, better-balanced, and have more reserves of explosive power to draw on during games. Lower-body work has been key to making the difference.

You may now be pushing for a first team place, trying to beat your own goal-scoring record or even be on the verge of representative honours.

It's now more important than ever that your technical work is complemented by further developing the lower-body strength, which has already helped give you an edge.

At Level 4, times are extended, distances are lengthened, and more repetitions are needed. The aim is always to take your test numbers up toward elite level. It'll be up to you and you alone: the physical challenge has to be matched by strength of will and an unflinching work ethic.

SINGLE-LEG SQUATS >>

- Balance on one slightly bent leg while your other leg is positioned slightly in front of your body.
- With your arms straightened out on each side to aid balance, start to bend the knee of your planted, balancing leg slowly, going as low as you can while still maintaining balance and control.
- Slowly straighten your knee again to return to the starting position. Repeat on your other leg.
- It's important to bear in mind that a player actually builds more strength on the way back up to his starting position than on the way down. Therefore, control and balance on the way back to the starting position are vital.

SINGLE-LEG WALL SIT >>

- Stand with feet shoulder-width apart against a smooth-surfaced wall.
- Slowly slide down the wall until both your knees and hips are at 90 degree angles.
- Slowly lift one foot off the ground until you can feel muscle tension in the planted leg.
- Keep the lifted foot raised for as long as possible before putting it back on the ground.
- Remain in the sitting position but rest for 30 seconds.
- Repeat the lift, using the other foot.
- Time how long you can hold on each foot off the ground.

Remember to be aware of any imbalance in strength between the dominant and non-dominant legs.
Work toward being able to keep each foot off the ground

for equal lengths of time. Any significant difference in strength can be lessened by increasing repetitions with the weaker planted leg.

BROAD-JUMPS »

A controlled broad jump is an excellent exercise for developing explosive strength, balance and coordination between upper and lower-body movements in young players.

- Stand behind a marked line on the ground with feet shoulder-width apart.
- Bend your knees and raise both arms forward in front of you.
- As you swing them back behind you, start to bend your knees. Swing your arms back out in front of you again and, as you do so, leap forward with both feet leaving the ground at the same time.
- Look to increase the power in your jump and measure it by how far your jump takes you.
- At the end of the jump, it's important to land as softly as possible with your knees bent and both feet alongside each other.
- Your knees should never be propelled ahead of your toes as this causes instability and the possibility of injury.
- Now look to perform 10 broad jumps in a row.

THE VERTICAL LEAP TEST »

If you're training at an academy or a well-funded club, you may have access to the technology, which measures both the velocity and reach of your vertical leap, giving you and your coaches an idea of the explosive power you're able to generate in your legs and lower-body.

It's not necessary to have access to that technology, however, for the Vertical Leap Test to be useful both as a measure and a way of improving your lower-body strength.

- Stand next to any wall and, with your feet completely flat, reach up with the hand closest to the wall and measure the highest point you can touch, ideally with a piece of chalk. Otherwise, you'll need to have someone with you who can do the necessary measurements.
- Keep the piece of chalk in the hand nearest the wall. Now let your knees bend and then jump upwards, using both your legs to generate power and your arms to help balance and propel. At the highest point of your leap, try to mark the wall with the chalk again.
- Measure the distance between the two chalk marks. That distance is your result.
- Repeat the test a few times, each time trying to leap higher and leave a fresh chalk mark on the wall.
- Repeat the test on a regular basis and compare measurements to chart progress.
- Repetitions of all other lower-body exercises will help to gradually improve your vertical leap test scores.
- The vertical leap test can be done off just one leg if you want to isolate muscles in just one side of the lower-body.

INJURY PREVENTION

At Level 4, tackles are harder, player contacts happen with more force, and extra strain is being put on muscles and joints by you having to cover more ground during games. You should have by now established an **INJURY PREVENTION** element in your fitness work. At this stage of your development, you don't want to miss games and training sessions, especially if they're due to avoidable injuries. Your progress can depend on you playing as often as possible. Of course, injuries happen. They happen to every player. But the very best players do all they can to lessen their impact.

Most injuries are suffered in the lower half of a footballer's body, particularly around important joints like the knee and ankle and within surrounding ligaments and tendons. Fitness work can help in two ways: first, by protecting and strengthening those areas to make injury less likely in the first place; and, second, by speeding up recovery from an injury if you're unlucky enough to suffer one. A good starting point for an injury prevention programme is simple balance exercises. These will strengthen and protect areas of contact during games, such as ankles, knees and hips, and also develop resilience in the connective tissues and muscle groups around them.

THE BALANCE DISK »

- You will need a balance (or stability) disk which can be bought for less than £5 online or on the High Street.
- Place one foot on the very centre of the disk.
- Now slightly bend your knee and raise your arms out straight beside you, to make a T-shape.
- Try to remain as still as possible, balancing for at least 45 seconds.
- You will start to feel the muscles and ligaments around your planted ankle start to burn/fatigue.

(This is exactly what you want: improving overall balance and, at the same time, strengthening muscles and ligaments surrounding the joints, making your body more resilient when the next tackle comes in.)

• Now change feet. Repeat 10 times on each foot.

BALANCE DISK PROGRESSION >>

1 >> Once you've mastered the static balance disk hold for a minimum of 30 seconds on each foot, progress using the same piece of equipment.

• Place one foot in the centre of the disk and step onto it as before. This time, though, once you're set, try to bend your knee, raising yourself 3 to 6 inches each time. The movement is similar to the single-leg squat.
• Repeat the movement six times, slowly enough to retain stability in the upper half of your body throughout.
• This will strengthen your glutes, hamstrings, and quadriceps as well as building resilience into hip, knee, and ankle.
• Repeat six times on the other foot.

2 >> Once you are comfortable with that sequence, put one foot onto the centre of the disk and assume the static position. Then ask a friend or teammate to throw a ball to you, gently enough for you to catch it without losing your balance.

• Throw the ball back and then lower yourself slowly on your planted knee as you would for a single-leg squat.
• Aim for 10 repetitions of this sequence on each leg.

BALL SQUEEZES »

As the number of passing and shooting repetitions increases due to training harder and more often, it's important to keep your adductor muscles (groin muscles) strong. Injuries to these muscles can be debilitating and lead to long-term issues. Ball squeezes combined with sit ups are key to keeping this muscle group strong.

- Place yourself in the sit up position with a moderately pumped up ball between your legs.
- Now engage your core and squeeze the ball for 2 seconds, then release for 1 second. Repeat this movement 20 times.
- Rest for 30 seconds.
- Repeat but, this time, squeeze for 5 seconds, then release for 4 seconds. Repeat this 10 times.
- Rest for 30 seconds.
- Finally, squeeze the ball lightly between your legs and keep it there while you perform between 15 to 20 sit-ups.
- Rest for 2 minutes. Repeat entire sequence a minimum of four times.

UPPER-BODY STRENGTH

At Level 4, **UPPER-BODY STRENGTH** becomes an increasingly important part of any young player's game, giving him the ability to shield the ball, ride tackles, and win his one-on-one battles, even against bigger and more powerful opponents. A young player needs to work hard physically to remain competitive. He'll have to improve his balance and coordination, learning how to time his challenges. But he'll also need to be physically stronger, particularly in his upper-body. By the time a young player reaches Level 4, his body is ready to train regularly with weights.

At a professional or semi-professional club, advice and guidance on weights-based exercises will be readily available. Free weights and resistance machines are both useful.

The widespread growth of gyms and fitness centres nationally means fully qualified expertise is readily available to every young player, including those developing outside the academy or college environments. Contact local gyms and ask what's available and, if at all possible, find a friend or team-mate to train with. This will be of benefit from a safety point of view and will also help motivate both of you as you challenge yourselves and each other.

Work with weights and machines in the gym, however, should be in addition to the calisthenics you've been doing at the earlier levels of the **COMPLETE ATHLETE** guide. It shouldn't be a replacement for them. Upper-body strength work, for example, based around using your own body weight should remain at the heart of your fitness programme.

The simplicity of the exercises means they can be performed almost anywhere and can be incorporated to run alongside other gym work or to tide you over between gym sessions. Simple doesn't mean any the less effective: calisthenics will continue to help you compete physically, build your confidence, absorb contact more readily, and retain your balance when challenged in possession. You're building on what you already know:

FULL PULL-UP »

- Grip an overhead bar with underhand grip with palms facing toward your body.
- Your arms should be fully extended. Ideally, you'll be high enough off the ground for your legs to be hanging straight down.

- Try and pull your body up slowly with the aim of getting your chin above the bar. The emphasis should be on using your arms and back to lift your body. Don't try to use any momentum generated by your legs swinging backwards and forwards.
- At the highest point, with your chin above the bar, your legs should be completely straight.
- Hold at the highest point for 5 seconds and then lower yourself slowly, maintaining control at all times.

PUSH-UP »

- Lie face-down with your palms under or slightly wide of your shoulders: fingers straight, legs straight and parallel.
- Straighten your arms, pushing your upper and lower-body up together in one smooth movement, back and knees straight throughout.
- Push up until your arms are straight then slowly lower again until your face, chest and knees are an inch or two from the floor.
- Perform as many controlled repetitions as possible before resting.
- Be very careful not to let your back arch as this will put strain on your back muscles and risks injury.

FUNCTIONAL (CLOCK) PUSH-UP »

- Start by positioning yourself on the floor as you would for a basic push-up. Perform a basic push-up.
- At the highest point of the push-up, with your arms straight and locked, move your right hand one shoulder width to the right, bringing your left hand across and adjusting your feet to balance in the new position. Then return your body to the floor to complete the push-up.
- Perform another push-up and repeat the sequence of movements at the push-up's highest point, again

moving to the right. This time, though, edge the right hand up slightly as well as out so that your body will move like the minute hand on a clock face.

- Repeat the sequence 12 times so that you arrive back in your original starting position, at 12 o'clock.
- Rest for 30 seconds before repeating the 12 push-ups, this time moving anti-clockwise by moving your left hand first at the highest point of each push-up.
- Just as in the basic push-up, form and technique are paramount. Don't arch your back or allow your bottom to stick up in the air.

DIPS »

- Use either a dip machine or two parallel bars set just wider than shoulder-width apart.
- Raise yourself onto the bars. Once in position, grip a bar in each hand, lift your upper-body and lock your arms straight. Your legs can be straight out beneath you or bent at 90 degrees.
- Lower your body through the bars until your arms create right angles either side. Keep your back straight at all times and look at a point on the wall opposite to make sure your head and chin are level.
- Lift yourself back up through the bars until your arms lock straight again.
- Repeat the sequence as many times as you can without having to use twists of the legs or torso to help your lifts.
- Be conscious of all the power you generate coming from the arms and upper back. Your legs and lower-body move as little as possible throughout.

FLEXIBILITY/MOBILITY

In a professional environment, a Level 4 player gets advice and guidance from specialists about pre-exercise muscle activation and stretching and recovery after exertion.

FLEXIBILITY AND MOBILITY are essential for any young player, not least in helping to prevent injury. The Sit and Reach Test is an effective and simple exercise for improving a young footballer's hamstring and lower back flexibility. It can also be used as a marker to assess flexibility and gauge continuing improvement. The exercise can be performed in any environment, making it useful for players working outside academy or college settings.

THE SIT AND REACH TEST >>

You'll need a box around 8 to 12 inches high. A shoe box is perfect. Use a ruler to mark out inch-divisions across the top of the box to measure your reach.

- Place the box against a wall with the top of the box facing upwards.
- Sit on the floor with the soles of your feet flat against the side of the box in front of you.
- Keeping your legs straight and flat on the floor, slowly stretch forward with straight arms and try to reach the box.
- Do this slowly and with control three times then, on the fourth stretch, reach as far as possible and hold for at least three seconds.
- Note the distance you reached using the inch-marks on the box. Work to increase the distance you are able to reach.
- If you cannot reach the box, ask someone to measure how close you are to the box. Monitor progress and increase flexibility until you can reach the marks on the box.

Guidance on flexibility and mobility can be found online if a player doesn't have access to professional advice. It's important at Level 4 to have a full-body stretching and mobility programme as part of a daily fitness regime, whether that's one set by club or college staff or one you develop for yourself.

YOGA

You will see massive benefits from any extra work you can do in terms of improving your flexibility. Yoga is a proven method, benefiting muscles and joints all over the body. Yoga can significantly improve your body's durability and its capacity for swift recovery after the intense exertion of training and games. The discipline demanded can also help develop mental resilience, as you focus on patient, careful movements very different from most of the other physical work associated with football.

Over the past 20 years, yoga has been introduced, in one form or another, into the fitness and conditioning schedules of the overwhelming majority of elite clubs worldwide. Every leisure centre and every gym in the country runs yoga classes at beginners and advanced standards. Finding one near you to join won't be difficult or expensive. If you prefer, there are online courses and TV shows which will be able to guide you through the basics and allow you to learn and practise yoga at home.

CORE STRENGTH AND BALANCE

Working toward becoming a **COMPLETE ATHLETE** has introduced the young player, at each Level, to improving **CORE STRENGTH** and **BALANCE**. At Level 4, the exercises learnt so far can either continue to function as a main programme or become useful additions to a programme set out for a player by his club or college. Either way, the effective functioning of core muscles is an essential component of fitness for strength, power and explosive movement. The core is the firm base from which larger muscles do their work of converting energy into football-specific movements and actions: kicking, jumping, sprinting and protecting the ball. Simple self-testing can identify any weakness in the core area. It may help to train with a friend or team-mate to check alignment of hips and buttocks during the exercises.

A PLANK >>

- Lie face-down on the floor. With elbows bent at a 90-degree angle, hands in a fist and shoulder-width apart, on the floor facing forwards, lift your body to balance on your arms and toes.
- Your body should be completely level and straight, at roughly shoulder height.
- No sagging or arched back as this puts concentrated strain on other areas.
- Think of the flat shape of a plank of wood.
- Now squeeze your stomach in and tighten while in plank position, keeping your body level.
- Hold this position for as long as you can.
- As you become comfortable with the plank, you can further challenge yourself. Once you've got into the plank position, raise one foot slowly off the ground, keeping your leg straight and aligned through the hip.
- Repeat with the other leg. You can also try lifting one arm at a time out straight in front of you.
- Bear in mind that the aim is always to avoid rotation in the hips or lower back, taking the weight in your core muscles exclusively.

A FUNCTIONAL PLANK >>

- Follow the same guidelines as above.
- Once in the plank position, slowly bend your left knee out beside you and move it up towards your left arm. The moving leg never goes above shoulder height.
- Slowly move back into plank position then repeat with your right knee moving towards your right arm.
- Repeat on both sides as many times as you can.

A FUNCTIONAL SIDE PLANK >>

- Lie on your side with your legs straight.
- Now slightly raise your body up onto your right forearm and elbow.
- Activate your core by contracting your abdominal muscles.
- Raise your hips until your body forms a straight line from your ankles to your shoulders. This is your hold position.
- Breathe deeply while holding this position.
- Now, keeping your legs together and parallel, slowly lower your right hip until the outer surface of your right thigh touches the floor.
- Slowly raise your hip to return to your hold position.
- Repeat as many times as you can.
- Repeat, raising yourself on your left forearm and elbow.

A MARCHING HIP-RAISE >>

- Lie flat on your back with your knees raised and bent at 90 degrees, feet flat on the floor.
- Keeping your back straight at all times, lift your hips as high as possible with only your feet and shoulders touching the ground.
- Now raise one knee toward your chest in a controlled marching movement.
- Repeat on alternate sides for as long as you can.

SPEED/EXPLOSIVENESS/AGILITY

To give yourself the chance to become a **COMPLETE ATHLETE**, you will need to work harder than anyone else. At Level 4, there is even more focus on speed and explosive movement. Every Level 4 player will need to be working on the three types of speed relevant in football: straight line speed, explosive speed, and lateral (side-to-side) speed.

As with all fitness work, the effort put in isn't just about today and tomorrow.

A young player is equipping himself now for what he hopes will be the 20-plus years of elite football which lie ahead of him. Straight line speed is the ability to get from point A to B as quickly as possible. Explosive speed is how quickly a player can take off in the first 5 yards of a sprint (explosive speed in football is multi-directional). Agility is the body's ability to get from point A to point B via multiple other points and moving in multiple directions.

The drills outlined here aim to develop speed over the ground for a young player. They also seek to promote his ability to stop/start and accelerate/decelerate in multiple directions of travel. The 30-yard sprint helps a young player improve straight line speed. The 5-10-5-5-10 shuttle runs help develop explosive speed and promote agility. The fast feet drill helps a player make quicker and sharper adjustments of his feet, enabling him to explode more powerfully into his sprints.

STRAIGHT LINE SPEED: 30-YARD SPRINT »

- Place 2 cones 30 yards apart.
- Run from cone 1 to cone 2 as fast as you can.
- When doing sprint work, it's important to rest for 8 times as long as the action has taken (for example, after a 6 second sprint you should rest for 48 seconds before going again).
- Time your sprint or get a friend or parent to time it so you can chart improvement.

The aim here is to train your mind to tell your body to run faster. This will only happen by continually sprinting as fast as you can. As the body becomes used to moving at a particular speed, it'll then be possible to push it to move faster. This will only be effective with the appropriate rest times of 8–1 between sprints. If you don't rest appropriately, you risk the sprints becoming just an endurance drill. This is counter-productive as your sprints will become slower the more you do. Our purpose is training the mind to recognise, get used to and then increase the body's maximum speed.

JOIN THE CONVERSATION!
For more fitness tips and how-to's, download the **COMPLETE ATHLETE** app now!

EXPLOSIVE SPEED: 8 TO 10-YARD MULTI-DIRECTIONAL SPRINTS »

- Practice 8 to 10 yard sprints in different directions by placing cones 8 to 10 yards away from you at different angles.
- Before each separate sprint, turn slightly away from the intended direction of travel (away from the next cone you're going to sprint to) so that each sprint begins with a turn in towards the cone you're heading for.
- Keep your body low at the start of each sprint and gradually come upright as you approach each cone in turn.
- Choose a spot in the distance and focus on this point while sprinting.
- Keep your body in line, arms pumping in a straight line faster than your legs (the faster your arms pump the faster your legs will move) and keep your head as still as possible.
- Don't let your arms and head flop side-to-side as this will reduce the efficiency of your explosive movements.

AGILITY: 5-10-5-5-10 SHUTTLE RUN »

- Set up five cones or markers, each 5 yards apart, in a symmetrical shape as below.

Δ

Δ   Δ   Δ

Δ

- Start in the centre and sprint 5 yards to the right cone.
- Then turn and sprint 10 yards to the furthest left cone.

- Sprint 5 yards back to the middle and then 5 yards running backwards to the bottom cone.
- Then explode 10 yards through to the top cone.
- Rest for six times longer than it takes you to complete the drill. Then repeat drill with your first sprint going to the left cone.
- When you get close to each cone in turn, try to start getting your body low to prepare it for a change of direction.

FAST FEET (3 POINTS OF CONTACT) »

- Place a single cone a couple of feet to your right and another the same distance to your left.
- Stand between these cones, lifted onto your toes, jogging lightly from foot to foot, ready to move.
- Keep your body facing forward through the drill. Only your feet move to the sides.
- Starting on your left side. Three positions: 6 inches to your left, 1 foot to your left, and next to the cone.
- While still jogging lightly, touch your left foot gently and quickly to each point in turn and back.
- Repeat the sequence on your right side.
- Repeat the sequence twice more on each side.
- At the end, explode into a straight or angled 10-yard sprint.
- It's important that your standing foot remains light and mobile while the reaching foot is active because it will be making small adjustments to help control the reaching foot and then be ready to jump off into the sprint.

JOIN THE CONVERSATION!

Improve your skills today! Learn more when you download the **COMPLETE ATHLETE** app.

ENDURANCE

ENDURANCE is the functioning of your heart and cardiovascular system to supply your muscles with enough oxygen to keep you running without fatiguing or breaking down. Low levels of endurance will result in lower amounts of oxygen in your blood and an inability to sustain the levels of intense physical activity football demands.

The best tests of endurance for Level 4 players are the Beep Test and the 30-second run. At Level 4, a multi-directional 30-yard run drill will be really useful, too. All function as exercises to develop a young player's stamina.

THE BEEP TEST »

The Beep Test is an endurance test: a series of shuttle runs between markers 20 metres apart, each run starting on a beep. It begins at level 1 and ends at level 20. For example, level 1 (not much more than a walk) has 10 runs and you have 8 seconds to complete each one between beeps.

At level 10, you have around 6 seconds between beeps in which to complete each 20-metre run; and so on. If you fail to complete the shuttles at any level in sync with the beeps, you will have failed that level.

Note the last level you completed: that's the level you achieved in the test. To provide your beeps, you'll need to download a Beep Test application to your phone or tablet. You'll also have to be able to measure, accurately, the 20 metres between lines for the runs.

- On a non-slip floor surface, place cones or simply mark lines 20 metres apart.
- After you press start on the Beep Test app, the recording will sound a beep for each 20-metre run and then sound a sequence of beeps to advise that you are moving up to the next level and that your speed will need to increase.
- Make sure one foot touches the line before each turn. And do not start to run until the beep has sounded.
- You should stop when you fall short of the 20-metre line two beeps in a row.
- Remember to note your last completed level (not the one you failed to complete).

THE 30-SECOND RUN »

- You need five cones and a timer, watch or phone with alarm function.
- Place the cones in a straight line, each 10 yards apart.
- Set the timer for 30 seconds and press start.
- Run to Cone 1 and then back the ten yards to your start position. Then run to Cone 2 and back the 20 yards to your start position. Keep working your way up the line of cones until you've reached Cone 5 and run the 50 yards back to your start position.
- If you get to Cone 5 before the 30 seconds are up, start from Cone 1 again and continue your way back up until the 30 seconds have run out.
- Now rest for 1 minute before re-setting the timer to 30 seconds again and repeating the runs. Look to complete six 30-second sets.
- Keep track of how many yards you cover in each 30-second set in order both to monitor progress and challenge your endurance capacity.

MULTI-DIRECTIONAL 30-SECOND RUN »

Set out five cones in an 'X' pattern as shown. You'll need to time each repetition of the drill at 30 seconds.

△2   △4

          △3

△1   △5

- The spacing between cones 1,2 & 3 is 10 yards between each cone. Likewise, between cones 3,4 & 5.
- Start the drill at cone 1.
- Sprint from cone 1 to cone 2, then sprint backwards to cone 1.
- Now from sprint diagonally to cone 3, then backwards to 1, then sprint all the way to 4.
- Sprint from 4 to 5, then backwards from 5 to 4.
- Now sprint diagonally from 4 to 3, then backwards to 4 and finally sprint all the way back to 1.
- Start the sequence again from cone 1 and continue until 30 seconds are up.

LEVEL-4 PERFORMANCE TESTS

LOWER-BODY STRENGTH »

• 15 full-range single-leg squats on each leg
• Series of 10 broad jumps of 78 inches or more
• Single-leg wall-sit held for 75 seconds on each leg

INJURY PREVENTION »

• Balance Disk: Progression 1, 25 dips on each leg

UPPER-BODY STRENGTH »

• Bent-arm pull-up held for 35 seconds
• 50 full push-ups in 60 seconds
• 1 full clock push-up set (1 clockwise then 1 counter-
  clockwise with no rest in between)

FLEXIBILTY/MOBILITY »

• Sit and reach test of at least 6 inches

CORE STRENGTH/BALANCE >>

- Plank for 2.5 minutes
- Functional plank for 1.5 minutes
- Side functional plank 40 reps, 20 per side, no rests
- Single-leg balance for 40 seconds with slightly bent knee
- Marching hip-raise for 2 mins with no rotation in hips or back

SPEED/QUICKNESS/AGILITY >>

- 30-yard sprint in under 4.1 seconds
- 8-yard multi-directional sprint in 1.1 seconds
- 5-10-5-5-10 shuttle run in under 6 seconds.

ENDURANCE >>

- Beep Test: minimum score of level 15
- 30-second run: 6 sets, each set to be completed to 50 yards + 20 yards
- Multi-directional 30-second run: Complete over 3 sets in 30 seconds, rest for 1 minute between sets

 # TECHNIQUE

By the time a young player reaches Level 4, he has proven himself a reliable and comfortable user of the ball. At this stage in his development, this will be challenged on a daily basis. The extra tempo, increased physicality, and added pressure all mean that it's essential for the young player to continue working on the technical elements of his game, now paying particular attention to those related to the demands of the position he plays in most regularly. That said, over the course of Level 4—during a single training session or game—the player must be ready for one or more changes in the position he's asked to play.

Flexibility with regards to the job he's asked to do for the team can prove a huge advantage for any developing young player. He may find himself called in to make up numbers or replace an injured player at a level or two above the one he's used to competing at. Other people's mistakes will be rarer. His own will usually be more ruthlessly punished.

Those steps up to a higher level of competition will often be determined by the team's requirements rather than being for the benefit of the young player's individual development. A young player's all-around knowledge and ability as a footballer will need to be as high as possible if he's to take advantage of any opportunity which comes his way.

PLAYER » *Our philosophy at Southampton at the time Alexander joined the club was to bring in boys who were technical, could do something with the ball and make things happen. Alexander was always small but he was technically good so his size wasn't an issue. But things can happen at a club: a new guy came in at Southampton and suddenly it was all about how tall they were. They were after the bigger boys, the boys born earlier in the year group. Lads would come on trial and get signed because they were 6 footers, never mind whether they could play or not.*

By the time Alex was 15, he was being played down an age group because he was smaller. Every now and again he'd play up with his own age group. I remember him saying, 'They're all giants! But when I pass them the ball, when I go for a 1-2, they don't pass it back to me.' I just said, 'That's because they can't. They're not good enough!' It was hard for him for a while, bigger boys getting picked in front of him. Especially at that age, it's easy for the boy and his parents to feel negative about being played down an age group. I just tried to be positive with Alex, getting him to keep giving it his best. And wait till he grew!

JOIN THE CONVERSATION!
Download the **COMPLETE ATHLETE** app now!

The thing is you never know who might be watching you play. When Alex was 16, he wasn't playing regularly for the youth team, there were other boys ahead of him. But he got a game in the FA Youth Cup, down at Brighton. The assistant manager Dean Wilkins was there. Southampton got beat but, afterwards, Dean actually said to me, 'Your boy did well. Kept going. Tried his best.' Apparently, he spoke to the manager, Alan Pardew, about Alexander and they had a look at him in training.

As an ex-player myself, I know what you can see in training: touch, vision, eye for a pass, excellent movement. They took one look at Alexander and said: Right, get him out of there. We'll have him to train with the first team. And he played for Southampton not long after that, in 2010.
—Mark Chamberlain

When Michael Owen and Wayne Rooney were growing up in schoolboy football, they were scoring 100 goals a season for their teams. Before they got taken into Liverpool or Everton, they'd have been playing for their school, for their local club, for a Sunday League team, and scoring goals every week.

If those same players were in academies now, playing best versus best every game, they wouldn't get anywhere near the number of chances, wouldn't score anywhere near that number of goals. It worries me a little bit. Owen and Rooney as boys were probably getting 600 chances a season. And learning to score goals. How will we develop those 'natural' goalscorers now? How many chances will an academy striker get in games every season? The same's true for midfield players, goal providers, wingers and so on as well. —Terry Burton

POSITION-SPECIFIC
TECHNICAL SKILLS

STRIKERS: HOLDING THE BALL UP UNDER PRESSURE / CONTROLLING FAST-PACED & AWKWARD PASSES / FINISHING UNDER PRESSURE » At Level 4, you will find yourself playing against bigger, stronger opponents who may have two or more years of experience than you. Holding the ball up effectively isn't simply about physical strength.

It's also about timing and technique, which enable you to get in front of a defender at the right moment to put you in control of the ball and the situation. Your body shape will need to adjust to keep the ball as far away from your opponent as possible, while maintaining your own balance in order to receive and control the ball, keeping it within a yard of you and thus putting you in charge.

Timed finishing drills are worthwhile in that they add an element of pressure to add to, or replace, the presence of a defender or defenders in the session. You need to continue to do extra work, however, with drills that encourage you to concentrate solely on the technical precision of your finishing at high tempo and pace.

STRIKERS / MIDFIELDERS: SHOOTING THE BALL WITH ACCURACY » When you move into full-time or open-age football, games become more demanding, both physically and technically. As a striker or midfielder, you may now find that your opportunities are limited: you may only get one or two chances to score during a game. Maintaining technical quality and accuracy is paramount, especially the ability to find the corners of the goal whenever possible. Try to avoid the temptation to risk composure, technique and placement for power.

MIDFIELDERS: WIDER RANGE & TYPES OF PASSES

>> Midfielders and wide players at Level 4 are expected to receive the ball and create opportunities in small spaces, working a route through congestion. You'll need high levels of game awareness along with the ability to shield and turn with the ball to get out from pressure. You'll also be expected to take opportunities to change the point of the attack. This means working on the widest possible range of passing techniques every day: passing through the lines, feathering passes over the top of defenses, and playing reverse passes to unlock tight defenses.

WIDE PLAYERS: ACCURACY FROM CROSSES >> At

Level 4, wide players will face experienced defenders who have studied the game and are playing as part of an organised defensive unit. Therefore, the areas you have to be able to hit crosses will become limited, demanding greater precision. Those optimum areas can also change from moment to moment as play unfolds.

You may need to be able to whip an early cross into the danger area between goalkeeper and defenders; or you may need to recognise that defenders have dropped back to cover that space and a cutback toward the edge of the 18-yard box has suddenly become your best crossing option. As well as practicing to ensure precision and pace with your crosses, be sure to work on your awareness of the positions taken up by defenders and the movement of your own strikers, helping you make good decisions as to which cross you need to deliver.

GOALKEEPERS: SAVES/DISTRIBUTION >> Level 4

goalkeepers will now find themselves one-on-one against players approaching with greater pace and power than ever before. Strikers are now able to find the corners of the goal with more consistent precision. Midfielders will be able to deliver set-pieces with greater accuracy.

When faced with challenges in the air, both the opposition and your own defenders are bigger and stronger obstacles. You may have the benefit of one-on-one work with a goalkeeping coach or you may need to try and find team-mates or friends who can help ensure you get regular practice across the whole range of goalkeeping skills: dealing with crosses, first and second phase finishing reactions, judging and closing down angles, body shape and body position in one-on-one situations, and being comfortable playing the ball to team-mates or away from danger with both feet.

DEFENDERS: PASSING RANGE/ONE-ON-ONES » When your team is out of possession is, of course, the most important part of a defender's game: you're expected to clear danger and win individual battles against strikers. In preparation for tackles and interceptions, the Level 4 defender works at keeping his body low and maintaining short, nimble stride patterns which will allow for sudden changes of direction in order to counter threats from any angle.

As well as snuffing out danger, modern defenders are also expected to be comfortable in possession. Short and long passing needs to be practiced: it's a great advantage to be able to switch play with long diagonals or play passes over the opposition's midfield and defensive lines. You will need to be consistently accurate with passes over five, ten and twenty yards. Daily repetitions in one-on-ones and with passing are both key to progressing as a modern defender.

JOIN THE CONVERSATION!
Study the techniques of the pros in the **COMPLETE ATHLETE** app!

PLAYER » It's important to be aware of the elements outlined above but every new technical skill you add to your game will rely on the techniques you've been working on for many years now. Those fundamentals remain the basis for everything you do as a player and need to be worked on both as part of your formal training schedule and outside it:

BALL CONTROL

BALL MASTERY/DRIBBLING

PASSING

SHOOTING

HEADING

AWARENESS

BALL CONTROL

- First and second touches
- Controlling the ball with all surfaces of the foot
- Direction of touch
- On the ground, bouncing, spinning and on the full
- Controlling while being pressured by opponent (awareness/pre-scanning)
- Controlling in confined and congested space (awareness/pre-scanning)
- Controlling to move forward with momentum

TECHNICAL TIPS »

- Lower your body and bend your knees slightly to encourage a soft and precise first touch.
- Do not lunge and stretch onto the ball as this will inhibit balance and quality of touch. Invite the ball

onto your foot (or any other part of your body) rather than meeting it with a stiff approach.

- Always try and get your body behind the ball. This will help you to protect the ball, stay balanced and keep your body in line within the width of your hips.
- When making contact with the ball, don't have your foot raised too high or it will connect with the top of the ball, pushing it into the ground. Don't have your foot too low, either, or it will connect underneath the ball and lift it into the air without you controlling that.
- Work on your awareness (pre-scanning) of what's happening around you before receiving the ball. Top players always have a picture of the other players on the pitch in their minds at all times.

The consistent quality of your first touch, your ability to control the ball with any part of your body on any part of the pitch is the foundation for everything you do. The quality of a player's first touch is probably the single most significant measure in setting the great player apart from the rest. You need to practice and challenge yourself every time you train.

BALL MASTERY/DRIBBLING

- Try keeping the ball within 5 inches of your foot as you move with it. This will allow you to change direction quickly in tight spaces without surrendering control.
- Try dribbling with the ball at different speeds. Draw in your opponent then beat him!
- Dribble with your head up if you can so you can see what else is going on around you.
- When you have the ball under control, try to manipulate it by touching it with all the different areas of your foot.

- Dribbling at full speed over larger distances, using both light and heavier touches on the ball.
- Being able to lift/scoop the ball over an opponent's foot while dribbling at high speed.
- Direct dribbling: recognising the shortest route to goal and dribbling with that destination in mind. Every successful direct dribble should finish with an attempt on goal.

TECHNICAL TIPS »

- Close control is paramount when you need to change direction quickly, under pressure or in a tight situation. Remember that 5-inch rule!
- Vary the speed and direction of your dribbling. This breaks up your opponent's stride pattern and undermines his balance. Those are the weaknesses you can capitalise on to beat him.
- Try and be aware of where you're taking the ball in order not to lose it and in order to use your skills most productively.
- Running too quickly with the ball can sometimes mean you lose control of it. Focus on control first and build up your running speed as you develop.
- Dribbling with your head down can take you into a crowd of opponents or even off the pitch altogether.

- As you build confidence in ball mastery, start to use your imagination and develop your own personal sequences of movement. The challenge is to complete these moves quickly but with efficiency and maintaining control.

At Level 4, you should have **COMPLETELY MASTERED**:

CRUYFF TURNS

DRAG BACKS

DRAG BACK AND PUSH

STEP-OVERS

SNAKES

TOUCH/FAKE STEP AND PUSH

TOUCH/ROLL, DRAG, STEP-OVER AND PUSH

TRIPLE-PACE MULTI-DIRECTIONAL DRIBBLING

PASSING

At Level 4, playing the game quicker and under more pressure from opponents, a player needs to develop his ability to vary the pace, direction and trajectory of his passes. Practice your range of longer **PASSING**, varying those elements as part of the drill. Work on fundamental elements of fitness, such as building lower-body strength, which will give you the physical power to deploy a full range of passes more readily.

With the game happening more quickly, your passing will come under pressure both in terms of the time you have on the ball and the space in which you're able to work. Quicker decision-making is crucial. Being aware of what's happening on the rest of the pitch (pre-scanning) can help you make the right decision—and make it faster—once the ball arrives with you.

The fundamental range of passing which you worked on at previous Levels remains the same and your game should continue to be built around mastering those techniques through constant practice:

- Inside foot pass
- Driven pass high and low
- Curved pass, high and low
- Feathered penetrating pass
- Low threaded penetrating pass between the lines pass
- Half-volley pass, inside foot, high and low
- Half-volley pass, driven with laces, low
- Volley pass, high and low
- Sharp link passes (one-twos and wall passes)

INSIDE FOOT PASS

- Try to make a good, clean, firm connection with soft instep of the foot with your hips guided toward the target.
- For a low pass, keep your follow-through low. To play a pass through the air, raise your foot on your follow-through.
- To keep the pass controlled, try to strike the ball with the soft instep so it doesn't clip your heel or your toe.

DRIVEN PASS

- Connect with laces tight against the ball. Short, punched follow-through with your hips facing the target.
- If you chop underneath the ball, you'll find it slices off in another direction to the one you intended.

CURVED PASS

- Connect with the ball using the inside of your foot on the outside of the ball. Shape your follow-through to describe the shape you want the ball to make as it travels.
- Always lift your follow-through to lift the ball off the ground. Keep your follow-through low if you want your pass to travel along the ground.
- Twisting your hips too sharply will make your follow-through take the pass beyond your target.

FEATHERED PASS

- A feathered pass is achieved by striking the ball a little less heavily so that it arrives at the target just as it loses pace and momentum.

LOW PASS BETWEEN THE LINES

- Passes between the lines are struck firmly enough to ensure they break the defensive lines but must also take into account the pace and direction of travel of the team-mate arriving at the ball.

HALF VOLLEY PASS

- Connect with the ball when it's just off the ground, within 2 inches of it bouncing, to give you maximum control over the pass.
- If you mis-time the connection and the ball is too far off the ground when you strike it, you'll hit underneath the ball and the pass will either slice or go too high.

VOLLEY PASS

- Get your body over the ball and connect in the middle of the ball, your laces guiding it downward to keep the pass controlled. Standing foot and hips should be pointed towards the intended target.

- Let the ball come onto your foot. If you connect too early, you'll hit the bottom of the ball and slice it. If you connect too late and strike the top of the ball, you'll push it into the ground instead of towards your target.

JOIN THE CONVERSATION!
Watch, learn, and communicate with the pros in the **COMPLETE ATHLETE** app!

SHARP LINK PASS
(ONE-TWOS/WALL PASSES)

- As well as relying on very accurate judgement of distance and pace, it's important to be balanced, with your body behind the ball, when making short, sharp link passes. This will help ensure you make the cleanest contact possible with the ball and also allow you to move onto a return ball with real explosive speed.

- Balance also helps you adjust quickly if the pass to you lacks precision or your teammate takes up an unexpected position.

'ROUND-THE-CORNER' PASS

- To perform this kind of pass successfully, when receiving the ball you will need excellent awareness of where your team-mates are positioned and where they are likely to face a challenge from.
- Adjust your body to ensure a good receiving angle which allows you to flick or re-direct the ball with the inside or outside of your foot, away from any incoming challenge and either into a team-mate's feet or into a space which is clear for him to run into to receive your pass.

SHOOTING

INSIDE FOOT

LACES STRIKE

CURVE

VOLLEY

HALF VOLLEY

'KNUCKLE' BALL

As well as mastering different kinds of shots, at Level 4 you'll need to make sure you've not only learnt the technical skills but are able to use them across a full range of situations you might face during a game:

- Opposed, where technical precision, decision-making and keeping your balance are all challenged.
- Unopposed, where your focus is on technical discipline and developing consistency.
- First-time
- Touch and finish
- Touch—set—finish
- Touch—set—fake—finish
- Inside the box
- From angles
- Outside the box

TECHNICAL TIP >>

When shooting, it's important that your hips are square to the target whenever possible as you follow through. Over-rotation of your hips on your follow-through tends to push the ball wide of its intended target.

INSIDE FOOT

- Body behind the ball, make a good strong connection with the inside of the foot. Transfer your weight through the ball with your hips angled toward the corner of the goal.
- Over-rotating your hips will tend to guide your shot toward the centre of the goal instead of the corner.

LACES STRIKE

First point of contact with the ball should be your laces right against the centre of the ball. Keep your follow-through below knee height and guide it towards your target.

- If the ball's first point of contact is the front of your foot and not your laces, this will mean you don't get a clean strike away and the ball will usually rise over the crossbar.

CURVE

- Similar to the curve pass, for a curve shot you need to connect on the outside of the ball with the inside of your foot. Shape your follow-through to describe the same shape you want your shot to make on its way to the target.
- Over-rotation of your hips or a loose follow-through may cause you to guide the ball wide of the target.

VOLLEY

- If possible, let the ball drop to knee height before striking it and connect with laces tight against the centre of the ball. Follow through on a high-to-low arc to keep the shot under control.
- Connecting underneath the ball—as you often do if the ball doesn't drop to knee height or below—will mean your shot flies up over the bar.

HALF VOLLEY

- As with the half-volley pass, it helps to strike the ball when it's as near to the ground as possible to ensure a clean, controlled connection.
- Allowing the ball to rise more than a couple of inches before striking it makes the shot much more difficult to keep low and on target.

KNUCKLE BALL

When connecting with the ball for this kind of shot, connect with the knuckle of your foot striking the lower part of the ball. Aim for the least possible amount of follow-through as you 'punch' the ball towards goal, keeping the connecting foot flat and straight.

- The intention is to make the ball move laterally in the air and dip without warning by striking it with an uneven part of the foot, the 'knuckle'.
- The trick is to connect with the 'knuckle' of your foot. Striking with the inside of the foot will not give the ball swerve and dip in the same way.

HEADING

HEADING is an important skill to master, particularly for attackers and defenders in the final thirds. Once making technically correct connection with the ball has been mastered, practice will ensure that power and direction are improved by the timing of that connection.

Daily practice is necessary if heading is going to be an important and decisive element in your game. The quality of repetitions is more important than their quantity.

CUSHIONED PASS HEADER

- As you approach the ball (or the ball approaches you), try to keep your eye on it and concentrate on making contact with your forehead. This will help you to avoid mis-timing connection and making connection with the top of your head.
- Don't follow through with too much momentum. The intention is to cushion the ball in the direction of the intended area or target.

HEADER AT GOAL

- When moving towards the ball with the intention of heading it, it's important to arrive at the point of contact with some momentum if possible.
- Always keep your eye on the ball. Use your neck muscles as your forehead connects with the ball to push the ball downwards toward the corners of the goal.
- Try to keep your eyes on the ball as you travel toward it. This gives you the best chance of connecting with your forehead rather than the top of your head, which would mean the ball bouncing upwards and over the bar.

DEFENSIVE CLEARANCE HEADER

- Try and get a run up towards the ball to generate some momentum.
- Keep your eyes focused on the ball all times and lift one bent arm across the front of your chest to protect your face.
- Try to generate power from the waist and spine, putting your whole body weight through the ball when connecting. This will to guide the ball upwards and away from you.
- Practice the timing and control of your jumps. Try to make sure you don't close your eyes. This is very important if you're going to avoid the ball hitting either the bridge of your nose or the top of your head.

FLICK HEADER

- A flick header is used to direct the ball toward a team-mate, toward the goal or into a dangerous area of the pitch. The idea is to keep the ball going forward, over or around defenders, when passing the ball isn't possible.
- For optimum control, the flick header is executed with the player looking skyward to ensure it's his forehead that connects with the ball.
- Rather than generating power behind the ball with full and front-on contact, try to let the ball skim off your head, redirecting its flight toward a team-mate, a dangerous area or even toward the goal.

4.5 LIFESTYLE

I think a lot of the boys at Football League clubs know that there's every chance that, at 18, they're going to be released and have to find their way into part-time football, into jobs or apprenticeships in other industries. But, during those two years as a full-time scholar, football sort of cuts them off from the real world. I was at a League Two club the other day where every single scholar was living in digs: away from home, away from everything they know. They're wrapped up in the football environment.

What happens if, after two years, they don't get offered a contract? If they're just out of the door, back in the real world? The game's a lot better now in terms of providing education and qualifications.

We go in and try to help develop life skills. But, even so, if you don't have people around to support you, being released can seem like a fall into oblivion. It's absolutely essential to have the tools you need to deal with that situation. I know I wasn't ready for it. When I was a kid, I played up front alongside Teddy Sheringham. Look at his journey. Then look at mine.

I was desperate to be a player. But, the way I look at it, I failed. After I was released, I took it badly. I suffered from depression. I didn't join a gang, exactly, but I found myself going out to bars, mixing with that crowd and getting involved in some stupidness. Found myself part of the pack, if you like. There were drugs around, drugs being sold. I wasn't involved but I knew these people. I used to DJ, and I remember one night, out in Woodford, a guy I knew got cut across the eye in a fight. In a matter of minutes, the people I knew were running about, chasing down the people who'd done it.

The next morning, I got a phone call: Were you in the car park after? Because someone's left a gun under one of the cars. Well, I'd been in the car park, packing up my gear. When I went back, the gun was still there. That was like a turning point for me: A gun? I was terrified. 'This is not you, Troy. This is not who you are or what you're about.' And, from then on, I slowly detached myself from that group and that world. But those were the five or six years it took me to get over having "failed" as a footballer. I know what the pitfalls are. —Troy Townsend

By the time he reaches Level 4, a young player will already have had to start coming to terms with big changes in the rest of his life. He may have become a full-time scholar at a professional club; he may have secured good enough results at GCSE to join a college programme; he may have decided to stay at school and take on the challenge of A Levels, in the hope that he can get onto a University degree course or football programme (in the UK or, perhaps, the US) in a couple of years' time; or he may have chosen to take the next step into adult life, finding a job or apprenticeship and graduating to open-age football in his spare time.

Each situation will be unique to the individual, not least whether or not he's now faced with living away from home or still being under the same roof as his parents. Whatever his circumstances, the Level 4 player will be challenged to combine his development in the game with fulfilling responsibilities in other key areas of his life, all of which can have a profound influence on his progress as a footballer. It's a balancing act that needs to be handled with courage, dignity and integrity.

FAMILY

SCHOOLWORK

SOCIAL LIFE

ROLE MODEL

LIVING YOUR SPORT

FAMILY

My personal opinion is that boys need to have a break from football. If they're involved all season, that already means they'll be training and playing for 10 months of the year. I'd always say, 'Over the summer, don't keep playing football. Play cricket, go swimming, go on holiday with your family or hang about with your mates!' My policy was always to give boys a proper break-eight or nine weeks-over the summer. —Tony Carr

As a young player progresses in the game, it becomes more and more important that he looks after his relationships with the people who've mattered most in his life. The people who still matter and will matter in the future as well. When football crowds in on top of him and a young man needs to escape the pressure, his **FAMILY** and friends are the ones who relate to him and identify with him as more than just "the player." When he wants to share his successes and his disappointments, who should he turn to other than those who best understand the journey he's been on? When he needs support, who can he best rely on to be there to offer it?

Since Level 1, a **COMPLETE ATHLETE** has been laying strong foundations for his relationships with his family and friends. It's vital that those relationships aren't now neglected as you enter new territory as an elite player and as a young man, especially if progression at an academy or college has taken you away from home for the first time.

The key is to communicate regularly, letting family and friends know what's going on, not only in regards to football but also with your academic studies and free time as well. It's a way to release the pressure that may be building up around you in a new environment, a way to keep an open mind and a sense of perspective. There will be some life-changing decisions to be made, new experiences and new professional relationships to be handled. The people who've been with you on the journey may still be the best people to turn to for guidance and advice.

Legally, an agent can't actually sign a boy until the year of his 16th birthday. But, if academies are looking at boys much younger than that, then you can be sure agents will be too. Trying to work out who the best players are, establishing contact with them and their parents.

There are some really good agents, of course. And there are some really bad ones, the ones who sign up as many boys as they can and then hope for the best, hope something drops into place for one of them so they can make some money. The better ones, though, will want to do their best for the individual boy. They'll have a plan, a pathway they see the young player following. And they'll do their homework on where might be the best place for him to develop and play. But how do you know? How do a boy and his parents make a choice? There's word of mouth, I suppose. Other boys saying, 'Oh, so and so really looked after me, got me a good deal.' You can go online and do a bit of research. It's natural to be wary.

We had a group of boys sign pro here the other day and, of course, their parents were here, too. One of the boys' agents came along, as well. He'd picked up Mum on the way down from London because he knew otherwise that she wouldn't be able to get here, a single parent, to watch her son sign. I think that tells you something about his attitude. I'd guess most of those boys had agents. When it comes to a first professional contract, an agent will usually be very useful for the player. Whether that's to advise on terms at the club the lad's attached to or whether it's to help him find somewhere else if the club end up letting him go. Much younger than 15 or 16, though, I'm not sure how useful a relationship with an agent's going to be. Unless it's as a way to stop other agents ringing Mum and Dad at all hours! —Terry Burton

JOIN THE CONVERSATION!
Don't miss out on all the conversation happening in the **COMPLETE ATHLETE** app. Join today!

SCHOOLWORK

Life at an academy is so different now to how it was for me as a young player at Arsenal. Everything's so scientific now; everything's measured. It's precise, machine-like. The style of play is very hard to replicate outside the academy environment: quick, one- and two-touch, always looking for the pass.

Back in the day, as a young player, I was just competing against other boys from England or other parts of the U.K. Now, there's a big foreign element at every top club's academy. The standard's high, and I think it's more difficult than it's ever been to get to the top. Maybe recognising that—and the reasons why—means a boy can still keep his enthusiasm for the game at whatever level he ends up playing at.

You don't want any boy to fall out of love with football and be lost to the game but you see it a lot: a boy has tried to make it as a pro, isn't able to, and then just stops playing football altogether. I worked for the Professional Footballers Association for a long time, working on coaching qualifications with young players at all sorts of clubs. That meant work they were doing outside of the commitments they had as young players. I saw kids released, and, at those moments, it felt to them as if their whole world had fallen apart. You track those boys, follow what's happened to them after they've left their clubs, and you find that too many of them have just drifted out of football altogether. They're not playing at all. —Paul Davis

Some young players at Level 4 have been given the opportunity, at college or at a professional club, to step into a full-time football environment. They'll be focussed on the prize of earning a professional contract and becoming a professional player. Of course, a young player needs to believe he's got a chance, believe that he's good enough and has what it takes to make a career in the game. That's what will drive him on to improve as a player every day.

At the same time, it's absolutely essential that he takes a step back now and again and reminds himself that, even having come so far, his chances of realising his ambitions remain very slim. That shouldn't undermine his commitment to doing everything he can to make a long-held dream come true. But it should remind him that he needs to pay equal attention to his academic studies, whether that's a B-Tech at an Academy or an Extended Diploma at college. If he's still at school, of course, he'll already know that a future place on a University programme, here or abroad, will depend on him working hard for his A Levels.

Properly preparing for a life in football should include preparing for a possible life outside football. Or a life connected to football in some other way other as a player. Having come this far, no young man should feel as if he's dropped off the edge of a cliff when, at 18, he doesn't find a club wanting to sign him on professional or semi-pro terms. Commit to schoolwork with the same energy and focus as you do your game, and you'll be guaranteeing yourself the future you deserve come what may.

With a teenage boy, the behaviour thing can be difficult. I remember when I was at school, everybody knew I played. It almost put me on a pedestal. Other kids would say, 'that's Troy. That's the footballer.' I thought I was different to other kids. Better, even, because I was good at sport and good at football. Teachers would let me get away with stuff, too. I was given pretty much a free rein at home: came in when I liked, got involved with girls too early.

I've tried to make sure it wasn't like that for my own sons. We had no idea if Andros would end up playing for a living but we were going to make sure he had all the tools he needed to give it a go. That meant not going out late, being quite strict, focusing on football. It's what I think I could have done with when I was a teenager: a bit of structure in my life. —Troy Townsend

SOCIAL LIFE

It goes without saying that, however strong-willed you might be, the people you surround yourself with will influence how you behave. Those people in your circle also affect how other people—scouts, coaches, and staff, for example—judge you.

It's your choice, so choose friends and acquaintances who have the right habits on and off the pitch. The margins for success are so fine when it comes to making it as a pro player or, outside the professional game, when it comes to playing for a team at the very top end of your ability. Being around the right kind of company might just prove to be a way for you to narrow those margins. Invest time only in people who you can trust completely, who share your values and recognise your hunger to realise your ambitions.

It's less of a problem while the boys are still at school. They're surrounded by their mates in that environment. They're not in that football "bubble" yet. But, at 16 or 17, when they step into an academy environment, things can change. They're focused completely on football. They spend more and more time with other players, get more and more immersed in that world.

Of course, it varies from club to club. Some are more down to earth than others. But some put quite a lot of pressure

on boys, even at a young age, to adapt completely to the footballer's lifestyle: looking after yourself, eating the right food, and everything else. It's a football culture.

In those situations, the boys' only release can often be talking to other young players. It's in those situations, I think, that egos tend to get inflated and boys can get disconnected from what else is happening out there. It can lead to a certain immaturity, boys not having any experience of dealing with issues other 17 and 18 year olds will be facing. When they do go out, it's with other players and you can see them trying to live up to the glamour and the limelight which come with being a young footballer.

They play on it and that makes them susceptible: to allegations of assault or sexual assault, perhaps, false or otherwise, or to becoming a target for blackmail because they're young and wealthy with a valuable career ahead of them. What happens right now can have a huge effect on their futures.

What's interesting is that, in other respects, the same boys can also be more mature than some of their peers. They may have left home—they may even have come from abroad—and be living with a host family. They may be more responsible than other 16 and 17 year olds because they're aware that they've got a lot more to lose. The law is the same for everyone but the repercussions for individuals can be very different.

A young player who gets caught up in an accusation of any kind of serious criminal behaviour? That can be his career over, right there and then. Very few clubs would take a risk with an unproven talent in that kind of situation. Boys need to be aware: even having the wrong kind of pictures on your phone—of a girl without her clothes on who's under 18, of a team-mate naked in the showers—can mean you're put on the Sex Offenders Register. The implications can be very serious. What club's going to come near you? —Kyle Phillips

We talk to boys about the kind of music they listen to: hip-hop, rap, grime and so on. We talk about the words to that music and the sexist, racist and homophobic content of some of it, the glorifying of violence and gang culture. There are people around a football club who might be deeply offended by that stuff. I can't tell a boy what to listen to at home but I can get him to think about what its impact might be in a football environment.

One lad said he'd been given a lift by an established player, a player who'd cost millions of pounds. And he'd been listening to the kind of music I'd been talking about. I had to explain the harsh reality of it: a multi-million pound player, it seems, can do pretty much what he wants. He's worth that much to the club. But if you step out of line as a kid, what are you worth to that same club? You've done nothing. They might just say, 'You're not for us.' Yes, you might go and look to play somewhere else but don't kid yourself: your reputation will have travelled ahead of you. It's harsh. But I have to be honest.
—Troy Townsend

ROLE MODEL

By the time a young player reaches Level 4, the die has probably been cast regarding the way he feels about himself and how he behaves towards others. On the pitch, his dedication, discipline, and hard work make him a player that others look up to and want to follow.

Those qualities should be equally clear and have a similar effect on people away from football, too, at school or college, at home or at work, or when out with friends and family. Without having set out consciously to make it happen, the young player is now a **ROLE MODEL** for younger siblings, friends, and fellow students; he functions as a leader off the pitch as well as on it.

This is only possible when a young man's values, developed at home and through football, are ingrained. Like your technical abilities, your integrity and good decision-making are now second nature. Instinct tells you, even when faced with adversity or difficult decisions, that you must do the right thing.

Being a natural leader—a role model—has an impact on your life in football, too. Every coach and manager, every scout and member of staff at every club wants to associate with players they know they can trust. And those are the people who can actually unlock the door to opportunities in the game, as you set out toward your football future.

LIVING YOUR SPORT

PLAYER >> Over the course of Level 4, there's every chance you'll discover where your passion for football is likely to take you. You've worked hard, devoted countless hours to improving as a player; enjoyed victories and been stung by defeats; met team-mates, coaches, mentors, and staff who you'll never forget. You've grown up through the game. What happens now?

It may be that the possibility of moving on to a career in football remains within reach. You may even have found a club and been offered a professional contract. If so, you've made it against all odds to the very top percentile in a ruthlessly competitive sport and equally competitive marketplace. It's at this point you'll begin to discover, though, the real demands made on an elite sportsman, a **COMPLETE ATHLETE**. Every day, now, is about improving, about gaining an advantage, about being an even better player. To stay in the game, you'll have to live football from here.

If, however, and for whatever reason, your journey feels as if it's coming to an end, don't forget what the game's already given you. Think about that and you can start to think about what football can do for you—and what you can give back to football—in the future.

You may need to work, to go on to further education, or you may have other commitments which feel more like your true vocation. So be it: you've been released; you've been accepted on a degree course; you've decided to become a referee or study for a completely different career in football, as a coach, a physio, a social media guru, or a Chief Exec. Unless injury's ruled you out, if you continue to devote your free time to improving as a player—becoming the best you can be and competing at the highest possible level—then who knows what can happen down the line? Living for football is an attitude to take on into the rest of your life.

I think, if we can, it's important to stay in touch with those players who feel football's not for them anymore, who find they have other demands on their time. It might be that they'd play five-a-side. It might be that they'd play at a different level where there wasn't the same level of commitment needed for training. Or, looking in the other direction, would they fit in at a club playing in a regional youth league like the Midlands Junior Premier, which aims to offer the highest level of competition in grassroots football, playing games against each other but also against development squads attached to pro and semi-pro academies?

Those clubs offer good facilities, good coaches and good players to play alongside and against. Certainly we should be pointing boys who drop out of academies towards that level of football. Pro clubs should definitely be communicating with the boys they release—and their parents—to say: This doesn't have to be the end of the journey. I'd really like us to find ways to keep boys in the game. At that moment they decide football's not for them anymore, can't we find a way to keep them involved, whether that's five-a-side or futsal or another kind of club? Make football fit around their lifestyle and the other demands on teenagers' time? You might find a boy who drops into another level of football but then bounces back: a kind of Jamie Vardy story, if you like. Or you might just find it keeps them connected to a game that they can enjoy playing for the rest of their lives at whatever level their ability will allow. —John Folwell

I'm honoured to be working in a job nowadays that means regular professional contact with some of the country's best players—the England squad—as they prepare for World Cup 2018 and individual elite footballers who are determined to improve by committing to extra training with me on top of what they already do at their clubs. They're not satisfied with 50 repetitions of their striker *drills each week. They want four or five times that many. It's a hunger that I think all the very top players share. They'll do anything to give themselves an advantage, to be better prepared to exploit any chance that comes their way in the rush and tumble of a game in the Premier or Champions League. They work hard—incredibly hard— all week in order to make what they need to do seem like second nature come the weekend. They cope with the pressure, and they always push harder to go further. They all have a desire that I think means, really, they are living for the game. —Allan Russell*

PLAYER » It can be quite a last-minute decision: I remember Gareth Bale having to go in to the club at the end of Year 11 and he had a sort of six-week trial to decide whether or not he was going to be offered a scholarship at Southampton.

I was lucky: they made a decision quite early with me, when I was 14, so I knew I would be leaving school and joining the academy full-time. My last year at school, I actually dropped two subjects so that I could go in and get experience of training with the scholars. It's something which happens more often these days, I think: boys getting more of their education at the club instead of in school. They have tutors come in and work with the players. For me, finding out about my scholarship early meant I could be prepared for it when it started. At that age—16, 17 years old—it can be difficult.

Teenage boys spending every minute of every day together. They're mates but, actually, they're competing against each other. You know, in your teens, there's a lot going on in your life anyway so, in the academy setting, it can get quite tense. You're not as in control of your emotions as you are when you get a bit older. Looking back, I think it was good for me that I was local.

I lived in Bournemouth so I could commute in on the train to the academy every day. It only took 35 minutes and then, when I was nearly 18, I got my licence and could drive it.

Most of the boys stayed at a place called The Lodge, which was a building that had been a hotel near the training ground but, by then, was just for the scholars. There were a couple of ladies who looked after everybody. Lads came from all over: Bristol, London, the Midlands, even abroad. We had scholars from Portugal. So, there was no way they could go home at night!

They were together all the time: competing against each other, training all day, and then going back to The Lodge and playing snooker or table tennis with the same group of lads. Some boredom, probably, some tension: it was pretty full on.

I was going home in the evenings and spending time with my family and other friends. I actually moved into my own flat in Bournemouth but spent a lot of time at home and round at a mate's house because I didn't much like being on my own. Anyway, it meant I wasn't so affected by things going on at the academy, like a couple of boys getting picked to play for the reserves or getting offered pro contracts while others weren't.

Being away, in a different environment, got me out of that bubble. I didn't feel the pressure building and building all the time like the boys who were together at the training ground. I think it's good that scholars nowadays are usually in digs, in family environments with a bit more structure, rather than in places like The Lodge.

It's hard: all these new demands and pressures on you when, really, you're still just kids. You're getting to the age where you can have a drink and go to nightclubs, outside influences that you have to balance against wanting to be a footballer, wanting to make it. The huge plus for me was having my family behind me. They always supported me, but never put pressure on me. Gave me good advice, 'yes, go out with your mates but, training tomorrow, don't be back late!' I like to think it's how I'll be with my kids. Might have to discipline them sometimes; question them; ask them if football's what they really want to do. But not put more pressure on them than they're already feeling. My parents were great in that way.

I'd been one of the first schoolboys in my group to be offered a scholarship, but I was one of the last scholars to be offered a pro contract. I had a lot of injuries during those two years. I'd be out injured, travelling in on my own for treatment, while other boys were playing and getting offered professional terms. They were moving forward, and I wasn't and it's natural to get a bit down in those situations. It was a testing time for me, looking back. But, at 17, I was a bit in my own little world, perhaps not realising exactly how much was at stake for me, so I didn't really worry too much or doubt myself. I was 17 and pretty immature and maybe that was a good thing! Taking things too seriously—and putting extra pressure on myself—could have made things worse.

During my first year as a scholar, I had an irregular heartbeat; I'd be peaking up at 230 beats per minute at rest. Even during the night, I'd have spikes in the rate. So, I had to have an operation to clear it up. I remember that being very frustrating: I didn't have any symptoms, just these spikes in my heartbeat.

At right around the same time, I was diagnosed with Ulcerative Colitis, the disease that kept Darren Fletcher out for so long when he was at Manchester United.

I don't know what caused that, although my diet back then was terrible, certainly compared to what it is now. Maybe that contributed to it. I was off for two or three months with it and then I'd have relapses, which meant taking steroids to settle it down.

I've spoken to Darren Fletcher about Colitis since. His was severe whereas mine was mild in comparison. The last test I had showed it's gone completely now. But there were times during my scholarship when I didn't want to even leave the house. I can remember games when I'd be getting cramps during the first half because I hadn't eaten. I wouldn't want to eat because that made it feel worse. I used to have to run off the pitch during training to go and use the toilet. All that was happening to me at 17, 18. I was diagnosed with Osgood-Schlatter disease in my knee at one point, too. So, my memories of my scholarship are that I had some very low periods with injuries and illness. But, at the same time, I was playing and growing up with mates; being a young footballer was fantastic.

Going full-time as a scholar, when your body still has so much growing to do, is a big change. Maybe my system couldn't handle it and that's why I got all the injuries and illnesses. You have to get to know your own body, learn how to look after yourself and how to manage pain.

You know, there were injuries I had which would stop me training back then, but, if I had them now, I'd probably just go out and play. I know how my body works and what it can handle now. I had to learn about balancing the way I lived with the demands of being a footballer, too. As a player and as a person, it just took me time to develop, both while I was scholar and during my early years as a pro. The kind of training didn't change so much, it was just that the load was heavier, working every day. We had a technical coach, a French guy named George Prost, who was absolutely brilliant with us. He was my Under-18 manager, too, so he was really important for me. He was a technical coach and I was a technical player. One thing we were less aware of back then, though, was the mental side of the game.

I realise now that's it's probably the most important part of being a player and there's much more attention paid to psychology these days. With young players, too, which is as it should be: if you're a scholar and your mentality isn't right, if you don't make the sacrifices and don't make the right decisions, those two years can be over in an instant. Players who have the talent but don't have the mental strength or the right people around them: suddenly, the career path can completely fall away. Suddenly, your chance has gone.

It's good that there's a lot more help with that side of things for young players now. I compare their situation to mine 10 years ago. First, they're being paid much more. We were on £80 a week. There's been the rise of social media. We had phones but they weren't camera phones. Probably because of the money, there are more distractions, more outside influences, even more pressures on them. We forget that they're still maturing as people. And they're still nothing like being complete as footballers yet, either.

I was at Southampton; we were a club in League One. What must be the expectations they have to deal with if they're at a top club, where it's an even more difficult path to get to the first team? I look at some young players now: Ben Woodburn here at Liverpool. He's so mature, so professional. I sometimes wonder whether, if I'd been a little more like him, I might have progressed a bit quicker.

But I had my own journey. I was neat and tidy, a technical player. I didn't have that more obvious talent like a Gareth

Bale or an Alex Oxlade-Chamberlain. I didn't play my first full season at Southampton until I was 21, which is why I think the Under-23 League now is such a good idea. Some players need that extra time to fully develop and mature. And it never stops: I've learnt new things, grown as a player, since I moved to Liverpool. And your life changes as well: moving away from home, getting married, having children. You always keep growing as a person, don't you?

All of that you probably have to find out for yourself. As a scholar, there'd be meetings now and again if someone had mis-behaved or kept being late, reminding us all about the principles of the club. Reminding us all we only had a certain amount of time to impress if we wanted to be pros. But it was a great life, being a young player at Southampton, and I always backed myself.

I thought I had something as a player and believed in my ability, believed that I'd get my chance eventually and earn a pro contract. When that happened, it was actually during the pre-season of what would have been my third year as a scholar. The manager, George Burley, saw me in training or in the reserves, and suddenly, I was playing in a first team pre-season game, ahead of all the other lads my age, other lads who'd already signed professional contracts. A couple of games after that and I'd signed a three-year deal. It all happened as quickly as that.

—Adam Lallana

IN LEVEL 5

It's been a journey. But you've reached Level 5, and, really, you're only just beginning. You are 18 or 19 years old and you may have been offered a first professional contract at the club where you completed your scholarship. You may have completed that scholarship but, without an offer from the club, you find yourself looking for a contract elsewhere. Perhaps you've already taken on the challenge of playing semi-pro—or further down the football pyramid—knowing that the chance may still come, as it did for the likes of Jamie Vardy and Andre Gray, to step back up into full-time professional football in the future; scouts and agents will still be watching your games.

Maybe you've moved on to University or Further Education, here or abroad, with the intention of entering the professional game, as a player or as a member of staff, after you graduate. Or you may have decided to find a job outside football and, like hundreds of thousands of recreational players, be happy to live for your game at the weekend from now on.

Whether your future in football means playing at a stadium packed with 60,000 fans or in front of one man and his dog at the local playing fields, the challenge is still there: be better than you were yesterday. Do whatever it takes to improve. If you've embarked on a professional career, you need to put every effort into making sure your first contract doesn't turn out to be your last. Every training session and every game counts more than ever from now on. If you're outside that environment, but want to keep the dream alive, be ready to take every opportunity that comes your way. The next might still be the one that changes your life forever.

Wherever this journey takes you from now on, working through the Levels towards becoming a **COMPLETE ATHLETE** will have given you many of the tools you'll need to find your way. First of all, you're a player. The best player you can be. As well, though, you're a leader and a role model for team-mates, for those coming up behind you, and for your family and friends.

The personal qualities, beliefs, and values you've worked so hard to develop will define you as a person now and for the rest of your life. Remain true to yourself and you can rest assured that others will see you in the way you'd wish to be seen, and will treat you with the respect you deserve. Keep working, keep improving, keep giving back to football. Remember what it's already given you. Whatever your destination now, great things can happen if you stay true to your love of the game.

PLAYER >> *There are players earning a good living playing football who don't really like the game. It just happens to be something they're good at. But I walk the dog sometimes at the weekend and see Sunday League players getting changed in freezing cold dressing rooms. Running out onto muddy pitches. And I think: Why are they doing it? It's because they're playing with their mates, having a laugh, enjoying that camaraderie. They'll still be mates long after they finish playing. Or maybe they'll be playing walking football some time down the line.*

But love of the game is what's kept them going. I just hope when a boy gets disappointed, doesn't get signed on for another season, he doesn't go out of football. I hope he's got a love of the game that'll help him bounce back. That circumstances or opportunity bring him back in. At whatever level.

Or, if not into playing, then into coaching, which is what happened to me. When I was told by Arsenal they weren't going to keep me, I didn't play for six months. It was such a knockback, I just couldn't face it. But a mate was doing a coaching badge—I was 19—and I went along with him.

I wasn't sure at all, but the guy giving the course, Roger Thompson, got me back into playing, non-League with Epping Town FC, as well as starting me off as a coach. I fell back in love with football because that one chance came along. —Terry Burton

JOIN THE CONVERSATION!

Sports performance is also influenced by preparation and proper mentality before games. Learn more by downloading the **COMPLETE ATHLETE** app.

5.1 ATTITUDE

A **POSITIVE ATTITUDE** is the foundation stone for any player's success, a quality that defines his approach to life on and off the pitch. As a professional player or a player aspiring to turn pro—or, come to that, as a player turning out on a Sunday morning, just for fun—your progress depends on your attitude. Realising your potential can be driven by focusing on and trying to demonstrate five key attributes which, together, sum up the idea of positive attitude:

RESPECT

SPORTSMANSHIP

TEAMWORK

PROFESSIONALISM

LEADERSHIP

RESPECT

At Level 5, you're now an adult player. You understand that controlling and channelling emotion is the secret to success, as opposed to falling victim to circumstances in which you've let those emotions run away with you. Key to that ability to control yourself is being sure at all times to demonstrate respect for others: coaches, match officials, team-mates and opponents. You will earn **RESPECT** in return. And you will learn, if you haven't already, the importance of respecting yourself.

In senior football, you need also to be showing respect to another group of people in football: supporters. At every level, of course, supporters are those who've helped you on your journey: family, friends, mentors, and youth coaches. They'll still be there for you now, whether you're playing at a packed Premier League stadium or at the local Rec. Respect will naturally accompany remembering what those people have done for you over the years: giving you practical help, offering good advice, being a person you could talk to without being judged.

At the top of the game—up and down the leagues in professional and semi-professional football—there's now a different kind of supporter to think about, too. Equally deserving of your respect are the hundreds or thousands of fans who pay in order to watch you play the game you love.

Don't take for granted the privileged position that puts you in. If you're asked for an autograph, a selfie or even a quick chat about last week's fixture, being gracious and friendly costs nothing in terms of time or effort. But it can have a huge impact on the supporter, particularly a youngster who's dreaming about following a path like you have into football.

At every club, supporters will be with you when you're winning games and scoring goals. Treat them with respect and there's every chance they'll still be there to support you when things aren't going so well. Of course, modern technology now means you can connect—if you want to—with supporters via social media: Twitter, Facebook, Instagram, Snapchat, and the rest. You'll soon find yourself with followers, very few of whom you actually know. Social media channels, though, are where those fans turn in order to feel they can get to know you.

Don't ever make the mistake of thinking that what you post or share just goes out there into the ether and disappears. For better or worse, one post can hang around for a very long time, via retweets and shares and by being picked up in the mainstream media. Your experiences and opinions matter to supporters, whether those fans are measured in hundreds or thousands or even millions, whether they come to games or they're watching on TV on the other side of the world. Just as you would in face-to-face contact, you need to be respectful at all times towards the people reading about you and watching you play.

It's in the nature of social media that, particularly when you or the team aren't having the best of times, comments posted online can seem disrespectful and rude. Even when they are, don't rise to the bait and respond in kind—that will only ever serve to make things worse. The vast majority of supporters will recognise the haters for what they are. And respect your strength of character in refusing to be undermined or unsettled by negativity and insults.

Most importantly, perhaps, it's worth bearing in mind that nothing should compromise what you do out on the pitch. That's ultimately where you'll be judged. Therefore, if you're not sure about anything to do with social media, don't hesitate to take professional advice, whether that's from staff at the club or a specialist outside.

And, if you don't enjoy that kind of online interaction or don't feel comfortable with it for any reason, then don't feel pressurised. You'll be better off not doing it. One great performance for the team, after all, counts for more than any number of posts on a social media channel.

SPORTSMANSHIP

Respect for yourself and for others is important. So, too, is respect for the game. That manifests itself in good **SPORTSMANSHIP**—playing football with integrity at all times. Good sportsmanship demonstrates strength of character and professionalism and can be seen when you observe some very familiar habits:

- Respecting the Laws of the Game and abiding by the decisions of match officials.
- Trying to bring out the best in your team-mates, on and off the pitch.
- Recognising and taking responsibility for your own mistakes.
- Demonstrating humility in victory and grace in defeat.

As a senior player, it's important to remember that football is a team game and that a team is successful only when all eleven players commit to the collective. Even as a star player or as team captain, you won't be able to win games on your own. Demonstrate good sportsmanship by giving credit to team-mates, coaches, and staff. Do your best to always acknowledge the efforts and performances of opponents, too.

PROFESSIONALISM

At Level 5, a player's **PROFESSIONALISM** isn't just defined by what he does over the course of the 90 minutes of a game. Professionalism is shown by the player's awareness that he represents himself and his team at all times. It's shown in his preparations for games and the way he behaves afterwards. And by the manner in which he conducts himself away from the football environment.

Values like respect, good sportsmanship, and an excellent work ethic are obvious at all times in a **COMPLETE ATHLETE**. He always leaves the best impression possible of himself and his team.

At the top end of the game, a player will often be called upon to demonstrate his professionalism publicly—speaking to the media, attending public functions, maintaining a presence online. Speaking to the media, especially straight after a game, can sometimes be very challenging.

The key is to remember simple guidelines which will help you deal with difficult moments and leave you not regretting any loss of control. What you actually say is often less important than the general impression of professionalism you leave with an interviewer and anyone watching or listening to you speak.

Firstly, remain polite and composed at all times: outwardly, at least, even if—inside—you're experiencing a strong emotional reaction to events on the pitch. In victory, try to deflect attention away from your own efforts and make sure you give credit, instead, to team-mates, to supporters and to the opposition whenever possible. In defeat, avoid the temptation to make excuses for yourself or your team.

Try to make sure you never single out individuals: team-mates, opponents, or match officials. Concentrate instead on finding positives in what's happened and commit publicly to working hard at putting mistakes right in time for your next game.

You've done everything you can to be professional in your approach to the game for as long as you can remember. That same attitude is necessary now whenever you're asked to represent your club and your team-mates in public. At elite level, guidance and advice should be available to you. If not, you should think seriously about finding it elsewhere. The best way to make yourself comfortable in those public situations is to take a professional attitude to them rather than resenting or avoiding having to do them. The professional footballer improves with training. That's as true in the field of public relations as it is out on the training ground.

Having a professional attitude to dealing with media requests and other public responsibilities isn't only important for players at the elite levels of the game, of course. It may not be an interview on Match of the Day, but giving the right impression even when you're just talking to the young reporter from the local free paper can have an impact on your career going forward. Certainly it's an opportunity to give people the right idea about yourself and the club you represent.

Even though you may not be launching a new footwear range in front of thousands of fans, be aware that every public appearance is an opportunity for the professional to make his mark. Talking to a local sponsor and behaving professionally in that kind of situation can make an enormous difference to both yourself and your club. The builder with his sign board by the side of the pitch may turn out to be the local businessman who ends up buying the club and becoming your future employer!

PLAYER » *I was a good player; certainly not a great player. I knew my limitations and so I worked as hard as I could to make the most of the strengths I had: work rate, professionalism, respect for the game.*

That's why some of my more gifted team-mates were out of the game or working their way down the leagues by the time they were in their mid-20s and some—much more talented than me—were no longer involved in the professional game at all. They had the ability—more ability than I did—but they didn't have the professional attitude they needed to make careers for themselves.

For me, it was all about football. Everything I did, I thought: How will this affect me as a player? Will it be the right thing to do for me as a professional footballer? I started thinking like that when I was very young. I thought like that all through 500-plus professional games. I still think like that now as I'm making my way in the game as a coach. —Allan Russell

LEADERSHIP

A **COMPLETE ATHLETE**, as well as pushing himself to improve as an individual, will also have established himself as a leader within his group, whether or not he's team captain. That's true, at Level 5, if he's playing at an elite professional club or for a Sunday League team with ambitions to move up through the local divisions.

Team-mates, coaches, and staff know they can rely on him. They look to him to help motivate and inspire the players around him. His strength of character and confidence rubs off on others, away from football as well as in the middle of challenging games.

At some point, it's likely that those **LEADERSHIP** qualities will attract the attention of people and businesses outside the player's immediate circle. There may be commercial opportunities that arise or it may simply be people seeing him as a spokesperson for the club he represents.

That circle of attention, in the modern game, is made wider by the impact of social media. It can work both ways: the player himself can use online channels to express his values and those of the team; a player's social media profile may attract interest from sponsors and supporters.

Whichever way social media becomes relevant, it's important the Level 5 player understands its potential impact on himself and the team he leads, as well as being aware of the rewards it can bring. There are plenty of commercial opportunities available to players with an active and popular online presence. It's also a very accessible way of establishing a rapport with the supporters who watch you play every weekend.

As mentioned previously, there's plenty of good advice out there on the subject, but very simple strategies can help a player take advantage of his online presence without it being able to undermine him in any way.

JOIN THE CONVERSATION!
Be a team player—join your team-mates in the **COMPLETE ATHLETE** app!

It's advisable to maintain separate professional and personal accounts. Professional accounts should be treated with care and diligence. Be true to yourself in so far as you want (and followers want) your personality to be reflected on these channels. But, at the same time, be conscious of expressing a positive outlook on your professional life whenever possible. And, if you're in any doubt about putting up a post, then you're probably best advised not to do so.

A player's unlikely ever to get into trouble for something he didn't say, after all! As in regards to responses to your posts, it's probably wisest to avoid any interaction 'below the line' on an outward-facing "professional" channel, irrespective of whether the comments are praising or criticising you, your club or anyone else.

At the same time as you maintain any professional channels, you may well want to have personal channels running, too. Those are private and personal to you. And they work in the same way as anybody else's pages, as a place to share experiences and memories, make plans, and share images and ideas with those you know and trust. You should look after those accounts in the same way as anybody else does to maintain control and accountability.

Social media can be another environment in which to demonstrate strong leadership skills, but it goes without saying that you must be very careful to keep the professional and the personal elements of your online life separate at all times.

1

2

3

4

5

5.2 PREPARATION

PLAYER » *I was always very aware that my career as a player was something that nobody else could take responsibility for. It was up to me to make the most of it. I hated the idea of looking in the mirror after a game and thinking I'd not played as well as I could have because I hadn't done as much as I could have on the training ground the week before. For me, to make sure I prepared properly, I got into the habit of asking myself questions every single day:*

- *What have I done in training today to make myself a better player in my position?*
- *Did I arrive at the training ground properly prepared, ready to go to work?*
- *Did I look after myself and get enough sleep last night?*
- *Could I have done extra work on my own position, done extra reps, after training? Or did I cut corners?*
- *Did I train at high enough intensity on a main training load day?*
- *On a day off, did I rest and eat properly?*
- *Was I brave, intelligent, and composed enough on the ball from Monday to Friday to be sure of being the same when it mattered on Saturday?* —Allan Russell

At Level 5, a player and those around him can start to be pretty sure of what they're going to get when they step out onto the pitch. The constant application to improving as a player—going beyond what's asked of you at every stage of the journey towards becoming a **COMPLETE ATHLETE**—will have pushed you toward the very top end of what you're capable of achieving as a footballer.

Going forward, all that hard work and effort will only be rewarded—from game to game and from season to season—by you being completely professional in preparing properly for every match, doing what you need to both beforehand and afterwards in order to be the best you can be over the next 90 minutes. Whether it's a schedule you design yourself or one in which some elements are laid down by your club, life as a top player is now broken down into two phases: "Match day Plus" and "Match day Minus." You should know exactly what you need to be doing on different days leading up to and immediately after your games: workloads, types of training, nutrition, hydration, mental focus, recovery, and the rest.

Many of these elements will already be familiar. You should already have good habits in place. From now on, your consistency of top-level performance will depend on you monitoring and improving what you're doing in specific areas of your **PREPARATION**:

TRAINING

NUTRITION

HYDRATION

RECOVERY

MENTALITY

TRAINING

At Level 5, now more than ever, it's imperative that you **TRAIN** with the same tempo and intensity as you play on match days. If you're surrounded by team-mates and opponents who've used a week's preparation to get themselves at the right pitch for the game, it's very unlikely you'll be able to just kick up a gear on Saturday in order to compete.

By now, the basic technical level of your game should be in place and training is about narrowing fine margins and making incremental improvements. If you've put in the work on the physical and technical aspects during the week, you should be able to trust those aspects of your game on a match day. You'll be freer to concentrate on the psychological element, which is often what makes the difference at the top level in football. If you're confident that your athleticism and technique won't let you down, you can focus on how to best make them count in your favour over the course of the next 90 minutes.

Self-development and self-improvement are vital even at the highest levels of football, where the difference between success and failure is often measured in tiny percentages. A **COMPLETE ATHLETE** continues to work alone or in small groups in order to give himself the edge. Either with a coach or on your own initiative, taking time away from the main group after training to work on specific technical or tactical issues can make a huge difference.

It's in that extra work attention can be focussed on individual details, in a setting where you can be more receptive to change and development. Every minute you put in as an individual will benefit you, but will also benefit the team as a whole.

NUTRITION

NUTRITION is a key element in modern football. Whether you have the services of a professional nutritionist available or you have to look after that side of your preparation for yourself, look to go beyond the standard advice and guidelines whenever you can.

As well as following a general programme of good nutrition, try and find out as much as you can about the specific needs of your own individual body: blood type, metabolic rate, any vitamin deficiencies, and so on. Paying attention to those elements on top of whatever else you're doing will have a tangible effect on you being able to maximise fitness and performance.

Eating the correct high-quality, nutrient-dense foods at the correct times can make all the difference—pushing you to be able make that last-ditch tackle or to get ahead of the defender to score a last-minute winner. Best practice in nutrition will help make sure that you don't find yourself cramping up on 85 minutes and desperate for the final whistle to blow. Nutrition is fundamental to high-level performance and to general good health, and is all about good habits. Never take short cuts on what and when you eat.

LEVEL 5 PLAYER NUTRITION GUIDELINES >>

Each individual has different macro-nutrient needs, based on height, weight, age, activity level and genetic background. The following macro-nutrient guidelines are based on age and estimated activity level for a Level 5 player:

- 45% carbohydrate
- 35% protein
- 20% fat
- No more the 7% saturated fat
- No trans-fat
- 38 to 40 grams of fibre per day
- No more than 150 calories per day from sugar
  (37.5 grams or 9 teaspoons)

HYDRATION

Proper and regular **HYDRATION** is an absolutely essential habit for a **COMPLETE ATHLETE**. Any player at Level 5 will have water on hand at all times and not just around his programme of training and games. He will also have worked out whether there's any need to be taking on fluids in the form of energy drinks enriched with minerals and electrolytes and, if so, when those drinks should be used instead of water.

HYDRATION AROUND TRAINING AND GAMES »

- Drink 16 to 20 fluid ounces (450 to 550 millilitres) within a 2-hour period before exercise.
- During exercise, drink 4 to 6 fluid ounces (120 to 170 millilitres) if possible and perhaps extra at half-time.
- After exercise, you'll need to replace 24 fluid ounces for every 1 pound (0.5 kilos) of body weight lost during exercise.
- 5 fluid ounces equal half a cup, 20 fluid ounces therefore equal a couple of cups.
- These figures are approximate. If you feel thirsty, you may already be dehydrated and need to drink straight away.
- Adapted from guidelines provided by the American College of Sports Medicine (ACSM).

RECOVERY

As well as replacing energy and nutrients lost during periods of intense physical exertion, a Level 5 player should think about **RECOVERY** after a game as also being the first step in preparing for the next.

REPLENISHING CALORIES & FLUIDS AFTER GAMES »

- Drink 24 ounces of fluid (not sugary drinks or alcohol) for every pound of body weight lost within a 2-hour period of training or a game. As a guide: 20 fluid ounces is about one pint. Look to drink that amount (or more) after your session or match.
- Consume around 30 to 35 grams of protein plus an equal amount of carbohydrates within the 30 minute recovery window. As a guide: 20 grams of protein is equivalent to about a single chicken breast or a can of tuna. 20 grams of carbohydrate is equivalent to a slice of bread.

SLEEP

At Level 5, **SLEEP** remains very important for general good health as well as for muscle recovery and repair. Inadequate sleep, whether that's not enough or poor quality, can have a drastic effect on your performance levels. You'll be less able to bounce back after periods of intense physical activity in training or in games and will therefore be less able to prepare properly for your next session or fixture.

According to the National Sleep Foundation, a Level 5 player should be getting a minimum of between seven and nine hours sleep every night. As an adult, it's difficult to generalise as regards how much sleep an individual requires. This makes it very important to listen to your own body and pay attention to how much it needs in terms of rest and recovery. It's possible to gauge how much sleep you need by monitoring how you feel each morning and during the day:

- Are you consistently productive, healthy, and happy after seven hours sleep each night? Or do you need more to feel consistently at your best?
- Do you wake feeling groggy and needing time to get out of bed? Or do you wake fresh and ready to go?
- Do you find yourself needing caffeine or craving high-fat and high-sugar content foods during the day?

Asking yourself those questions and then adjusting your sleeping habits accordingly can make a big difference to your ability to perform. Getting enough of the right kind of sleep is part of finding your way towards achieving a professional balance between the demands of your work—your football—and you enjoying the rest of your life. Traditionally, this issue is of particular concern around Christmas and New Year and over the summer holidays. Both team-mates and family and friends may be putting pressure on you to loosen up and socialise more than usual. Of course, team spirit and relationships outside football are important and very much worth putting time aside for. But, when it comes to Christmas and New Year parties and events, for example, it's important to remember that the lines dividing success and failure are as fine at that time of year as at any other.

Looking after your body and getting enough sleep are important in making sure you perform at your best across what is usually a busy time for fixtures in the UK. It should be possible to balance the demands of family and friends with those of your football career.

It's worth remembering that one late night—and one sub-par performance put in as a result—can cost your team points or you a place in the starting line-up. Every game and every training session counts: what sets elite players apart is that they're ready for the next one every time. Which means they've slept well enough to be sure that they can put in the extra yards, the extra reps, and the extra minutes the following day.

JOIN THE CONVERSATION!
Don't miss out on additional tips on recovery and proper hydration from coaches and professionals in the **COMPLETE ATHLETE** app!

MENTALITY

Becoming a **COMPLETE ATHLETE** doesn't simply demand that a young player trains for harder or for longer. As well as making sure his body's ready to cope with the workload of training and games, learning and practicing the right kind of **MENTAL PREPARATION** is also important in ensuring he performs consistently at the upper limits of his ability. At Level 5, focus becomes an increasingly important part of mental preparedness. More and more elite players and sports organisations are incorporating mindfulness, meditation, and other similar practices into their training regimes.

According to neuro-scientist Dr Kristen Race, PhD., an expert on brain-based mindful solutions: Mindfulness helps train the prefrontal cortex, the part of the brain that creates a calm and alert state of mind, which helps us stay focused, avoid distraction, and perform at our best. Practicing mindfulness is not easy but, like everything else involved in developing as a player, the more you train the better at it you'll become. And the more dramatic its impact will be. Dr Race proposes the following ways for sportspeople—or anybody else, for that matter—to begin practicing mindfulness:

- Engage in mindful breathing every morning—as well as immediately before games or training sessions—to create a calm, clear state of mind. Sit comfortably, close your eyes, and start to take deeper breaths. Inhale fully, exhale completely. Focus on each breath entering and leaving your body. Start with five minutes of this "mindful" breathing and build up from there.

- Conduct a "body scan" which can help release tension, quieten the mind, and develop awareness of your body in a systematic way. Lie down on your back, with your palms facing up and legs relaxed. Close your eyes.

Start with your toes and notice how they feel. Are they tense? Are they warm or cold? Focus your attention here for a few breaths before moving onto the sole of your foot.

- Repeat the process as you travel from your foot to your ankle, calf, knee, and thigh. Bring your attention to your other foot and repeat the process. Continue to move your attention up to your hips, lower back, stomach, chest, shoulders, arms, hands, neck, and head. Maintain focus on each body part in turn and any sensations you're aware of specific to that limb. If you're aware of tension anywhere, try to imagine that tension being released as you exhale.

- Pay attention to and try to take control of your internal dialogue in the build-up to games. This will allow you to shape your mental state before you need to perform. Focus on what you can do positively rather than dwelling on potential negative outcomes. Rather than: 'I hope I don't miss the target,' talk to yourself in positive terms, 'this is how I'm going to score today.'

5.3 FITNESS

However hard you've worked and trained to give yourself the advantage as a player, at Level 5, in senior football, you'll now need to put it all to the test. This is where your body will be fully and most brutally challenged for the first time in your career. You'll need to keep practicing, developing new levels of general and football-specific fitness, if you're going to be competitive. You need to be stronger than your opponent. You need to be faster, more explosive, more flexible. You'll need to achieve your highest-ever levels of endurance to be able to perform from first minute to last.

As well as committing to whatever **FITNESS** programme your club puts in place for you, it will be of enormous benefit to you as a footballer to keep engaging in the exercises and tests which have been set out already at previous Levels on your path to becoming a **COMPLETE ATHLETE**. Aim now to be able to push well beyond previous targets and capacities. To improve as a player day by day. Bear in mind that muscle memory needs daily repetition. Neglect of more than four days will start to affect your strength, flexibility, and fitness.

At Level 5 you should be stronger, more explosive, healthier, and better balanced than ever before. You're staying fit during crucial winter months, getting more technical repetitions and training time because of it, and seeing the difference on the pitch during games. Staying fit and healthy, training and playing regularly, you can generate meaningful momentum in your career. With that comes confidence and resilience, and the opportunity to realise your potential and stand out from the crowd. Strength isn't simply about size and muscle mass. You need to combine strength with mobility and lightness of touch. You need to be agile, explosive on your feet and able to last the full length of a game.

Strength is only an advantage when it's deployed correctly. Timing of contact and of physical challenges is the key. A player weighing 60 kilograms can out-fight an 80 kilogram opponent if he understands and controls the strength he's developed and works on each day. Strength is only a decisive factor when it's combined with other elements of all-round athletic fitness, such as balance, flexibility, and speed.

LOWER-BODY STRENGTH

Stronger legs and lower-body have made you faster over the first five yards. You're generating the power to outjump opponents. You're stronger in the tackle and stronger, too, in your ability to use your body as a shield to control and protect the ball before dribbling or passing to influence play. Single-leg squats are now easier, your balance is near-perfect. Explosive multi-directional bursts of pace allow you to get out of tight spaces, in and out of possession. Those attributes will help you continually raise your performance levels. Your progress can be checked using tests you're already familiar with.

UPPER-BODY STRENGTH

You may now be playing against players anything up to ten years older than you. You may be skillful enough to compete against them. But are you strong enough? Can you protect the ball from them? Are you balanced as you run and play? Upper-body strength is vital if you're going to make the most of your technical ability. Coaches, scouts, and managers will all be watching you closely at this stage of your career. They'll be very conscious of how well you're able to exploit your physical attributes—your strength and your fitness—during the course of games, to win your 1 v 1s and give yourself and your team the edge in close-fought situations.

CORE STRENGTH

At Level 5, you should be in better shape, physically, than you've ever been. Your levels of fitness give you the opportunity to deploy your technical skills from first minute to last in every game. Your body needs to be resilient in the face of challenges—fair and foul—which are part of every match. Avoiding heavy challenges, as well as rapid changes of direction in order to dribble, sprint, or pass the ball, mean generating torque through individual muscle groups from moment to moment. The power for those movements comes from **CORE STRENGTH**. Any weakness in that area will also leave you at much greater risk of picking up injuries during games.

LEVEL 5 PERFORMANCE TESTS

LOWER-BODY STRENGTH »

- 16-18 Full range Single-Leg Squats on each leg
- Series of 10 Broad Jumps of 85 inches or more
- Single-Leg Wall-Sit held for 90 seconds on each leg

INJURY PREVENTION »

- The Balance Disk: Progression (1), 30 dips on each leg
  Progression (2), Hold with eyes closed for 30 seconds, no dips

UPPER-BODY STRENGTH »

- Bent–arm pull-up held for 40 seconds
- 55 full push-ups in 60 seconds
- 1.5 Clock push-up set (1 clockwise, 1 anti-clockwise, then 1 more clockwise)
- No rests between

FLEXIBILTY/MOBILITY »

- Sit and reach test of at least 8 inches
- Practicing yoga at Advanced level

CORE STRENGTH & BALANCE »

- Plank for 2+ minutes
- Functional plank for 2 minutes
- Side functional plank 40 reps, 20 per side, no rests
- Single-leg balance for 60 seconds with slightly bent knee
- Marching hip-raise for 2 minutes 30 seconds with no rotation in hips or back

SPEED/QUICKNESS / AGILITY »

- 30-yard sprint in under 3.9 seconds.
- 8 yard multi-directional sprint in 1.0 second
- 5-10-5-5-10 shuttle run in under 5.9 seconds

ENDURANCE »

- Beep Test: score of level 17 or above
- 30 Second Run: 6 sets, each set to be completed to 50 yards + 20 yards
- Multi-directional 30 sec run: complete over 3 sets in 30 seconds, 1 minute rest between sets

JOIN THE CONVERSATION!
For additional drills to improve speed, mobility, and agility, be sure to check out the **COMPLETE ATHLETE** app. New video content is continually updated!

5.4 TECHNIQUE

Playing senior football at Level 5, you're now analysed and judged on every first touch, every pass, every shot at goal and every decision you make on the pitch. You have built up a sound technical base to your game over the past decade and more. You're comfortable receiving, protecting, and using the ball. To make a real impact on games, however, and to use your talent consistently at the highest possible level, a new element has to become a part of your training regime, both in club sessions and in the work you do away from that environment.

Achieving technical excellence under the pressure of match conditions means much more of your training needs to be taking place in the same high-tempo, high-intensity conditions you experience in games. You need to ensure that you're training with a daily position-specific technical programme in mind, one which exposes you to the pressure of match conditions whenever possible.

Being a professional player, excelling at the top end of your ability, depends on you performing the basics of the game to the highest and most consistent standard possible. Everything you do in extra training sessions at Level 5 should be match-related. This readies your mind to make the right decision in a split-second and empowers your body to fulfil that intention time after time.

All your technical work should be done with these match-related elements in mind:

- Improving potential weak areas in your game, particularly those exposed or identified in your previous match.
- Reinforcing the strongest elements of your game, with a view to how those can be used to gain an advantage over an up-coming opponent.

- Extra technical work done at a ratio of 70 percent equal to or above match tempo and intensity (this should be opposed work) and 30 percent at a slower tempo to exaggerate awareness and discipline in your technical execution.
- All technical work should be performed in the area of the pitch where it will relate to match conditions.

In an ideal world, mastery of technical skills will be liberating for you as a player, giving you the confidence and capability to approach the game with the freedom and spontaneity which you enjoyed when you first started playing the game. As well as consistency and discipline, it's important to remember that the element of surprise—your ability to do something unexpected—may be the difference between winning and losing a tight game.

The highest possible technical standard will be required of you. Achieving it will only be possible by continual work, adapted to the demands of your position on the pitch, in the key areas identified throughout your journey towards becoming a **COMPLETE ATHLETE**:

BALL CONTROL

BALL MASTERY/DRIBBLING

PASSING

SHOOTING

HEADING

AWARENESS

PLAYER >> When you talk to young players, you can tell a lot. You know the ones who look you in the eye and take in every word are the ones who are willing to immerse themselves in the culture of a professional football club. The ones who don't, it's going to take a bit longer for the penny to drop, if it ever does.

But the ones who listen are giving themselves the best chance possible of making it. That said, you keep an eye out for a maverick, too, a boy who's technically excellent, who when you suggest a way of doing something in a particular situation might say, 'Well, no. How about I do this instead?' And he's got the ability to do things his own way. He can do something a coach can't teach him. He's found his own solution.

It's easier when you're in the academy, developing players. There are some who are good technically and tactically but might not be strong enough physically. There are others who can compete physically but will need time to adapt to the tactical demands of the game.

You manage that, you give them time. It's about being patient, like Manchester United were with Tom Cleverley: he was technically excellent but needed to play down a year when he was 15 and 16 so he got game time and had the chance to catch up physically. By the time they're with the first team, though, you have to know you can send players out on a Saturday and trust them to do what needs doing in every aspect of the game. —Rossi Eames

5.5 LIFESTYLE

At Level 5, a footballer has at least a decade of working tirelessly at his game behind him. Now, as you begin to feel the pressure to perform at your best, week in and week out, the importance of what you do in the rest of your life needs to come into focus. Everything will need to be aimed towards a successful career at whatever level of football you've reached; key to that will be balancing your commitment to the game with taking ownership of the responsibilities which you face away from the training ground and dressing room:

FAMILY

SCHOOLWORK

SOCIAL LIFE

ROLE MODEL

LIVING YOUR SPORT

Every Academy manager will tell you he's had great, skilful players on the books who just haven't been big enough. They haven't been strong enough. The modern game's tough and so you've got to think carefully about how long you give those boys to develop. We had Leon Britton at West Ham: really good player, fantastic attitude and great to have around the place. A lovely young man, too. But I remember talking to Harry Redknapp about him when he was manager and Harry had to say, 'Look! He's so small. How can I put him into a game up against a giant like Patrick Vieira?' We let Leon go. I'm really pleased, though, that he picked his career up in the lower divisions and found his way into the Premier League. Still doing great for Swansea, Leon's had a fantastic career.
—Tony Carr

FAMILY

If I was sat in front of a young player now, I might say, 'if you get married, look at pre-nuptial agreements; don't sleep around; think about your future and your career.' I'm not here to give advice on family planning. I'm here to advise on what can happen when things go wrong.

Sometimes I wish I could speak to players' parents as well as to them. These boys are in extraordinary situations often and aren't prepared for them. In my experience, the ones who do the sensible thing are often the ones with a stable family situation behind them, which they've been able to learn from, rather than having parents who are happy for their son to swan about because they see him as a future superstar who's going to be their meal-ticket for life. The family environment is just as important as the football environment, I think. —Lois Langton

When you were young and really had no idea where a journey in football might take you, someone was there to wash your kit, tie your laces, and drive you to training. Someone was there on windswept Sunday mornings to watch and support you from the touchline. Your family was there at the very beginning and should still be beside you now, an integral part of your life.

They were there when it mattered. Make sure you're there for them now. Set aside a specific time each week to talk to your family, by phone, Skype or FaceTime. Keep them in touch with how you're doing and what you're doing. If you're lucky enough to still be living nearby, make a point of visiting whenever you can.

- Make the effort to attend family events whenever possible.
- Let your family know they're important to you and that you appreciate the part they've played in your life.
- You may now be in the public eye as a professional player or you may just be playing locally while getting on with a career doing something else. Either way, remember you represent your family's history and values. Do what you can every day to make them proud.

As you approach your late teens and early 20s, it may be that you're in a relationship and looking toward starting a family of your own. If you've broken into the professional game, you need to be aware that a career in football can put very particular pressures on you.

In terms of family law, I usually talk to boys who are between the ages of 17 and 23. We're discussing relationships, marriage, and having children; so once you're old enough to be having children is when it becomes most relevant. With young elite footballers, there can be almost a disconnection with the outside world and the rules that apply there.

More so the higher up you go: at the very top clubs, the boys are cocooned, someone's there to take care of everything for them, whereas you go into a Championship club and, even though the boys are really well looked after, it feels somehow more down to earth, more connected to the real world.

If you're at a big club, an Arsenal or a Chelsea or a Manchester United, the aspirations are so high. They have the first team players as role models; they see that success and that's where they're aiming to get to. And to be an 18 year old footballer can seem like a very glamorous thing to other people, to the outside world. If those guys are out at a night club, they've got a little swagger about them and it's not unusual to find that there are girls almost throwing themselves at them. Of course that brings problems with it, for footballers and for aspiring footballers. Clubs don't always take responsibility for educating players about relationships and so they need to take responsibility for their own actions.

I have to say that, when I go into speak to young players at clubs, they're always very well-behaved, very respectful. Even the one or two who are lounging around to start with, wondering why they're there, get pretty engaged pretty quickly. Talking about family law, I'm trying to get them to think about the future, of course, and so there may be things they haven't thought about: that once you've been married, divorce means dividing up assets; if you have a child after a one-night stand you may well need to buy that child a house to grow up in. Usually, about halfway through our talk, they'll say, 'I'm not going to get married!' And, by the end, they're saying, 'I'm not going to have any children either!'

The boys are often too young to have really thought about what relationships can mean in the future and the impact a divorce or a fling can have on a career. A lot of what we talk about can come as a bit of a shock to young players, but I'm always surprised how intelligent the questions they ask are. If we're talking about divorce, for example, there'll always be one hand goes up and he'll say: So what about pre-nuptial agreements? Or a boy will ask what happens if the girl he marries is the one with more money: Does that mean everything's turned around? They pick stuff up, from other players, from the press, and the questions they ask are often more intelligent than the questions I'm asked by my adult clients! —Lois Langton

SCHOOLWORK

At Level 5, unless you're at University or on a college scholarship somewhere, you've probably put your schooldays behind you. You may be thinking that you'll never have to write another essay or sit another exam ever again. Don't forget, though, what your time as a student has given you as you've grown up into a life in football. In 10 or 15 years' time, your playing career at the highest level you manage to reach will be over.

Distant as that prospect may seem right now, when it happens you'll feel as if you're having to pick up the pieces and start all over again. Because of that, enrolling on courses and continuing to study now can be a great investment for the future. If football's all you ever want to do, then now may be the time to start looking into a future career in coaching, sports science, or the media. The discipline and powers of self-motivation you've developed on the way to becoming a **COMPLETE ATHLETE** will serve you well as a student, too.

PLAYER >> *I always liked football: playing it, watching. I can still remember going to my first game at Chelsea: we beat Newcastle 1-0. Mark Stein was playing for Chelsea; Andy Cole was playing for Newcastle. I ended up at college in Aylesbury, playing for the college team. I wasn't much good, but I worked hard and I was captain. I moved into senior men's football with Amersham Town, where a couple of my mates played, and it was the making of me. As a coach, anyway! My first full season, I was in the reserves and I was at every training session and at every game. But I didn't start once; I was always on the bench. I didn't play a single minute. I never got a word of encouragement or feedback from the manager that whole time. It was a shock, coming from the professionalism of my gymnastics training into amateur football. But I fell* in love with the whole football thing: match days, banter, being with the boys. It put some fire into me, and I started watching the game from a coach's perspective: from the bench! The chance came up to do a degree in Sports Science at Leeds Metropolitan University and I jumped at it.

During my time at University, I got involved with coaching at Leeds United—community projects, the ladies team— and ended up working at the development centre in Chapeltown, quite a tough part of the city but a hotbed for football. It's where Aaron Lennon and James Milner began their careers. I loved working with young boys who were all dreaming of becoming players, some of them coming from real difficult home backgrounds.

We'd pass the best ones on into Leeds United's academy. Eventually, I came back to London and started working for Barnet, at first as a performance analyst, coaching the U13s and then running the club's college programme: boys training as a development squad while studying for BTECs.

One of the first cohorts I worked with was Jamal Lowe, who'd been released by QPR but soon moved up to Barnet's youth team and is now playing for Portsmouth in League One. It was another chance for schoolboys—released by clubs or playing grassroots football—to prove they had what it took to become pros. —Rossi Eames

JOIN THE CONVERSATION!
Join us today for further tips, advice, and conversation by downloading the **COMPLETE ATHLETE** app!

SOCIAL LIFE

So, a young player from a big London club, is out with a group of players, the U23 squad. Only one or two faces anyone would recognise. They head into a nightclub and get an area roped off as VIPs. Of course, that immediately sets them apart. Nobody would have known who they were but now other people in the club want to find out. The next thing, one or two irate fans have found their way behind the ropes and started having a go. A brawl ensues and the bouncers call the police who arrive and just pull people out and arrest them. The end result is a player charged with assault and, from that moment, his career's hanging by a thread. —Kyle Phillips

As mentioned previously at Level 4, the people you surround yourself with will influence your own behaviour as well as helping to define you in the eyes of others. Your choice of friends and the choices you make about how to spend your free time can have a significant impact on your career. The margins between success and failure are slim. Having a long career is as difficult and precarious as starting one in the first place. While you're playing at the top of your game, it's important to remember that what you do away from football can make a big difference when it comes to what you achieve in the game.

PLAYER » *I grew up on a housing estate in the East End of Glasgow, a part of the city with a reputation for being particularly tough. I wouldn't have swapped it for anywhere: I learnt lessons there that I'll never forget; from mates my age who loved football like I did; from watching a younger crowd who knew my younger brother; and from older lads who you had to treat with due respect. You had to learn to be tough yourself if you were going to get by without anyone giving you a hard time.*

Until I was 17, I was training with Glasgow Rangers: three nights a week, a game at the weekend and sometimes another in midweek. I realised pretty early that, at one of the biggest clubs in Scotland, if I wasn't up to the mark then there'd be plenty of other lads ready and waiting to take my place. That meant that, when I had pals who were out drinking and messing about, I knew I had to keep my distance, even if they were putting me under pressure to join in.

I had friends who were good footballers but didn't have the discipline and focus that kept me going. I remember one lad—we would both have been around 20—who could definitely play but who lost his way as a teenager. I hadn't seen him in a while and, by this time, I'd probably played about 100 league games in Scotland. His first words to me were: 'I wish I'd been more like you and got my head down when I was younger.' He hadn't found a club but had been accepted onto a college soccer scholarship in the USA. That would have been a great move but there were routine background checks which were done before he left Glasgow and they turned up a conviction he'd had as a teenager—stupid, really. Just a night out with some pals, too much to drink and an arrest for damage to property after they'd vandalised a couple of cars. He couldn't get a US visa.

I was so disappointed for him: a route into professional football—his second chance, if you like—was snatched away because of being in the wrong place at the wrong time as a 16 year old. In the end, the dream died for him and he dropped out of football altogether. We all make mistakes and we have to learn from them. But in football the stakes can be so high: if you let peer pressure and the wrong kind of social life sweep you up, you can lose it all in an instant. My dad was forever saying to me, 'Allan. Fly with the crows and you'll get shot with the crows.' I kept that in mind throughout my professional career. —Allan Russell

There are all sorts of places for a young player to go to for the wrong advice! Agents, management teams, even coaches and senior players. Or family and friends away from football. If I'm involved with a case on behalf of a young player, I do everything I can to make clear that, like any other person, he has to take responsibility for what's going on.

It can be difficult: the player may have people around him giving him conflicting advice; he may have an agent telling him he's going to take care of everything for him. He may have people close to him who may well believe they're doing what's best for him, who believe they know everything about everything and can make things hurry up and just go away. But, if it comes to a court case, I'm working on behalf of the player and nobody else. I need to look him in the eye. Make sure I know exactly what's happened and that nothing's being held back from me that could turn up later in court and undermine what we're trying to do. There's a place for professional advice: education so a player knows what can go wrong; being there when things do go wrong; and then doing everything possible afterwards to mitigate the circumstances for the player himself and for his club. —Kyle Phillips

ROLE MODEL

PLAYER » *Just because you're a sportsman, it doesn't mean you don't have a view, an opinion. In fact, people are going to want to know what you think. Things can happen so quickly in football. Take an example: I was at an U23 fixture a couple of seasons ago, Spurs versus Manchester United. Marcus Rashford got about five minutes as a substitute. That would have been October. By February, he's scoring twice against Arsenal on his Premier League debut at Old Trafford. Circumstances pushed him through and, suddenly, everybody wants to know everything about him: Who is he? What's his background? What kind of lad is he? Suddenly, Marcus is absolutely in the spotlight. People are looking for stories about him.* —Troy Townsend

A life in football means a life lived in the public eye. And that's not just for elite players at the very biggest clubs in the game. Everyone's got a camera phone and a social media account. Whatever you do, out on the pitch or anywhere else, can be uploaded and broadcast in the public domain in a couple of seconds. That can mean trouble for you, trouble for your club and trouble for your friends and family. The only answer is to take your responsibilities seriously and behave with the integrity you've developed along the journey to where you are now. Respect others, respect yourself, and remember who and what you represent.

You think of yourself as a footballer. Just a footballer. But, if other people are interested in watching you play, you can be sure they'll be interested in everything else about you, too. Especially for a young player, the idea of setting an example to others—especially to children—can seem like an extra pressure in a situation where there are enough pressures already as you try to move forwards in your career.

You can't hide, but you can try to make the right decisions. Try to do the right thing. You can support charities and help the community around you in all sorts of ways. A little time and a little effort can often be enough to see you setting the right kind of example, for team-mates, for supporters, and for family and friends.

LIVING YOUR SPORT

What happens if a boy who's been involved for 10 years, who's been dreaming of a professional career, finds himself without a scholarship at 16? Or a boy who gets through a scholarship but doesn't get a contract somewhere? I'd like to say to that young man: You're feeling down right now but try to remember what the game's given you. And what it can still give you.

Think about the friendships and the enjoyment to be had from football going forward. Think about the possibility of using the experience you've had to put something back into football, into your local community. Find the level that's right for you to keep playing, the highest level you can, whether that's National League or Sunday League.

Stay in the game because the game can still give you so much. And you can still give so much to the game. I sometimes say to kids I've been coaching who've just lost a game, who are down or having strops: Look, if I'd said to you before the game that you were going to lose 3-0, would you have still played the game? Every single time, they say back to me, 'Yeah. Of course we would.' Well, it's the same thing now.

If I told you, when you first started playing football that you weren't going to be able to go on and have a professional career, would you still have wanted to play

football? Was it all about being a professional or was it about trying your best and enjoying the game? A professional career should always grow out of a love for football. Then, if you don't make it, you'll still be left with that love. There's every chance you'll still be playing the game. —John Folwell

PLAYER » When I was young I trained with Charlton, between the ages of 14 and 16 I was at Lilleshall, which was a kind of national centre of excellence back then. The best young players in England. It's closed down now. Joe Cole, Michael Owen, Sol Campbell, Andy Cole—the list goes on! They all went to Lilleshall. I was up there between 1997 to 1999 and, towards the end of my time, I had a decision to make about where I was going to go on to next.

Nowadays they call it an academy scholarship, but then it was called a YTS. Even though I was a schoolboy at Charlton, I'm an East London boy. West Ham had just won the FA Youth Cup. I'd watched the game; the stadium was packed and lots of friends who I'd played with at District level were in the team. It was an easy choice. Why would I not want to go to West Ham? It ticked every box. I have to say that, as soon as I signed for the YTS, I knew I was with the club but that, really, I was on my own. It's a case of every man for himself: the aim is to get into the first team. You're there to get into the first team; the academy's there to produce first team players for the club. My mentality was always: I'm here now and I'm going to do whatever it takes. I was always ready to do that bit more work than the player next to me.

All of us young lads started together, but it was only one by one you might get a chance to train with the first team, move up from the U17s to the U19s or the Reserves. And I knew you only got your chance by doing it in games, *whatever level you were playing at, all the way to the first team. I wouldn't call it arrogance. I'd call it confidence. Even at 16 I was sure that, if I was in the first team, I'd score goals. I'd stay behind after training every day and practice, practice, practice.*

Even when I was 16, I tried to have the mentality of a first team player. Nobody had to tell me to do that. I might have been playing in the youth team but, every day, I was preparing myself for the first team, preparing myself to score goals in the Premier League. Ian Wright, Frank Lampard, Trevor Sinclair, Paolo di Canio: those guys were staying behind after training and, even though I was still so young, I wasn't scared to just go over and join in their finishing sessions. I remember once, when I was still just 17, Harry Redknapp pointing to me and saying to the senior players, 'That's how you finish!'

Football's a team game but you have to be single-minded. You have to be prepared to stand out from the rest. You have to be prepared to do everything you can to be ready when it's your turn in the first team. I always took on board as much as I could from the coaches; I wanted to improve. It was never a case of turning up for training and going through the motions. I used to wake up every morning looking forward to training, to being better and to scoring goals. As far as I was concerned, I had to train as I was going to play. If I trained at 100%, I knew that when it came to the weekend, for the U17s or U19s, I'd always produce. The manager, Harry Redknapp, used to watch some of the games. He'd always get the results. I convinced myself that, if I kept scoring goals at this level, it'd only be a matter of time before I got my chance.

All I ever thought about was playing football. The contract side of things never really mattered to me. I was just obsessed with scoring goals. I can't speak for anyone else. Maybe there are kids whose motivation in the game is buying a nice car. Of course at West Ham I saw the cars some of the lads had: Paolo di Canio had an old style Jaguar, Joe Cole had a two-seater Mercedes; the car park was full of Range Rovers!

But my motivation was simple. We'd play our game at hadwell Heath on a Saturday morning and then go down to Upton Park to watch the first team play in the afternoon. I'd just sit there, looking, thinking: I want to be out there. Scoring goals. Showing this crowd what I can do. And, you know, if you can't imagine something, it can't happen. I was like a sponge, watching everything the senior players did. I'd watch Paolo di Canio doing extra work in the gym; I'd look at what the players were eating; I'd ask loads of questions.

Everything I did, all the practice, was about making sure that I wasn't a player who needed a few chances to score. I wanted people to trust me: give him one chance and he'll score. When I was still only 17, I started training more often with the first team. Finishing with both feet, movement: those things came naturally to me by then.

I was still small but that was something I could work on in the gym and with my diet. That's all part of development. I'd watch Ian Wright videos night after night, watching the runs he made, watching his movement. I was obsessed, really! My mum would tell you: I'd sit at home dreaming about scoring goals in the Premier League. And, deep down in my heart, I knew I could do it. I made my West Ham debut when I was still 17. I trained all week and then, the day before the game—against Walsall in the old Worthington Cup—the manager just said to me, 'Oh, you're on the bench for tomorrow night.' You can imagine: I was buzzing. Even if I didn't get on, sitting on the first team bench was a big thing for me.

As it turned out, I got on about 6 or 7 minutes from the end. All I wanted to do then was score and the chance came to me: we won 1-0. Maybe it was that night that Harry Redknapp made up his mind about me and decided to send me down to Bournemouth on loan for the season. That year at Dean Court, he used to come to the games, watching me develop. He didn't have to do that; it made me feel sure he had a plan for me. Harry was fantastic for me.

At West Ham, I suppose I'd always felt a little protected. Even though I was around the first team, I was the young one and I felt like the coaching staff were looking out for me. At Bournemouth, 18 years old, I really felt on my own for the first time. Exposed to everything. West Ham had had to pay a lot of money to Charlton as compensation when I left; I'd scored on my debut at West Ham; I suppose there was quite a bit of hype around me: eyes on me, pressure. I had to produce here. I had to score goals. But the truth is I just love playing football. So I got my head down, worked hard, ignored most of what was being said about me.

I ended up setting a Bournemouth club record, scoring in ten consecutive games. I think mentality is everything. Even when I was scoring goals at Bournemouth and things were going really well, I just felt like I needed to keep my foot down: keep going, keep going! It was an amazing experience.

For the first time, I was playing against men every week. Playing with men, my team-mates, who'd look at me as if to say: Give him the ball. He's going to score for us. These were hard-working guys. Honest, grafting, putting it in every day. They were married, had kids. Had mortgages to pay and I didn't even know what a mortgage was back then! And they were giving me the responsibility for scoring the goals.

I'm old school probably: I've always thought hard work gets its reward. And that's what happened when I came on loan to Bournemouth. It really helped me develop. Little things like having to wash your own kit. Bigger things like being in a dressing room with grown men who were ready to tell you when you did something wrong in a game. It toughened me up. This was League One football.

I was small; people were smashing me; I had to stay calm and not react. I had to be brave and keep trying to do the right things. It was about being positive. I've always said that, if someone tells you you're not good at something, then go away and practice until you're better at it. Whatever you're good at, master it. Look at Michael Jordan: the best, but he used to practice every day. The coach couldn't get him off the court. Anywhere around the box, I want to know what I need to do and be able to do it. Rehearse it and rehearse it until it becomes instinct.

Young players nowadays can sign a first contract and, straight away, they're earning money like their mums and dads have never been able to. You're doing something nobody in your family has ever done before. If you're going to make sure that first contract isn't your last contract, you need to keep your feet on the ground. It's so important to have the right people around you. What's got you this far is hard work: playing for your school, playing for your district, playing for youth teams. Suddenly, you get there: a professional contract.

Why would you suddenly stop there? Why would you stop working hard? You can't ever be satisfied. The only time to be satisfied is when you've finished playing. That's the time to sit down and look back. You've had a great career or you haven't, but what you have to be able to say to yourself is, 'I did my best. I did everything I could.' I've known kids who were at clubs, got released and, for them, it was the end of the world. Maybe they even stopped playing. I had my own way of dealing with setbacks, though. If a coach didn't pick me, I'd say nothing out loud, but I'd be thinking to myself: One day I'll show you that you made a mistake with me. I can remember, while I was at Lilleshall, I got left out of an England youth squad. I was just 16 and still small, but it hurt me being left out. If I saw that coach now, I'd say to him: You helped me. You put fire in my belly. It hurt me at the time, but I went on to represent my country, didn't I? 50-plus caps, 20-odd goals, playing at tournaments?

I'd say to any kid that you've got to use setbacks in a positive way: do better, bounce back. You know, it's like my mum says: Only God can dictate your future. His plan for you is the only one that counts. If someone knocks you down, you have to get up again, like a boxer in the ring. You can't let an opponent decide on your future. Fight on. I always say, 'In football, a lot can change in 90 minutes.'

You have those moments in your career. Your whole life can change and, because of that, you've always got to be ready. Trying your best to always be switched on and focused. Whether you're a young boy on trial or a senior player hoping for an England call-up, you never know who might be watching the game you're playing right now. I don't really know where it all comes from. My work ethic, I guess, is down to my family. My mum's been a single parent. And further back, too: my grandparents coming over from the Caribbean, working hard to build a home. I think it's in the East London mentality: if you want something, you've got to go and work for it.

I don't want it easy. I want to have to work for what I can achieve. That way I feel good about it when I get there. It's in my mind that, if I have a good game on a Saturday and score my goals, I'll know exactly what it was I did *in training during the week to make it happen. If I work during the week, I get my reward at the weekend.*

When I came back from Bournemouth, all I wanted to do was score goals in the Premier League. I was sure I could do it, even though I was only 19. I remember a game at Ipswich where I came on for Paolo di Canio, and, as he came off, he gave me the captain's armband. I don't know if I was supposed to give it to someone else, but I just put it on! I scored and we ended up winning 3-2.

It was one of those afternoons when everything changes. It's an amazing feeling. I've had it all through my career, the buzz of scoring a goal but also knowing that other people are thinking, 'If we need a goal, if JD gets a chance, he'll score it for us.' I still have that feeling, as much as I did when I was a teenager. I think when that goes away it's the time to stop playing.

I'm 34 now. People probably think, at that age, you should be slowing down, you won't be as sharp as you used to be. But I go back to how I was when I was young, wanting to be different to the boy next to me. Why can't I be as quick, as sharp, at 34 as I was at 25? Even back as a youth team player, I was always trying to do things that would mean I had a long career: looking after myself, eating the right things. For 4 or 5 years, I worked on my own with a fitness coach, a French guy named Tiberius Darau, who said to me, 'This is hard but the work we're doing now will put 5 years on the end of your career.'

I always wanted to be playing into my 30s. And not just playing: I wanted to be playing with the same intensity and still scoring goals. Here I am. 34 and still in love with the game. —Jermain Defoe

APPENDIX 1

LAWS OF THE GAME

To play the game properly at any level, it's important to understand the rules by which football is played and to stick to those rules. There are 17 laws of football which are the standard for any professional or international match played (and, for the most part, cover any game at senior grassroots level). Here's a brief summary. The detailed Laws can be downloaded from FIFA's website.

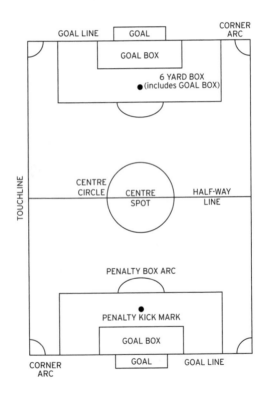

LAW 1 >> THE FIELD OF PLAY

Football can be played on either grass or artificial turf, but the surface must be green in colour. The pitch must be rectangular in shape and distinctly marked by two short goal lines and two long-touch lines. The pitch is divided into halves, separated by the halfway line, which runs from the midpoints of each touchline. At the midpoint of the halfway line is a marked centre point surrounded by a lined center circle with a radius of 10 yards. Opposing players are not allowed to enter this circle during the possessing team's kick-off. The length of the touch line must be greater than the length of the goal line.

REGULATION LENGTHS ARE:

- Touch line: Minimum 90 meters (100 yards), maximum 120 meters (130 yards).
- Width (goal line): Minimum 45 metres (50 yards), maximum 90 metres (100 yards).
- At each end of the pitch is an 8-yard-wide goal centred along the goal line.
- Six yards from each goal post along the goal line and six yards out into the pitch (perpendicular to the goal line) is the goal box.
- Extending 18 yards from each goal post along the goal line and 18 yards out into the pitch (perpendicular to the goal line) is the penalty box.
- In each of the four corners of the pitch is a 5-foot-high corner flag.

LAW 2 >> THE BALL

The ball must be spherical in shape and made of leather or another comparable material. Its circumference must be in the range of 27 to 28 inches. This rule is only applicable for official sanctioned matches, as youth leagues often employ the use of a smaller ball that is better suited to children.

LAW 3 >> THE NUMBER OF PLAYERS

Matches are generally played by two teams of 11 to a side. The goalkeeper is included in the 11-player total. If a team cannot field at least seven players at kick off, the game cannot be played. Teams of fewer than 11 a side can often be seen in youth leagues, where smaller teams are used as a developmental tool. FIFA-sanctioned matches are generally limited to three substitutions per match, although this varies from competition to competition.

Most youth leagues allow an unlimited number of substitutions, which must also be listed on the game card prior to the beginning of the match, otherwise those players are ineligible. Substitutions may only enter at the halfway line, with the referee's approval, and after the player being subbed off has left the pitch. The goalkeeper may be substituted with anyone on the pitch or any eligible substitute on the bench during a game stoppage.

LAW 4 >> THE PLAYERS' EQUIPMENT

All players are required to wear a jersey, shorts, shin guards, socks and boots. The socks must cover the shin guards entirely. If the referee deems a player's equipment unsatisfactory, the player can be sent off until the issue is remedied.

LAW 5 >> THE REFEREE

The referee is the authority on the pitch, and his word is law. If you question a referee's decision, you can be disciplined further simply for dissent.

LAW 6 >> THE ASSISTANT REFEREES

The assistant referees are primarily responsible for assisting the referee in performing his duties: signalling with a flag when a ball goes of play, when a player is fouled, or when a player is in an offside position.

LAW 7 >> THE DURATION OF THE MATCH

A football match comprises two 45-minute halves, with extra time added for each at the referee's discretion. The halves are separated by a half-time period not to exceed 15 minutes. The extra time generally corresponds with the referee's estimate of how much time was taken up due to substitutions and injuries. Although games do have an allotted time limit, it is ultimately up to the referee as to when to end a match.

LAW 8 >> THE START AND RESTART OF PLAY

Kick-off is generally determined by a coin toss, whereby the winning team can either choose to start with the ball or choose which goal they would like to attack. The losing team is then given whichever choice the winner does not elect to take. Kick-off occurs at the start of each half and after each goal scored, and is taken at the centre of the halfway line. If a team scores a goal, the opposing team is given the kick-off to restart the match.

LAW 9 >> THE BALL IN AND OUT OF PLAY

The ball is out of play when it fully crosses either the goal line or the touch line. It is also out of play if the referee stops play for any reason. If, for any reason, the ball strikes the frame of the goal or the referee and remains within the goal and touch lines, it is still in play.

LAW 10 >> THE METHOD OF SCORING

A goal is scored when the whole of the ball has crossed the goal line within the frame of the goal. At the end of the match, the team with the most goals is the winner, barring the circumstances in which extra time and/or a penalty shootout is taken to determine the result of a drawn game.

LAW 11 >> OFFSIDE

When the ball is played forward by the attacking team, an attacking player receiving the ball while in his opponent's half must be level or behind the second to last defender (the last typically, but not necessarily, being the goalkeeper). However, this rule only applies if he is involved with the play. To get a better understanding of the offside rule, please refer to a detailed explanation of the Laws.

LAW 12 >> FOULS AND MISCONDUCT

A DIRECT FREE KICK is awarded when a player:

- Kicks or attempts to kick an opponent
- Trips or attempts to trip an opponent
- Jumps at an opponent
- Charges an opponent
- Strikes or attempts to strike an opponent
- Pushes an opponent
- Tackles an opponent
- Holds an opponent
- Spits at an opponent
- Handles the ball deliberately

If any of these are fouls are committed by a player in their team's penalty area, the opposing team is awarded a penalty kick. INDIRECT FREE KICKS are awarded if a player:

- Plays in a dangerous manner
- Impedes the progress of an opponent
- Prevents the goalkeeper from releasing the ball from his/her hands
- Commits any other unmentioned offense

YELLOW CARDS are awarded as a caution or warning to a player and can be issued for the following offenses:

- Unsporting behaviour
- Dissent by word or action
- Persistent infringement of the Laws of the Game
- Delaying the restart of play
- Failure to respect the required distance when play is restarted with a corner kick, free kick, or throw-in
- Entering or re-entering the field of play without the referee's permission
- Deliberately leaving the field of play without the referee's permission

RED CARDS are used to send a player off the pitch and can be issued for the following offenses:

- Serious foul play
- Violent conduct
- Spitting at an opponent or any other person
- Denying the opposing team a goal or an obvious goal-scoring opportunity by deliberately handling the ball (the goalkeeper being an exception)
- Denying an obvious goal-scoring opportunity to an opponent moving towards the player's goal by an offense punishable by a free kick or a penalty kick
- Using offensive or abusive language and/or gestures
- Receiving a second caution (yellow card) in the same match

LAW 13 >> FREE KICKS

Free Kicks are broken down into two categories: direct and indirect. A direct free kick can be shot directly into the opponent's goal without touching another player. An indirect free kick is indicated by the referee raising his hand before the kick is taken. An indirect kick can only go into the goal if it has subsequently been touched by another player before it enters the goal. The ball must be stationary for both types of free kicks.

LAW 14 >> THE PENALTY KICK

A penalty kick is awarded either when a defensive player fouls an attacking player or commits a handball in his own team's penalty area. The ball is placed on the penalty spot (12 yards from the centre of the goal), and all players on both teams must remain outside the penalty box before the penalty kick is taken. They may enter the box immediately after the kick is taken. The goalkeeper may move horizontally along the goal line before the shot is taken, but he may not come off the line until the ball is struck.

JOIN THE CONVERSATION!

For advice from coaches and professional athletes, check out tips and techniques in the **COMPLETE ATHLETE** app!

LAW 15 >> THE THROW-IN

A throw-in is awarded to the team out of possession when the team in possession plays the ball out of bounds over the touchline. While taking a throw-in, a player must release the ball with both hands simultaneously and keep both feet firmly planted on the ground. If these conditions are not met, play is stopped, and the throw-in is given to the opposing team. Players are not allowed to score directly from a throw-in.

LAW 16 >> THE GOAL KICK

A goal kick is awarded when the attacking team plays the ball out of bounds over the defending team's goal line. After the ball is out of play, a defender or the goalkeeper may place the ball anywhere within the six-yard goal box and kick the ball back into play.

LAW 17 >> THE CORNER KICK

A corner kick is awarded to the attacking team when the defending team plays the ball out of bounds over its goal line. The ball is placed within the corner quadrant and is kicked back into play by the attacking. A goal can be scored directly from a corner kick.

APPENDIX 2 »
SPORTS NUTRITION GUIDELINES
FOR PLAYERS

All of **COMPLETE ATHLETE** sports nutrition guidelines were provided by Courtney M. Sullivan, founder of Nutrition for Body and Mind. Sullivan is a Registered Dietitian certified by the Academy of Nutrition and Dietetics and a Certified Personal Trainer recognized by the National Academy of Sports Medicine. Below are more detailed guidelines as well as suggested meals and recipes developed by Sullivan. Nutrition is key to enhancing athletic performance.

Young players with incomplete or inadequate diets may have insufficient fuel for games and training sessions. They can suffer from nutrient deficiencies, which lead to fatigue, a compromised immune system, or a susceptibility to injury. Such weaknesses will be reflected in the quality and consistency of their performances. Proper intake of macronutrients and micronutrients is necessary to help maximise sports performance. Critical micronutrients include calcium, iron, folate, vitamin B6, and zinc.

CALCIUM

Poor calcium intake can lead to decreased bone mass and increased risk of stress fractures and possible bone-related injuries. The adequate intake of calcium is 1,000 mg per day. This is particularly important in adolescence when a boy's bones are growing. For younger boys, up to 10 years old, 700 mg is sufficient. As with most micronutrients, the recommended intake should be reached with a healthy balanced diet and without the need for supplements. Milk is the most obvious ready source of calcium.

IRON

Important for its oxygen-carrying capacity, iron also plays a major role in the energy metabolism of carbohydrates, proteins, and fats. Young players with an iron deficiency anemia, are at risk of athletic performance being undermined by fatigue, impaired immune function, and/or impaired cognitive function (i.e. reasoning, memory, attention, and language). Foods that are rich in iron include red meat and enriched cereals and grains, coupled with fruits and vegetables that are high in vitamin C, which aids in iron absorption.

FOLATE AND VITAMIN B6

Both are critical for amino acid metabolism. Good sources of both are enriched grain products, fish, liver, and potatoes. Spinach, broccoli, lentils, and asparagus are good sources of folate. A vitamin B-complex deficiency can lead to fatigue, muscle soreness, and loss of cognitive function.

ZINC

Zinc plays a role in more than 300 enzymatic reactions in the body. It is also critical for wound healing, tissue growth and maintenance, and immune function. Good sources of zinc in a balanced diet are beans, nuts, whole grains and dairy products. Dietary protein enhances zinc absorption and plays an important role in muscle recovery.

MACRONUTRIENTS

An increase in energy expenditure will require an increase in the regular and balanced intake of carbohydrates, protein, and fats. Either at your club or privately, it's to be recommended that you consult a professional nutritionist to discuss your personal macronutrient needs, based on your height, weight, age, and activity level.

Activity level is measured by the time (how long you exercise), type (the training program you're currently in), intensity (low, moderate, or high), and frequency (how often you train and/or play). After analysing those factors, your estimated calorie burn will be established.

Current research is suggesting that an increasing percentage of players are not consuming enough total calories, as well as total carbohydrates, in comparison to the amount of calories they burn. Fluid intake is often inadequate as well, which alters the hydration status of young players. Therefore, as stressed elsewhere in **COMPLETE ATHLETE**, it is very important to practice a pre- and post-workout nutrition regimen and re-hydration program.

CARBOHYDRATES

For players, poor carbohydrate intake results in inadequate glycogen stores and fatigue, which compromises performance and forces your body to break down its own protein stores for fuel (through a process called gluconeogenesis). Carbohydrate is the preferred fuel source for athletic performance. Carbohydrate needs are based on body weight and intensity of activity.

• 3 to 5 grams of carbohydrates per kilogram of body weight for very light intensity training.
• 5 to 8 grams of carbohydrates per kilogram of body weight for moderate or heavy training.
• 8 to 9 grams of carbohydrates per kilogram of body weight for pre-game loading (24 to 48 hours prior).
• 1.7 grams of carbohydrate per kilogram of body weight for post-game refueling (within 2 to 3 hours).

PROTEIN

Protein is essential for muscle-building and lean-muscle maintenance, repair, and/or gain. It is important to note that an adequate protein intake and inadequate total calorie intake will inhibit protein balance, and can still cause lean muscle breakdown. It's crucial that players consume adequate total calories and protein to avoid this problem and maintain a healthy body weight. Vegetarians and vegans should be sure they're consuming adequate plant proteins.

On the other end, consuming excess protein can lead to dehydration (it puts strain on the kidneys), weight gain (your body will store as fat any excess protein that is not utilized), and calcium loss. Current advice is that footballers will need to consume between 1.4 grams and 1.7 grams of protein per kilogram of body weight per day.

FAT

Fat is essential for light-to-moderate intensity exercise and for absorption of the fat-soluble vitamins. Low-fat diets are not encouraged. Adequate heart healthy fats such as monounsaturated and polyunsaturated fats should make up 20 to 30 percent of your total calories. Lowering the amount of saturated fat and trans fats (the unhealthy fats) is definitely to be encouraged. Ideally, your diet should consist of less than 7 percent of your total calories coming from saturated fat and preferably no trans-fat.

FLUID

Maintaining proper fluid balance is critical to athletic performance and, specifically, to avoiding early fatigue and heat exhaustion. Signs of dehydration include dark urine, small urine output, muscle cramps, increased heart rate, headaches, nausea, and vomiting.

- Be sure to consume 16 to 24 ounces of fluid for every pound lost via sweat during exercise.
- For activities that are less than 60 minutes, hydrate with water.
- For activities that are greater than 60 minutes, you can hydrate with a sports beverage containing 6 to 8 percent carbohydrates to restore electrolytes and energy.

GENERAL GUIDELINES >>

All players should consume five or more balanced meals spread throughout the day, every 3 to 4 hours. Eating every 3 hours helps to maintain your metabolic rate, lower-body fat percentage, lower serum lipid levels (cholesterol), decrease stress hormone production, lower insulin response, and improve glucose tolerance (especially if you are pre-diabetic, are diabetic currently, or have diabetes in your family history). Meals should be eaten 2 to 3 hours before training or games, and snacks eaten 1 to 1.5 hours before training or games. Eat when you're hungry to prevent lean-muscle breakdown and stop when you're full to prevent feeling sluggish. Listen to your intuitive eating cues, which will help to do the following:

- Maintain blood sugar and insulin control
- Regulate appetite
- Improve concentration
- Gain lean-muscle mass
- Enhance muscle in the recovery process (i.e., repairing and rebuilding of muscles)

- Eat breakfast within 30 minutes of waking up to prevent lean-muscle breakdown, increase energy and concentration, and maintain good blood sugar control. Choose whole grains, fresh fruit, and lean protein.
- Eat well-balanced meals and snacks, consisting of

carbohydrates, lean proteins, and heart-healthy fats.
- Drink a protein shake or eat a snack or meal that has equal amounts of protein and carbohydrates within 30 minutes after a training session or game.
- Choose fresh, whole foods when possible, instead of processed foods that are packaged or refined, to increase nutritional value. Especially avoid foods that are high in sugar or trans fats.

MEAL PLANNING

BREAKFAST >> It is the most important meal of the day. Don't ever skip it. You are coming from an overnight fast and will wake up with low blood sugar because of that. Breakfast literally means to "break the fast." You need to focus on eating breakfast within 30 minutes of waking up to prevent lean-muscle breakdown, increase energy and concentration, and maintain good blood-sugar control.

Start your morning with 8 to 12 ounces of water with a squeeze of lemon wedge to rehydrate and reduce stomach acidity. Choose whole grains, fresh fruit, and lean protein. Although many breakfast choices are focused around carbohydrates, it is important to include a good source of protein for lean-muscle gain and maintenance.

EXAMPLE BREAKFAST MEAL >>

1 to 2 scrambled eggs (free-range and/or organic), 1 slice of whole grain toast with avocado (spread on top of toast). Add some sliced tomatoes on the side and a cup of low-fat cottage cheese or yoghurt (for added protein, as needed). If you're trying to gain weight, adding a protein shake is also ideal with breakfast.

SNACK >>

Choose a snack consisting of lean protein, fresh fruit, and a whole-grain carbohydrate. You can add essential, heart-healthy fat as needed.

EXAMPLE MID-MORNING SNACK >>

One medium-sized organic apple (i.e., size of a tennis ball) with 2 tablespoons of natural almond butter or peanut butter and 1 cup of nonfat or low-fat plain Greek yogurt. Optional: add sprinkled cinnamon and half of a cup of blueberries to mix with your yogurt.

LUNCH >>

Eat a well-balanced meal, consisting of carbohydrates (whole grains, not refined white flours or sugars) and lean proteins, with a portion of fresh or steamed vegetables and heart-healthy fats (omega-3s).

EXAMPLE LUNCH MEAL >>

3 to 4 ounces of boneless, skinless lean chicken breast; half to 1 cup cooked brown rice; and a portion (1 cup) of steamed mixed vegetables or green vegetable of choice (e.g., broccoli, asparagus, Brussel sprouts, courgettes, etc.). Add a piece of fresh fruit, such as a medium-sized orange (size of tennis ball) on the side.

SNACK >>

Choose a snack consisting of a lean protein, a fresh vegetable, and a whole-grain carbohydrate. Avoid consuming foods high in fat, or excessive amounts of fibre or protein, before your training or game, because these foods are slow-digesting. Your body needs foods that are higher in carbohydrates, which yield readily available energy for working muscles and which also contain a high nutrient/water density to increase hydration.

EXAMPLE AFTERNOON SNACK MEAL »

1 slice of whole grain toast with a spread of hummus (1 to 2 tablespoons); 2 thin slices of turkey, with sliced cucumber and tomato on top. You can eat this open face or add another piece of whole grain toast for additional carbohydrates. This depends on your current age, macronutrient needs, and training regimen.

DINNER »

Eat a well-balanced meal consisting of carbohydrates (whole grains, not refined white flours or sugars) and lean proteins; also add fresh or steamed vegetables and heart-healthy fats. (omega-3s)

EXAMPLE DINNER MEAL»

3 to 4 ounces of lean protein (e.g., fish, chicken, turkey, etc.), half to 1 cup cooked quinoa or baked/sweet potato with the skin on, and a side salad (e.g., kale/spinach/or mixed greens with chopped tomato, garbanzo or kidney beans, shredded carrots, chopped broccoli, avocado, feta cheese, and a light balsamic vinaigrette).

POST-ACTIVITY (WITHIN 30 MINUTES) »

Consume a protein shake or balanced intake of protein and carbohydrates to repair your muscles overnight and restore glycogen that was used during your training session or game, so that you are prepared to go again tomorrow. (See the protein-shake recipes that follow for recovery nutrition.)

NIGHT-TIME SNACK »

The myths that you should not eat after 7 pm or that you should not eat 2 hours before bed do not apply to you. You are a footballer and therefore need to fuel your body properly to optimize your athletic performance.

EXAMPLE NIGHTTIME SNACK »

1 to 2 tablespoons of almond butter or natural peanut butter, with .5 cup organic raspberries or strawberries on the side. Optional: Add 1 cup non-fat plain Greek yogurt

HYDRATION

- 14 to 22 ounces (2+ cups) 2 hours before exercise.
- 8 ounces 10 to 20 minutes before exercise.
- 6 to 8 ounces every 15 to 20 minutes during training.
- 16 to 24 ounces (2 to 3 cups) for every 1 pound lost within 2 hours after activity
- Sodium (Na) 0.5 to 0.7 g/L in exercise lasting more than one hour to avoid risk of hyponatremia (low sodium can have dangerous effects on the body)
- Drink fluids with carbohydrates and electrolytes if exercise is longer than 1 hour, for improved performance and decreased fatigue

Consume 24 ounces of fluid for every pound lost via sweat. Pay attention to internal cues (e.g., headaches) or external cues (e.g., urine color) to monitor hydration status. If you have a headache, you are most likely already >10% dehydrated. Your urine should be light yellow in colour or clear. If it is dark yellow or brown, you are dehydrated and need to increase your fluids (and overall electrolytes, including sodium, potassium, calcium, and magnesium) drastically.

PHYSICAL/MENTAL EFFECTS OF DEHYDRATION

• Decreased muscle strength, speed, stamina, energy, cognitive processes
• Increased risk of injury

BENEFITS OF ADEQUATE FLUIDS

• Decreased heart rate, perceived exertion.
• Increased stroke volume, cardiac output, skin blood flow, and improved athletic performance

ADDITIONAL TIPS AND TRICKS »

AVOID "BOTTOM-HEAVY" DIETS This is defined as eating anything over 60 percent of your total daily caloric intake in the afternoon or evening (anytime between 3 pm and 10 pm). The timing of your meals will affect your body composition.

For example, studies show that a player who consumes a "bottom-heavy diet" will have a higher body-fat percentage than another player who consumes his meals throughout the day, every 3 to 4 hours (even if both players are consuming the same total calories and following the same training regimen). You need to eat to fuel your body when your body needs the energy for optimal metabolism, for lean muscle gain, and to maximise performance. You may already be skilled in football but mastering your nutrition can help take you to the next level.

JOIN THE CONVERSATION!
Nutrition advice and tips are also available in the **COMPLETE ATHLETE** app—download it today!

AVOID PACKAGED, PROCESSED, AND REFINED FOODS WHICH ARE HIGH IN SUGAR OR TRANS-FAT

These foods are high in preservatives and artificial ingredients that our bodies do not process well and may cause an upset stomach. These foods may provide convenience and quick energy, but they will ultimately lead to a "crash" or feeling of fatigue about one hour after consumption due to the quick rise and fall effect of your blood-sugar levels.

Artificial trans-fatty acids are an unhealthy fat added to foods to increase their shelf life and Best Before dates. Be sure to look at the ingredient list below the nutrition facts label for "partially or fully hydrogenated oils," which means there is trans-fat in the product and it should therefore be avoided. Trans-fat raises your LDL (bad cholesterol) and lowers your HDL (good cholesterol), which can increase your risk of heart disease, stroke, and type II diabetes.

TIMING OF MEALS (FOR LEVELS 1-5) >>

Eating smaller and more frequent meals is ideal for proper digestion, metabolism, and lean-muscle weight gain. Eating frequently yields high energy and stable blood sugar levels. Waiting too long between meals can lead to lean-muscle breakdown and weight loss. Players with poor nutrition are more prone to injury, especially during periods of growth and development or when their bones are strengthening or becoming denser.

NUTRITION REGIMEN: NIGHT BEFORE GAME

Avoid greasy or fried foods that are high in fat. Avoid high amounts of sugar, or refined carbohydrates, which can also make you feel sluggish. "Carb loading" is not necessary. Instead, eat a balanced meal containing lean protein, whole grain carbohydrates, and steamed vegetables. Add a protein shake for dessert (if needed).

MACRONUTRIENT SUGGESTIONS

CARBOHYDRATES >> Higher fibre foods (i.e., lower Glycemic Index), such as whole-grain bread, brown rice, whole-grain pasta, (or gluten-free versions), beans, starchy vegetables (e.g., corn, peas, potatoes), quinoa, and cereals.

PROTEINS >> Chicken, turkey, or fish (e.g., wild salmon, tuna, trout, mackerel, or sardines, which are high in heart healthy omega-3 fatty acids).

FATS >> Low-fat cheese, nuts/nut butters (e.g., natural peanut butter or almond butter), avocado, seeds, oils (e.g., extra-virgin olive oil, canola oil, grapeseed oil, flaxseed oil).

VEGETABLES >> All green vegetables are preferable.

DINNER MEAL BEFORE GAME #1

PROTEINS >> Boneless, skinless chicken breast
(portion: 3 to 6 ounces, depending on age and weight)

CARBOHYDRATES >> Brown rice (portion: .5 to 1.5 cups cooked, depending on age and weight).

VEGETABLES >> Side salad with organic spinach leaves, chopped cucumbers, carrots, tomato, and a light olive oil and vinegar dressing

PROTEINS >> Ground turkey (portion: 3 to 6 ounces, depending on age, weight etc)

CARBOHYDRATES >> Baked potato (1 medium-sized) with a dollop of low-fat Greek yogurt instead of sour cream (optional) or brown rice/wholemeal pasta (portion: .5 to 1.5 cups cooked, depending on age/weight etc)

VEGETABLES >> Steamed broccoli and mushrooms (portion: 1 to 2 cups, depending on age/weight etc)

NUTRITION REGIMEN >> MORNING OF GAME

Avoid high fat or high protein foods on the morning of a game. They are more difficult for the body to digest. Carbohydrates provide the best source of readily available energy for the body. Dairy products can be tolerated in a small amount, but when consumed in larger amounts can cause stomach upsets. Your body will always use carbohydrates as its first source of energy.

MACRONUTRIENT SUGGESTIONS

CARBOHYDRATES >> Lower fibre foods (higher Glycemic Index), cream of rice, oatmeal with 2 grams of fibre or less, rice cereal (dry), bread (with 2 grams of fibre), or plain bagel

PROTEINS >> Eggs/egg whites, protein shakes (made with whey protein, pea protein, vegan protein, hemp protein, etc.), low-fat plain Greek yogurt

FATS >> Nuts/nut butters (e.g., peanut butter, almond butter, cashew butter, sunflower-seed butter), seeds, avocado

FRUITS » 1 medium-sized piece of fresh fruit (e.g., banana, apple, kiwi, peach, pear, nectarine, plum, etc)

Peanut butter (or almond butter) and jelly (or honey) sandwich on whole-wheat bread with a sliced banana

1 cup low-fat, plain Greek yogurt with .5 cup organic blueberries, or a banana with 1 cup low-salt/low-sugar wholegrain cereal. Avoid high-fibre cereals which will cause an upset stomach.

NOTE » Greek yogurt contains 20 grams of protein per cup and healthy probiotics, which increase immunity and aid in proper digestion. It is important to get the low-fat or non-fat version (to avoid the high saturated-fat content) and plain (to avoid the 20 to 22 grams of added sugar in the flavored varieties.)

CAFFEINE

Caffeine has been proven to be one of the best ergogenic aids and is known to help players train harder and longer. Caffeine stimulates the brain and contributes to clearer thinking and greater concentration. If you like coffee or tea, consume caffeine at least 1 hour before training or a game.

RECOMMENDATION » 1 to 3 milligrams per kilogram of body weight. Do not consume caffeine in the form of energy drinks or colas because they have concentrated sources of sugar, which cancel out any health benefits. Coffee and green tea are natural sources of caffeine and provide a high antioxidant value. Make sure to only add a dash of honey, agave, or milk. Do not add sugar.

HYDRATION

- 14 to 22 ounces (2+ cups) 2 hours before exercise
- 8 ounces 10 to 20 minutes before exercise
- 6 to 8 ounces every 15 to 20 minutes during training
- 16 to 24 ounces (2 to 3 cups) for every 1 pound lost, within 2 hours after training
- Sodium (Na) -0.5 to 0.7 g/L in exercise lasting longer than one hour to avoid increased risk of hyponatremia (low sodium can have dangerous effects on the body)

* Drink fluids with carbohydrate and electrolytes if exercise is longer than 1 hour, for improved performance and decreased fatigue.

Consume 24 ounces of fluid for every 1 pound lost via sweat. Pay attention to internal cues (i.e., headaches) or external cues (i.e., urine color) to monitor hydration status. If you have a headache, you are most likely already more than 10% dehydrated.

Your urine should be a light yellow color or clear. If it is dark yellow or brown, you are dehydrated and need to increase your fluids (and overall electrolytes, including sodium, potassium, calcium, and magnesium) drastically

PHYSICAL/MENTAL EFFECTS OF DEHYDRATION

- Decreased muscle strength, speed, stamina, energy, cognitive processes
- Increased risk of injury

BENEFITS OF ADEQUATE FLUIDS

- Decreased heart rate, perceived exertion
- Increased stroke volume, cardiac output, skin blood flow, and improved athletic performance

TRAVEL NUTRITION >>
FOODS TO EAT WHILE TRAVELLING

- Make your own nut trail mix with nuts (choose from almonds, pistachios, pecans, walnuts, hazelnuts, Brazil nuts, cashews) and dried fruit (choose from cranberries, raisins, apricots, blueberries, goji berries, acai berries, mango pieces)

- 100 percent whole-wheat bread, with all natural peanut butter or almond butter (optional: add a sliced banana and raspberry jam)

- Granola bar (choose one that is higher in protein and carbohydrate, and low in fat, because fat is slower digesting and will not provide the quick energy you need for training/your game)

- Dry cereal (containing more than 3 grams of fibre per serving) can be eaten dry or with half cup almond milk

- Healthier chips/crackers: Pitta chips, brown rice chips, soy flaxseed chips, vegetable chips, popcorn chips, edamame crackers, bite-sized pitta crackers (mix any of these with hummus, yogurt chive dip, spinach dip, fresh salsa, or homemade guacamole)

- Drinkable yogurt or single-serving Greek yogurts (if eaten 2 hours before game)

- Crackers with a spread of almond butter or peanut butter on top

- String cheese (if eaten 2 hours before game)

- Beef jerky or low-sodium turkey jerky with no nitrates or preservatives added

- Fresh portable fruit (i.e., apple, banana, pear, peach, nectarine, apricot, orange, blood orange, tangerine, plum, grapes, kiwi, berries, etc)

- English muffin with wheat wrap with almond butter or natural peanut butter

- Multigrain, sesame seed, or 100 percent whole-wheat bagel with part skim mozzarella cheese or reduced-fat vegetable cream cheese (can replace with a spread of hummus or Greek yogurt if eaten within an hour or two of being prepared)

- Cooked quinoa (place in large container and snack on with veggies)
- Yogurt-covered raisins or pretzels
- Hard-boiled eggs
- Build your own sandwich: Whole-grain roll or 2 slices whole-wheat bread with lean protein (sliced turkey, chicken, or ham), 1 slice low-fat cheese, mustard or hummus, lettuce, tomato, and avocado
- Almond butter and jelly/raspberry preserve sandwich on wheat bread for breakfast/snack on the go
- Whole-wheat pretzels (dip in all natural peanut butter for sweet and salty taste)
- Meal replacement shakes (made with water or coconut water and whey protein

NOTE >> Shakes require a mixer/shaker to blend the protein and beverage

MILK PROTEINS >> Whey and casein stimulate muscle protein synthesis and prevent muscle breakdown

HIGH-PROTEIN SHAKE RECIPES

Add natural whey protein or plant-based protein (pea protein or vegan Vega) powder to any of the following smoothies that don't already include protein powder. You can alternate between the following milks and milk substitutes: non-fat organic milk, 2 percent organic milk, or unsweetened versions of almond, coconut, hemp, or rice milk.

TIPS TO INCREASE CALORIES INCLUDE » use a larger serving of the nuts or nut butters and seeds or seed butters. To reduce carbohydrates, use a smaller serving of fresh or dried fruit (bananas, dates, etc). To increase fibre and nutrients without adding calories, add more leafy greens such as kale or spinach.

THE ENERGIZER

- 8 ounces unsweetened coconut milk
- .5 banana
- 2 tablespoons hemp seeds
- 1 to 2 tablespoons chia seeds
- 2 dates
- Sprinkle of nutmeg

NUTRITION FACTS » 400 calories, 16 grams fat (mono- and poly-unsaturated fat), 25 grams carbohydrate, 13 grams fibre, 18 grams protein (add 10 grams protein powder as needed to make it 28 grams protein total)

- 8 ounces unsweetened almond milk
- 1 scoop whey or pea protein powder
- .5 cup non-fat plain Greek yogurt
- 2 tbsp. almond butter
- .5 banana
- Sprinkle of cinnamon

NUTRITION FACTS >> 350 calories, 20 grams fat (mono- and poly-unsaturated fat), 14 grams carbohydrate, 5 grams fibre, 43 grams protein

BERRY BLAST

- 8 ounces unsweetened almond milk
- .5 cup blueberries
- .5 cup raspberries
- .5 cup blackberries
- 1 ounce raw, unsalted walnuts
- 1 tablespoon ground flaxseeds

NUTRITION FACTS >> 400 calories, 18 grams fat (mono- and poly-unsaturated fat), 30 grams carbohydrate, 18 grams fibre, 10 grams protein (add 10-20 grams protein powder as needed to make it 20-30 grams protein total).

IMMUNE BOOSTER

- 8 ounces unsweetened coconut milk
- 1 scoop pea protein powder
- 1 cup chopped kale
- .5 cup frozen mango chunks
- 2 dates
- Slivers of fresh ginger
- Sprinkle of coconut flakes

NUTRITION FACTS » 360 calories, 8.5 grams fat (mono- and poly-unsaturated fat), 35 grams carbohydrate, 10 grams fibre, 37 grams protein.

ANTI-INFLAMMATORY

- 8 ounces coconut water
- 1–2 teaspoons maca powder
- 1 teaspoon turmeric powder
- .5 avocado
- .5 cup frozen pineapple chunks
- .5 cup frozen organic blueberries
- 1 cup spinach leaves
- Touch of mint

NUTRITION FACTS » 260 calories, 13 grams fat (mono-unsaturated fat), 31 grams carbohydrate, 14 grams fibre, 8 grams protein (add scoop of protein powder, 20 grams, to make 28 grams protein total)

- 8 ounces coconut water
- 1 banana
- .5 pear
- .5 cup chopped cucumber
- 1 cup chopped kale
- 1 fresh squeezed lemon
- Touch of coriander
- Sprinkle of cayenne pepper (optional for spice/heat)

NUTRITION FACTS >> 240 calories, 0 grams fat, 37 grams carbohydrate, 8 grams fibre, 7.5 grams protein (add scoop of protein powder, 20 grams, to make 28 grams protein total)

ANTIOXIDANT

- 8 ounces unsweetened coconut milk
- .5 cup strawberries
- .5 cup blueberries
- 1 banana
- .5 cup shredded carrot
- 1 cup spinach leaves
- 1 tablespoon goji berries

NUTRITION FACTS >> 340 calories, 4.5 grams fat (mono-unsaturated fat), 45 grams carbohydrate, 25 grams fibre, 9 grams protein (add scoop of protein powder, 20 grams, to make 29 grams protein total)

BLISS

- 8 ounces unsweetened vanilla almond milk
- 1 scoop vanilla whey protein powder
- 1 tablespoon cacao powder
- .5 banana
- 2 dates
- 1 ounce cashews
- Sprinkle of cinnamon and nutmeg

NUTRITION FACTS >> 375 calories, 20 grams fat (mono-unsaturated fat), 30 grams carbohydrate, 12 grams fibre, 35 grams protein

JOIN THE CONVERSATION!

Find more ways to live a balanced life-style in the **COMPLETE ATHLETE** app!

ACKNOWLEDGMENTS

We'd like to extend a special thanks to Gary Jabara for his vision and dedication to making this book possible. He was a real driving force behind the Complete Athlete project.

Thanks to Arsene Wenger, Tony Carr, Ian Marshall, Tony Roberts, John Folwell, Paul Davis, Paul Clement, Terry Burton, Mark Chamberlain, Wendie Oxlade-Chamberlain, Lois Langton, Kyle Phillips, Rossi Eames, Troy Townsend, Steadman Scott, Tony Goldring, Jermain Defoe, Andre Gray, Tosin Adarabioyo, and Adam Lallana for their readiness to share experience, advice and expertise in order to help young players navigate their own journeys in football.

We thank the promising young players who agreed to be in the photo sections for this book and we're also grateful to Scott Heavey for his excellent photography.

To all the athletes who reach out to someone with a little guidance, help, advice or support: you're using your sport for good and acting as role models, whether you realise it or not. You inspire us.

And, finally, to all the parents who love their children and only want the best for them: this book is for all of you, as you seek to support your sons in the best ways possible as they grow in the sport. You are helping them become independent and self-sufficient young men. Thank you for caring enough to do everything you do!

Join Mia Hamm, Walid Khoury & Ziad Khoury alongside Don Yaeger, in *Complete Athlete: Women's Soccer.*

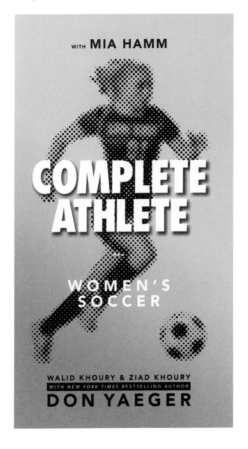

Available by downloading the **COMPLETE ATHLETE** app in the App store or via Google Play.

Also available in paperback at Amazon.
www.MyCompleteAthlete.com